The Mongwande Snake Cult

A Case Study in Contextualization

Sveinung Johnson Moen

/VTR
Publications

Bibliographic information published by the Deutsche Nationalbibliothek
The Deutsche Nationalbibliothek lists this publication in the Deutsche Natio-
nalbibliografie; detailed bibliographic data are available in the Internet at
http://dnb.d-nb.de.

ISBN 978-3-941750-88-3

VTR Publications
Gogolstr. 33, 90475 Nürnberg, Germany, http://www.vtr-online.eu

Unless otherwise stated, all Biblical quotations are from the New International
Version, © 1973, 1978, 1984, 1990 by International Bible Society.

Printed by Lightning Source

Table of Contents

Figures and Tables

Figures

Tables

Preface

Sveinung Johnson Moen is a Baptist pastor and missionary who has spent ten years at the pre-independence period in what is now the Democratic Republic of Congo, and subsequently eleven years in South Korea. At the age of eighty plus he has started higher theological studies at the International Baptist Theological Seminary at Prague, Czech Republic, where we met. At this high age he arrives at a rare accomplishment: to write an academic analysis of his missionary experiences in DRC Congo between 1951 and 1961 when the turmoils around independence obliged all missionaries to leave the country. He reflects on his missionary experiences in the light of today's missiological insights, particularly with regard to the necessity for contextualization. The political developments in this corner of the world have not permitted him to visit the Congolese church during the process of writing as he had wished and as it would have been also desirable from a scientific point of view. This scientific drawback is somewhat made up for by the recent information on the actual state of contextualization in the Monga region which he has received by means of correspondence with the church president and with other Christians from the region.

Sveinung Moen chooses to treat in this book a fascinating topic, the Mongwande snake cult, which he has already presented from an anthropological perspective in his book *The Mongwande Snake Cult* (2005) published by the Swedish Missiological Institute at Uppsala. Not satisfied with merely an anthropological presentation, Sveinung Moen presents in this book a comparative theological and anthropological analysis of the phenomenon submitted to the International Baptist Theological Seminary. This book is a shortened version of that text. Based on the comparative analysis, Sveinung Moen reflects on a better Christian contextualized practice, missionary and ecclesial, in the context of Mongwande culture. In the course of this reflection, Sveinung Moen comes up with very original and profound thoughts and proposals on the subject. This book is, in my knowledge, the first publication on the contextualization of Christianity in the face of a snake cult. I congratulate Sveinung Moen for this exceptional accomplishment at this stage of his life. I will always have feelings of great respect for him.

May the Lord who has led him as a missionary to RDC Congo and to Korea, and who has given him all the energy, health and strength for this academic work, give him an entire satisfaction about his great accomplishment and bless the rest of his life abundantly!

Hannes Wiher

Abstract

This present work consists of experimental thoughts and ideas. I have made use of a great specter of elements that seemingly may not belong to the subject, but in the end are influential in the subject matter. I have thouroughly (critically and analytically) gone through all the basic words in their native tongue (seven laguages) in order to define their deep meaning. I have done this with the intention of avoiding superficiality. Controversies and loopholes are deliberatedly left due to the fact that I could not stretch the thoughts and elements further.

The work is an investigation into the problem of contextualization. Through my reflections, summed up in the figures and tables of comparative evaluation, I analyze the source culture and the receiver culture comparatively. Contextualization should try to find a point of contact. If any contention arises as to the interpretation of facts, the biblical view should prevail. I am not defending either liberal or conservative theology. I consider myself being a practical theologian who tries to find the best solution to the problem that emerges when two cultures are encountering each other.

Acknowledgment

I cannot let this text go for printing before I take the occasion to thank Dr. Hannes Wiher for his eminent and competent guidance in my project. He became my mentor par excellence and I do extend my warmest regards and thanks to him for supervising my work over the past five years. He provided me with books, articles and clippings in order to elaborate the project.

Dr. Wiher has encouraged me as the process of writing went on and his proposals on the subject matter have been more than welcome. I am sure that I wouldn't have been able to accomplish the project without his assistance. I am hereby extending my gratitude and thanks to him

The second person that also helped me along the route is my son, John Ernst Moen. As the computer is not easy for elderly people, I had at times difficulties in working with it. Here John came to assist me. If it weren't for him, I would have had a very hard time with the use of the computer. John gave me also good advice concerning the project itself. I am so thankful to him, and I am also thankful to the rest of my family who stood by me at all times.

From the bottom of my heart, thank you all!

Halden, September 20, 2011
Sveinung Johnson Moen

Chapter 1
Introduction

1.1 Background

After graduating from the Norwegian Baptist Theological Seminary, which I attended for four years, and a subsequent year of "studies of the Belgian Congo" in Brussels in 1952, I left in 1953 for the Belgian Congo, now the Democratic Republic of Congo, with the Norwegian Baptist Mission. I stayed there until the turbulences of the independence forced the missionaries to leave the country in 1961.

While working in the Monga area as a missionary, I stumbled upon the snake cult phenomenon. It was more coincidentally than anything else. But, from 1953 on, I started studying the phenomenon which held a dominant position in the beliefs and practices of the local people. This gave rise to many questions relating to the Christian mission, especially its encounter with the snake cult. It was not an easy task to delve into the reality of the cult, its roots, its dimensions, its liturgy and its strong grip on the people's devotion. To gather information about the cult through interviews turned out to be rather difficult. The silence surrounding the worship was almost absolute, and I had to work meticulously and patiently in order to gain the people's trust and subsequent access to their closely guarded secrets. Most of the missionaries reacted with great animosity towards the snake cult. Not only was the cult in their view a work of the devil, but its artefacts were zealously burnt and destroyed. My mission agency did not encourage any kind of cross-cultural ministry.

Upon returning to Norway, I was frequently asked questions about the snake cult by both missionaries and other people. Professors, teachers and staff of the Museum of Cultural History, University of Oslo, were particularly interested. Professor Dr. Axel Sommerfelt of Oslo University became my mentor and I wrote *The Mongwande Snake Cult* (2005) under his auspices. The book is an anthropological study. Therefore, I was forced to sacrifice the more theological aspects of the subject matter. For this reason, I want to undertake this book, trying to sound the depths of the rich religious aspects of the Mongwande culture and to investigate the possibility of contextualizing Christianity into a society dominated by a phenomenon so seemingly apart from the western world as the snake cult.

1.2 Scope of the Subject

In this book, I deal specifically with three key subjects: the concept of contextualization and the phenomena of the snake cult and the twins. The snake cult in question is the one practiced among the Mongwande living in the northern part of the Democratic Republic of Congo.

Worshipping snakes is known from all over the world from time immemorial. From the Uroboros, the snake in Greek myths that embraced the earth, to Midgårdsormen, the snake in Nordic mythology which did the same, to the snake goddesses on Crete, the examples are many (Cooper 1978/1993:254). The snake has also some importance in the Old Testament (Stallman 1996:3.84-88) and appears in the NT (Bietenhard & Budd 1986:1.509-510). The Mongwande, who are the subject of this book, call the snake *ngbo*. They believe in God, *Nzapa*. Everything happens according to his will. However, he is a distant divinity and the Mongwande relate very little to him. Instead, they relate more to *ngbo*, the snake. The snake represents power or a power sphere. It is an omnipresent god. But it is at the same time an ordinary, crawling serpent (Kebanga 1951:61).

The snake cult is a large topic covering all aspects of human life. What characterizes this particular snake cult is its connection to twins. They are considered to be children of the snake. They are considered a manifestation of the snake in the real world and as such are also considered snakes, and concomitantly, a threat to the established order, in particular, the chief. They cause chaos in the structure of the world. Just like the twins are regarded as snakes, so also are their parents: the mother is a snake mother (*ta-ngbo*) and the father is a snake father (*to-ngbo*). Families with twins stick together in times of both joy and sorrow. As mentioned, the twins are considered to be snakes, i.e. animals, and they are looked upon as such until the name giving ceremony. Then, on that day, they are given human names and thus released from their status as animals and become humans. Ceremonies of this kind can take place at various lengths of time after birth, from a couple of days to several months. This name giving ceremony restores the old village order.

Another element indicative of the Mongwande snake cult is the absence of the concept of sin. This means that forgiveness in the biblical sense is non-existent. Hence, the idea of salvation from an eternal perdition or salvation into heaven has no meaning for a Mongwande. Religiosity for the Mongwande is about the here and now. What comes tomorrow nobody knows. Their cosmology does not extend beyond the real world around them (Moen 1961). This does, however, not mean that it lacks a spiritual dimension. It just means that their spiritual dimension is precisely that: an extra dimension in and of the here and now.

The consequences of this kind of thinking however is that there is no need for reconciliation or justification, neither for sanctification nor glorification.

Consequently, contextualizing the Gospel in relation to the snake cult in Monga presents some specific challenges. All contextualization does. But based on the above, particularly when we consider that the Mongwande does not have a biblical concept of sin in his culture, we will need to introduce the concept or knowledge of sin and the dangers thereof and thereafter guide him to the hope of salvation through grace. As mentioned above, the snake cult consists of many elements. But since the name giving ceremony is so central in the snake cult, we will focus on that practice when we discuss the need of contextualization of the Christian message in the context of the snake cult. I will study the religious behaviour of the followers of the snake cult in the relation to both Hiebert's model of contextualization (1985/2006) and Kraft's model of culture (1979/2005).

I will also look at the aspects of the snake cult as it is filtered through the translation model as well as the anthropological model of contextualization (Bevans 1992/2008). I will briefly deal with the question of how to teach the Mongwande about sin before I continue with the name giving ceremony.

Hiebert says in his model that one must commit oneself to the eternal truths of the Bible, both the missionary as well as the new convert (Hiebert 1985/2006). It seems that we must work at two levels. Firstly, we shall have to introduce the "law" in order to get them to understand that there is something we call sin. The apostle Paul says he did not know what sin was except through the law (Rom 7:7ff). Secondly, we have to teach them that one can be free both from the law and sin through grace and faith (Rom 5:17, 20ff; 6:7ff; 8:2ff). Kraft's model of culture (2005:157) may prove helpful in these regards. It deals with how to reach the deep-rooted worldview and with changing it so that the concept of sin gets planted in the deep-rooted level of the consciousness. This can be done by applying ourselves as Christians to live out the Gospel. That is why our conduct of life is so important. But we must also do what Jesus did, namely challenge the basic values of the local culture by asking questions or telling parables when necessary. The rite that is primarily linked to sin and forgiving of sins is of course the Lord's Supper. Referring back to Hiebert's model, I will attempt to show how his suggestions dealing with the modification of rites and ceremonies, or even adding new ones, may be applied.

I have talked about the concept of sin and its absence in the Mongwande culture. What then about the name giving ceremony? How does it relate to sin? The ritual is entrenched on the deep-rooted psycho-cultural level. But it is at the same time a visible manifestation of faith which can be reached on the surface level (Kraft 2005:86-87). It is also visible or accessible to the extent that it can be attained by the help of the efforts suggested by Hiebert. In other words, though it is true that we have to work on deep levels as shown by Kraft, the ceremony itself can be reached on a more surface level as implied by Hiebert's model. So, having committed ourselves to the authority of the Bible, one can see whether there is a respectful and effective way of dealing with this ritual or not. I choose once more to take my point of departure in the Bible. On Mars Hill in Athens, Paul took as his point of departure the Athenians' own image of god and taught them about the Only True God (Acts 17:22ff). Perhaps we can in the same way base our starting point on the name giving ceremony in an attempt to say something about the salvation in Jesus Christ. My own fieldwork showed that the battle between nature and culture, order and chaos is evident in the snake cult (Moen 1961). This battle is visible from time to time and particularly frightening for the Mongwande when twins are born. It is a threat that must be warded off through the name giving process. The point is that it means however that the Mongwande have, to a certain degree, ideas of renewal and re-creation of peace and quiet in the village (Moen 2005:58). If for example the missionary could get the local people to see the connection of sin on the one hand and chaos or danger on the other, it would be possible to see the name giving ceremony as a rite like baptism, something which restores order and safety. The result of this might lead to conversion and salvation. If we return to Hiebert's model, we see that it is possible to justify or modify rituals that originally belonged to the Mongwande and give it a Christian content and meaning. When the new converts have done this modification, it is time to take a step further. Because, it may simply not be enough just to modify a pagan ritual, turning it into a Christian one. A name giving ceremony can contain several elements that may be considered unbecoming for a Christian. For example, such things as paying homage to the snake, offering of hens, etc. Therefore, this ritual must be evaluated in its entirety by the congregation together with the missionary. Perhaps the name giving ceremony must quite simply be substituted by baptism (Hiebert 1985:90).

1.3 The Problem

Missionaries coming to the Monga area faced a lot of problems when they encountered the local people. The Mongwande worldview is quite different from the Western worldview. I will define the term worldview in more detail below. In the eyes of many missionaries, the gap between the church and the Mongwande religiosity was unbridgeable. Nevertheless, the missionaries stood their ground and tackled the problems as best as they could.

The Great Commission (Mt 28:19f) gives a mandate to missionaries, in fact to all believers, to preach the Gospel, and seems to exclude making scientific research among the people with whom they work. However, it has become more and more self-evident that we must work together with people, not against them, if we want to succeed in our task. This topic will be expounded upon below in connection with critical and uncritical contextualization (Hiebert 2006). Thus, investigation and research have been proven to be far more effective tools, far better than condemnation and contempt for local religious traditions. Earlier, the Christian kerygma brought by the missionaries had more the air of a commandment than anything else. When locals turned to Christ, they were told that each conversion should be followed up with a full cleansing of old traditions and customs. Pagan thought had to be relinquished and heathen objects should be thrown away into the river or sea or be burnt (2Cor 5:17). In other words a form of uncritical contextualization was being practiced.

I found the situation unworthy and unfair for the converts and far too condescending towards the local population and their inherited traditions. Tension was building up between the representatives of Christianity and the worshippers of the indigenous religion. This is the crux of the contextualization issue. How do we make the Gospel palatable in the Mongwande culture where the snake is so venerated, without compromising or loosing the truth of the word of God? Shall we go all out and accept uncritically any and all aspects of the host culture or must we adhere to maintain certain biblical teachings as unnegotiable? Is there any limitation to contextualization?

1.4   Aim and Objectives

The aim of this book is twofold: firstly, a desire to investigate and clarify as much as possible the phenomenon of the snake cult among the Mongwande people, and secondly, to try to make the subject more understandable for missionaries and the church and to other people who might have a vested interest in the matter. I hope to be able to present a workable approach to a better contextualization of the Christian faith in the Mongwande culture and thereby help missionaries, aid workers and the local church or any others who might feel the need to learn more about and delve more deeply into the Mongwande culture. I pray that this book can give some guidelines how to work more effectively and respectfully with the Mongwande people, who seemingly stand so far apart from the western world.

Within these two main tasks the focus will be on the following objectives:
1. Investigate the Mongwande snake cult.
2. Evaluate the different models of contextualization.
3. Investigate the snake concept in Scripture.
4. Evaluate the Mongwande culture in the light of the Bible.
5. Propose a better contextualized practice of the evangelical church in relation to the Mongwande snake cult.

1.5 Outline

The above questions will be dealt with in the following way:

Ch. 1: Cultural analysis of the Mongwande snake cult. What is the meaning of the snake cult?

Ch. 2: Method of contextualization: Which models of contextualization are faithful to the Bible?

Ch. 3: Biblical analysis: What biblical concept(s) is/are concerned with the Mongwande snake cult?

Ch. 4: Evaluation of the culture in the light of the Bible: What continuity and discontinuity exist between the Mongwande culture and the Bible?

Ch. 5: Contextualized practice: What would be a better contextualized practice of the evangelical church? What biblical form(s) could translate the meaning of the Mongwande snake cult? What evangelical reaction does the evaluation of the Mongwande snake cult incite: acceptance, refusal, tolerance, modification, creation of something new? In other words: If the snake cult has to be discarded, what would be a possible functional substitute?

1.6 Methods

The anthropological analysis is primarily based on my original field work which I undertook between 1951 and 1961 (Moen 1961/2005). The quantitative aspects of my work included some 55 objects used in the performance of the snake cult, all of which were donated to the Museum of Cultural History, University of Oslo, on January 27th, 2002. The more qualitative work includes: observations of cult séances, cult songs, snake songs, incantations, rituals, interviews with medicine men and participants. My intention is to use the anthropological work which I have done as a basis for the theological presentation below. Needless to say that the anthropological work and the theories and models of contextualization will be scrutinized in the framework of theology. Languages, religious practices, social and cultural aspects of the Mongwande society will be studied and filtered through theology, biblical truths and contextual models. The literature survey will cover books like *Le culte du serpent chez les Ngbandi* by Basile Tanghe (1926) and *Aspects de l'organisation du monde des Ngbandi* by Louis Molet (1970).

For the biblical analysis I will primarily use selected word and concept studies, exegetical studies and techniques of systematic theology in the perspective of redemptive history. For the evaluation of culture in the light of Scripture, exegetical and anthropological tools will be used. For the historical presentation of the Norwegian Baptist Mission in the Congo, I will build on historical sources, using the archives of the Norwegian Baptist Union and my personal experience. Hopefully, I will arrive at a conclusion outlining a better contextualized practice.

Chapter 2:
The Mongwande Culture

2.1 Introduction

The objective of this book is to make a cultural analysis of the Mongwande snake cult. I will attempt to define and describe some of the various forms and meanings of the Mongwande culture. Furthermore, I will try to provide some answers with regard to the dimensions of this society, and delve into the Mongwande world of animism. The focus will be especially on the Mongwande religious life, particularly on the snake cult.

Before we delve into the topic, it might be in place to come with a little caveat. One should be wary of immediately equating culture and its various expressions of religion as such, or in this case, the local snake cult. Not all culture is religion, but one can perhaps assert that all religion is culture in that it is a cultural expression for those devotees who have the belief pertaining to that particular religion and who carry out its rituals. The point is that the Mongwande culture encompasses all Mongwande people. Naturally, the snake cult did not extend to all of them. Not all of them were followers of this particular path. Still, the cultural expressions are so old, engrained and common to many Mongwande that they often overlap. It is often very difficult to see where a snake cult ritual is no longer a snake cult act, but a Mongwande cultural expression used by the general population, for example divination, healing or blessing. Still, the rituals and cultural expressions of a snake cult witch doctor is very Mongwande, for a lack of a more scientific term. Therefore, I will often refer to them interchangeably. The only main difference regards, for example, the object of their veneration. Though the Mongwande had a concept of god (*Nzapa*), as far as the devotees of the snake cult were concerned, *ngbò* "the snake" was their god; he was the object of their veneration. The economic and social aspects of the Mongwande culture will also be briefly treated.

To put this into perspective, it might be useful to consider Charles H. Kraft definition of culture. Kraft states in his book *Appropriate Christianity* (2005) that culture is made up of "cultural forms." Forms are the customs, patterns and structures in which we live and move and have our being. In language we find cultural forms. Beyond language, material objects such as chairs, pencils, cars, and dishes are cultural forms. So are non-material items such as ceremonies and practices. Forms, then, are the vehicles of culture, religion and worldview. Any given form can be the vehicle of more than one meaning (Kraft 2005:155-156).

In describing the Mongwande society, it might also be helpful to turn to the American anthropologist Elman Service who classifies societies into four different categories such as mobile hunter-gatherer groups, segmentary societies, chiefdoms and states. On the organization of segmentary societies, Colin Renfrew and Paul Bahn say (2000): "Segmentary societies operate on a larger scale than mobile hunter-gatherer groups and they usually consist of farmers based in villages – permanent sedentary communities" (Renfrew & Bahn 2000:194). In that they have left their migratory life behind and dwell in permanent villages the Mongwande communities are sedentary societies. They are also chiefdoms in that they are governed by a chieftain with his council of elders. Hence, there is a principle of ranking and a difference in social status between individuals. The office of chieftain is a blend of lineage and appointment. The villagers know of each other and come together once in a while to discuss matters of importance, yet none of them dominates or is subservient to the other. Hence, the power structure among various villages is more of a segmentary nature than a centre-periphery one.

I will attempt to investigate the Mongwande society in the light of these definitions. I will also discuss the Mongwande religious life and attempt to determine whether the snake cult is to be clssified as formal or informal religion or as animism, particularly in the light of what Lothar Käser says about the matter (Käser 2004:19-29). All, of this is done with a view towards a better contextualization of the Gospel.

2.2 Geography, Political Structure and Social Life

The Mongwande live in the northern part of the Democratic Republic of Congo, and along a narrow strip in the southern part of the neighbouring state, the Central African Republic (Burssens 1958:20). The Mongwande, also called Ngbandi, moved into these areas probably in the beginning of the 18th century, perhaps from southern Sudan. Today, they live on both sides of the border. The arrival of the Europeans into these regions at the end of the 18th century put an end to the Mongwande conquests. In this book, we are dealing with the Mongwande who live up north within the border of the Democratic Republic of Congo. The term Mongwande probably stems from the word Ngbandi meaning "the big one." They do not consider themselves Bantus but Sudanese, something they are really proud of. There are many variations of the root word Ngbandi such as Mogwandi, Mongbandi, Mongwandi and Gbandi (de Clerq 1912:231-353). Their migratory journey from Darfur, Sudan, seems to have taken place alongside the renowned Azande tribe, at least according to their own account.

In colonial time (1908-1960), the Congo was divided into five provinces. Each of these was divided into districts, which were organized in territories, and these again in chiefdoms. Monga, the village where I lived, was a chiefdom. As mentioned above, chiefdom was a matter of lineage and appointment. The chieftain was usually selected from a chieftain family and then chosen or approved by the Belgian authorities (Maessens 1952:12-13). The chieftain was in charge together with a Belgian senior government official from the civilian administration.

The social life of the Mongwande was varied and entertaining. There was dancing, singing, and on a smaller scale, fables and fairy-tales were told. Apart from their origin myths, however, they did not have an extended recount of tribal history. If stories were produced, they were ordinarily linked to the dances. The participants in snake dances danced in a line writhed and wriggled along like a snake. There were quite a few songs. In the section "Snake Songs" below, I am going to take a closer look at some of the songs collected by Basile Tanghe and myself (Tanghe 1926:40-60; Moen 2005:59-92).

2.3 Village, House and Family Structure

Village in Mongwande is *kodoro* and in Lingala *mboka*. The Mongwande live in villages numbering 20 to 50 families, in smaller enclosures, or in big compounds accommodating several thousands. This is especially the case for the so called river-people, the riparians. A Mongwande house carries its own identity (Carsten & Hugh-Jones 1993). Ordinarily, there are two types of Mongwande houses: round and rectangular. The most common house is the round one. It expresses simplicity in grade and means, while the rectangular ones represent higher social and better economic status. They are for the rich and people in high position. The houses were usually beautifully decorated, with for example plants, flowers, geometrical shapes such as circles or even representations of human forms or animals like the writhing snake. The house becomes a prolongation of the people dwelling in it. The individuals in the village are intimately bound together. The responsibility of the villagers for one another strengthens the morality of the community. The houses were placed so that they formed a circle. In fact, that circle was the natural theatre for the Mongwande cultural events. A camp fire in the middle of the encampment created the right atmosphere for the popular performance.

Marriages were arranged by the parents. The practice of marriage gift was not originally considered as selling or buying wives, but rather a compensation for lost labour power and loss of rights in her fertility within the bride's family (Maessens 1952:8). Parenthood is the basis of African society. The biological family is the primary social unit. But this "biological cell" is too weak to maintain itself. Therefore, the village, or better yet the community, is there to support both the new born baby and the family. This pattern is practiced at Monga. Some anthropologists speak of patrilinear and matrilinear societal models in Africa. I observed in Monga that the patrilinear model was custom-ary. The father is the head of the house and if he passes away, his eldest son inherits the power and the privileges that follow (Maessens 1952:6). The ruler of the house is always the male. The wife takes over when there are no more males left.

As already mentioned, the patrilinear family structure is common in Monga. The inheritance descends through the direct (vertical) line from father to son. In the case where both the father and the elder brother are missing, the inheri-tance passes on to the younger brother (the indirect horizontal line).

The Mongwande distinguish between two types of marriages: monogamy which is widespread, and polygamy which mostly appears among rich people. Polyandry was not practiced in the Monga area. One may also distinguish between two practices of marriage: endogamy (the wife is chosen from the same social group as the husband) and exogamy (the wife is selected from other groups than the social group of the husband). We are facing here old traditions and customs that the missionaries have to deal with in the imple-mentation of contextualization. The question of polygamy for instance cannot be ignored, but neither can it be accepted in light of the biblical view. The missionaries will have to engage themselves together with the host church to find a solution that is acceptable to both parties. There must be a critical en-gagement for both of them.

There are many kinds or methods to be used in acquiring a wife:
1. Abduction is one of these. This is not used today but as a symbol.
2. Exchange is another where the partners exchange women without any payment involved.
3. Prestation is the third one, meaning that someone has to pay for a bride by manual work like Jacob for Rachel (Gen 29:16-20).
4. Payment is the fourth. The bride has to be paid for. The payment might be regarded as a symbol or also a gift. In most cases I know of, the payment has been a compensation for lost working power.
5. Preferential indicates that the husband to be must choose his wife among people who are somehow related or tied to the bridegroom's family in a special way.
6. Levirate: levirate marriage is marriage between in-laws.
7. Sorority is marriage between a widower and his sister-in-law.
8. Optional marriage happens in more primitive circles.
9. Indissoluble monogamous marriage. It is a sort of magic-religious cult. It is a definite indissoluble eternal union. The two conjoints believe in rein-carnation and they will meet again in a new incarnation when time comes.
10. Blood relationship. An association sealed by magic-religious rites (adap-ted from Maessens 1952).

2.4 Language

The two languages the Mongwande of the Uélé territory normally speak in their daily life, and fluently I might add, are Mongwande and Lingala. Mongwande is their mother tongue. It has roots in the Sudanese dialects. According to H. Greenberg's classification of the African languages, Mongwande belongs to the Adamawa Eastern subgroup of the Niger-Congo language family (Greenberg 1963). The other language is Bangala, which is a grammatically well constructed commercial language and is today called Lingala. The Mongwande language is quite different from Bantu languages in its vocabulary and syntax. Mongwande has for example a prefix only in plural: "a-"

Example: Singular: *keke*   "tree"   Plural: *akeke*   "trees/sticks"

Singular: *gwa*   "slave"   Plural: *agwa*   "slaves"

Some nouns change from singular to plural.

Example: Singular: *dzo*   "man"   Plural: *adzi*   "men"

The adjectives are generally at the head of the nouns, sometimes behind. Diphthongs are obsolete, and if two vowels come together, they are each pronounced separately. The core of the syllables consists of vowels. Names and the nouns generally end in vowels. The past tense is obtained by the auxiliary word *ngo* and the future by the auxiliary *ande*. The length of time in the past perfect is expressed by the auxiliary *ndo*. The word *ne* indicates the accomplished mode (de Clercq 1912:110-112).

There are particularities in the Sudanese languages which B. Tanghe uses to explain the snake cult and the ability to differentiate the action with more verbs than we do. He insists that this is a way of Sudanese thinking that has prevailed in the Mongwande language. I am not sure about this argument and will deal with it later in the book. Mongwande is relatively rich in words with, for example, an array of names for snakes. *Ngbo* is the group name for snake. The Mongwande also have names for each species such as *konga, mbito, siri, masi, kodoro. Ngbo* is furthermore a name that covers other subjects. I will return to this question when I discuss the idea of *ngbo*.

The second language is Lingala. Lingala is a *lingua franca* that joins the different folk groups together. Lingala comes from the Bantu language -*ngala*. Lingala contains today many words from other Bantu languages as well as French and is well constructed. But Lingala has only one single name for snake (*nyoka*), which covers all different kinds of snakes. The word for the soul of the ancestors is *tolo*, a word which appears in connection with the snake cult and Mongwande religiosity (Burssens 1958:129-151). I will keep to these two mentioned languages.

2.5 Health, Education and Welfare

The health and welfare situation in Monga left much to be desired when the missionaries arrived in the 1920s. If people could afford it, they turned to their medicine man. My observations of the medicine man made it clear that his assortment of remedies was quite large. He knew generally a great deal about herbal medicines. There is no doubt that he helped people to the extent that his abilities allowed him. But in most cases, he lacked knowledge and medicine. It was only when the Belgians and the missionaries from different Christian missions entered the scene that real medical assistance could be given. The Norwegian Baptist Mission offered medical treatment already from the start in 1920. The Mission built dispensaries on the premises of the mission stations and provided medical staff and medicines. The plan was to build a hospital fully equipped with medical staff and to provide medicine. The medical doctor arrived in 1955, but the construction of a hospital was never realized, as the turmoil of the struggle for independence (1960) hindered the plan (Moen 2005). During the colonial period the Belgians provided the colony with an adequate health care and welfare system. Hospitals, clinics and dispensaries were established and furnished with medical staff. But social assurances such as old-age pension, retirement pension and unemployment insurance were non existent except for some private companies. There is an array of illnesses in the northern part of Congo such as malaria, filariasis, Congo fever, anky-lostomiasis, all kinds of abscesses and festering wounds, smallpox (extin-guished in 1972), tuberculosis, sleeping sickness, leprosy, polio, Ebola fever (a viral disease that suddenly emerged at Ebola river within the Mongwande border in the second half of the 20th century), not to mention kwashiorkor. As of today, it seems like the medical situation in the Democratic Republic of Congo is rather unclear.

Before the arrival of the Belgians, there was the practice of bringing past ex-periences, history and information on to the next generation. Some of the in-terviews I conducted indicated that the Mongwande possessed knowledge of the past which had been brought to them from elderly people. The Belgians introduced schools offering six years of primary and four years of secondary education, leading up to university level. The Louvain University in Leopold-ville, now Kinshasa, was well known, with campuses at Kisangani and Lubumbashi. The Norwegian Baptist primary school at Monga centre grew rapidly and could boast 1536 pupils by 1953-1954. It had a large staff of teachers and an extensive school activity scattered in the district. Dormitories were also built in order to accommodate pupils who were far from their home. The opportunity of learning became very popular in the Congo. People loved books. I remember one of my evangelists embraced and kissed the Bible I gave him. And people who attended classes were called "people of the book" (*batu na buku*). The Mongwande had a special talent for languages. Most people spoke at least two languages, Mongwande and Lingala, and many spoke even three or four: their own tongue, Lingala, French, and a neighbour tribe's language. They were good students in humanities as well as in vocational studies.

2.6 Economic Life

2.6.1 Natural Resources

The main economic resources of the Democratic Republic of Congo are its mineral deposits. Copper in the Shaba region was especially a source of desire for the Europeans. But also other types of minerals were found in the Shaba and Kivu regions such as cobalt, zinc, manganese, coal, silver and gold. Diamonds occur in the Kasai-Oriental and Kasai-Occidental regions. There are gold deposits in Haut-Zaire and Bas-Zaire. There are other natural as well as energy resources in the Congo, e.g. waterfalls and forest reserves that cover 55% of the country. The forest is considered to be the largest in the entire African continent. Hunting in the forest and fishing in the rivers contributes to the local diet. The country's hydroelectric resources have an estimated potential of 13% of the world's potential capacity and 50% of Africa's potential capacity (Encyclopaedia Britannica 1988).

After having made an overview of Congo as a whole let us now focus on the Upper Congo around Uélé, Bili and Bomu rivers. These areas are not so rich in natural resources. This might be the reason why people have settled along the river banks and are named the riparians: "people of the rivers." The riparian right gives all owners of land contiguous to streams, lakes and ponds the right over the water. Part of Mongwande economy is based on that right.

2.6.2 Agriculture and Industry

The primary economic enterprises in the Uélé and Yakoma districts are agriculture, hunting, fishing and collecting insects, especially ants. The men cut trees and clear the field for raising crops. At the time I was there, cutting trees was done by simple means. They cut the trees at knee-level and left the trunk lying on the ground to dry. The underwood was cut down and burned after a while. Following this operation, the women entered the field clearing it and tilling the soil for raising crops. Each family possesses its own property, *elanga na ngai*, meaning "my field." Peanuts, rice and cotton are sown in the same field together with other plants. Large amounts of banana, maize, manioc, cotton, oranges, avocado, grapefruit, papaya, melon and mango are cultivated. But mainly peanuts, cotton and coffee are put up for sale.

The traditional occupation was hunting. But as game successively disappeared in the forests, this activity declined. To go out hunting with the Mongwande is an experience one never forgets. They carry their nets, spears, arrows, bows and home made rifles, which ordinarily were made of water pipes and pieces of wood. The world's oldest dog race, the *bazinzi*, was part of the hunting team. However, I never saw the necessity of these dogs as they did not seem to understand the concept of tracking prey. There was seldom enough prey for sale so we devoured it in the *mboka* "village."

If twins were born in the village, special hunting and fishing raids were arranged. Arrangements were made by the intervention of the twin's mediator, the medicine man, hoping to attain the big catch. The entire village participated in the happening. Men and women went to the river where they formed a sort of ring or pool with their nets. They then threw *dawa makasi* "strong medicine" into the water. This drug was so strong that the fish was rendered unconscious and floated to the surface. The people believed the fish to be dead. Tightening their nets so the aperture got smaller, they scooped up the fish with their bare hands and threw the catch in the baskets and buckets. According to Tanghe, both fishing and picking ants were activities under the protection of the snake (Tanghe 1926:8-14). Singing and dancing to the honour of the snake were performed before and after the capture. I am personally in want of this type of observation, but I have heard about it. On the other hand, catching fish with *dawa makasi* "strong medicine" was almost commonplace to me. As mentioned earlier, the Monga people kept the secret of their local religious notions very much to themselves, and if possible out of reach of the Europeans.

Arts and crafts were poorly developed although the Mongwande were well known for certain excellent products such as swords and knives from their domestic industry and smothery. The production of iron, wood work, basket work, copper, fibre, skin and ceramics was done according to the simplest method possible. But even so the items were well made. In the olden days, they made shields from ropes that were very artistically interwoven. Nowadays, the most common products are mats, baskets, sifters, cooking pots and vessels. They also mastered a variety of diagonal, square, doubled and reinforced plaiting. When it came to hewing out boats and canoes, they surpassed their neighbours. As smiths they excelled and were great artists. They loved to tell me that they were smiths long before they entered the regions of Monga and Yakoma. The production of all these articles formed, along with ordinary daily wage labour and trade with their neighbours, the basis of their economy.

2.6.3 The Question of Development

Why do we call some countries developed and others underdeveloped? We talk about high per capita income and low per capita income. Countries with high per capita income are called developed countries and countries with low per capita income are called underdeveloped. It looks like the underdevelopment lies in the fact that they have not yet succeeded in making full use of their potential economic growth. The natural riches in the Congo are enormous. However, the peoples in the Congo have been exploited over a long period of time. And today, for example in the Kivu district, businessmen are making fortunes by transporting truckloads of Congolese resources right across the border from the Congo to Rwanda, while the Congolese people are powerless to do anything about it and the UN seem unable to intervene. In our Monga region, a similar scenario is being played out between the Congo and Uganda.

The income will naturally be low in comparison to the so called developed countries. The differences are therefore not so much in natural conditions, but more in the economical and institutional organizations. Development of an infrastructure and organizational framework (market system, administrative machinery, international trade, foreign investment, technological and organizational innovations) would enable an underdeveloped country to make a fuller use of its domestic resources. It was very little of this kind in the Democratic Republic of Congo and even less of it in the Upper Congo or Mongwande land. And now, due to years of war and its concomitant pillaging and plundering, keeping the Congolese from ever gaining control over their own resources and developing them into viable raw materials and industries, there are quite a few structures that must be built in order to establish and secure a stable and sound economy. And it goes without saying that a pivotal ingredient in this is peace.

2.7   Religious Life of the Mongwande

2.7.1   Introduction

My observations and fieldwork showed me that the daily life of the Mongwande in the Congo-Oubangui territories is permeated by numerous magico-religious ideas. In fact, they dominate the social, political and economic life of the people. A Mongwande believes in a Supreme Being. He would look at you with awe if you insisted that God didn't exist (Tanghe 1925:435-438). Their Supreme God is in Mongwande *Nzapa* and in Lingala *Nzambe*.[1] The overshadowing idea though is that he is a far away, supreme power who reigns according to his own will. He has created the world, i.e. he has brought forth all the things and objects that the Mongwande observe in their surroundings.

---

[1] In what follows, the abbreviation (m) stands for Mongwande and the abbreviation (li) stands for Lingala.

Yet, the Mongwande have no cosmogony, at least not in the western way. *Nzapa / Nzambe* is the sole creator of all things in this world. He sustains the entire universe. He is the source of life and the cause of fertility of women. He has also created the great spirits that are the origin of the Mongwande people. In spite of this knowledge, this Supreme Being is not an object of direct veneration, but he may be reached by supplication, for example at the morning prayers. All that happens in this world happens because *Nzapa* wants it that way: *Nga ó Nzapa* (m) / *paka Nzambe te* (li) "it is all the will of God." The fundamental belief is that this celestial force possesses authority and power to accomplish his divine resolutions. He is not to be tampered with. *Nzapa* (m) / *Nzambe* (li) has no representative on earth. There is no need for a mediator between God and man in Mongwande religious thinking. Nor is there any sin of which to be cleansed either. Hence, there is no need for any reconciliation with God. These are Christian concepts, and as such are not part of an animistic religion like the Mongwande snake cult. However, it becomes a challenge when a missionary is faced with such a religion and finds himself having to explain biblical concepts such as sin and reconciliation. I will return to this below. Suffice it to say that critical contextualization, not to mention Paul's pedagogical approaches when dealing with various groups of non-believers, for example the Athenians on Mars Hill, are important tools when it comes to explaining Christian concepts in local cultures. According to the Mongwande, no one knows where God lives, what he looks like or what shape he has. Therefore, there is no logical reason for constructing a temple for a God whom nobody knows anything about.

In the following discussion, we will interweave practical observations of the Mongwande religious life with general considerations on folk religious concerns in order to deepen our analysis of Mongwande culture and religion.

2.7.2 Meaning of Life and Death

The meaning of life and death is a problem for most people. The formal religions try to give meaning to life by answering questions of an ultimate reality: about nature, the cosmic world, humankind and the individual. Folk religions give people a sense of meaning by answering their questions concerning life and death, sorrow and joy, sickness and daily tribulations. Questions pertaining to the meaning of life are numerous. Most people speculate about who they are, where they have come from and what they are to become. Why are we here on earth? One thing that gives meaning is a sense of connectedness. A strong link between humans is pivotal. Again we have the link within the family and in relation to God, land and people. In addition, people may get a sense of usefulness through work, not to mention a sense of ownership through possessions. There could even be meaning in death through for instance belief in an afterlife. Meaning is found in the growth of a person into full maturity and in the reality of salvation.

There is no doubt that the believers in the snake cult find meaning therein. Even though the cult does not offer eternal salvation, it offers to improve the earthly situation, both physically and spiritually.

2.7.3 Human Well-Being and Misfortune

The main concern of folk religion is the well-being of the inhabitants on earth, not eternal life in heaven. Many beliefs and activities are designed to gain blessings here and now. When people are striving for a good life but misfortune occurs, most people do not stand by in despair doing nothing. Rather, they seek to ensure success and overcome crisis. The first step is often to find the right belief system to explain the situation (Hiebert et al. 1999:133).

When we read the snake songs below, we see that the snake brings mostly misfortune. It is very seldom that it brings happiness to the family or to the village. When twins are born into a family, nobody is happy. This situation is remedied partly by the intervention of the snake itself through medicine men (kòkòrò, m) and medicine women. The mourning usually lasts until the name festival takes place. It seems like the snake cult phenomenon is an attempt at explaining twin births. The birth of twins was a mystery to the Mongwande. And the only way of explaining it was to blame it all upon the snake. According to Mongwande thought, the snake had been flicking its forked tongue in front of the woman during the act of copulation (Yanzere 1959).

There are several systems that can be used to explain the miseries or misfortunes that befall people, such as religion, medicine, science or philosophy. The Mongwande chose to explain everything in terms of the snake. Their selection of this system of explanation is a collective one, but individuals can also hold their own views and beliefs. The means of generating well-being are many. Some, as mentioned above, find meaning in work, others in planting or even hunting. A purpose of choosing a belief system is to guard oneself against unknown and unforeseen events.

People all over the world believe in the power of blessing to bring good fortune and of curse to bring misfortune. In fact, blessings and curses are linked. In the Mongwande culture, this is also the case. Curses cause misfortune. They are imprecations calling evil upon offenders and enemies. On the other hand, blessings bestow rewards and riches upon a being, be they deserving or no. Oaths are also powerful when used and pronounced correctly. However, oaths are mostly directed towards oneself.

There are many causes of misfortune: natural calamities, diseases, wars and conflicts, for example. Some believe that calamities and misfortunes are caused by sin, deities, ancestors or evil spirits, while others explain misfortunes in purely natural terms or offer more scientific explanations (Hiebert et al. 1999:156). Still others believe in the power of destiny. They may adhere to esoteric directions like astrology with their horoscopes, and believe that a person's life is predetermined by fate. Voodoo, magic, both white and black, or simply luck, good or bad, are also means of explaining life's twists and turns. The notion that some people possess an inner evil strength is quite common, such as evil eye, evil mouth or evil touch. Hiebert et al. present a Christian response to this aforementioned desire for the good life and protection from misfortune. The Christian response is the belief in a trinitarian God who promises help in time of crises which allows developing a theology of suffering. In a sinful world, God may use suffering and misfortune to lead people closer to him. The doctrines and ministries mentioned above may serve as strategies when confronted with local people who seek to explain and alleviate their daily plight. They give guidelines as to how the church can serve as a holistic healing and teaching ministry (Hiebert et al. 1999:162-168).

2.7.4 Guidance and the Unknown

People often plan their day in order to avoid dangers or unexpected occurrences. However, in their struggles with the unknown, some make use of their knowledge of the unknown to come to grips with the future. The methods used to obtain guidance vary greatly. One set of methods spring more or less from within the believer himself. Dreams, visions and trances are often used to seek guidance or predict future occurrences. Other means involve seeking information and help from the dead, which is called necromancy (Hiebert et al. 1999:177).

Divination can include more mechanical methods of obtaining guidance, when instruments or objects are used. People seek a diviner who plays the role of an intermediary between the seeker and the unknown. Usually different divination methods are used. The diviner reads and interprets the answer which he conveys to the client. It might be anything from Tarot cards to tea leaves. In the context of the snake cult, the *mbeti* "tripod" was often used. The size and the shape of the *mbeti* could vary, but they were more often than not made out of wood. One piece of wood would be halved yielding two surfaces that could readily fit against each other. These surfaces would be smoothed out such that they could be rubbed against each other in a circular fashion, much like grinding your thumb against your index finger in the case of smaller *mbeti*, or applying a coat of polish on to the hood of your car in the case of larger ones (Moen 1961).

We find Christian responses to these various practices and other forms of magic in the Bible (Ex 22:7,11; Rev 21:8). But it is imperative that one does not misconceive God's will. He has therefore put before us general principles, which can be found in the Scriptures.

2.7.5   Right and Wrong

What is wrong and what is right? According to Hiebert, all societies have their own notions of basic order and the world is organized according to this basic order. Hiebert raises critical questions as to what the foundation of the belief in good and evil is. Before coming up with the Christian response, he deals with sin as basic disorder (Hiebert et al. 1999:198-203). In most societies, sin must be repaired. Some form of restitution must take place. Sacrifice or restoration is the answer if one has committed a crime or has sinned. Other analogies to sacrifice are homage, gift-giving, communion, eating and drinking together and having common meals. All these practices serve to restore relationships.

Among other things, pollution is a breach of the cosmic order accepted by most societies, and is regarded as evil. The purification of these kinds of disorders is met by rituals. "Purity and holiness are central in the Bible," Hiebert maintains, and he goes on to describe different themes such as sacrifices and reconciliation, righteousness, holiness and sin. He maintains also that there is a difference between culturally and biblically defined sins. So when he talks about salvation, he means, as I understand him, salvation from biblically defined sins. The terms right and wrong must be dealt with in the light of the Bible, and here we clearly see the critical contextualization model applied. A particularly heinous sin is according to John 16:8-11 not believing in Jesus. The quoted passage emphasises also that Jesus is the only one who brings justice and repairs wrongdoings in the world. We are doing the right thing when we believe in Jesus and the wrong thing when we turn away from him. As mentioned above, the Mongwande do not have a concept of sin in the way Christianity teaches. They don't have a concept of hell and certainly don't see the link between going to hell in the afterlife due to committing evil acts in this life. Because they have an embodied spirituality, and because spirituality is seen as part of reality in the here and now, the closest one can come to describing sin in a Mongwande sense would be in terms of doing good or bad things. The act of experiencing good or bad fortune may also be seen as being a consequence, sometimes immediate, of having insulted a god or disrespected your neighbour. In any case, such an act was seen as part of the here and now reality and did not have any bearing on one's afterlife. The challenge for a missionary would then be to contextualize the concept of sin. I will delve more into this topic below.

2.7.6   The Mongwande Concept of Sin

As mentioned above, the Christian way of looking at the notion of sin is strange to the Mongwande. The Hebrew word *hata'* and the Greek word *hamartia* both mean "to miss the target." Western Christians may be stretching the use of the Greek word a little bit more than originally intended. For the OT, sin is a relational and a legal concept for the behaviour that misses the goal and is against the norm (Wiher 2003:181-185, 317f). Western theologians have usually emphasized the legal aspect with the meaning of "guilt toward God" demanding penitence. The Greek words *adikia* or *kakia*, are the way I see it, not so much God-centred as the abovementioned Greek expressions (Kittel and Friedrich 1985:44-53, 267-335). Today the word sin has different connotations than just to "miss the target."

A Mongwande, however, does not acknowledge any sin towards a God he doesn't know anything about. The dualistic separation of material and immaterial world is incomprehensible for the Mongwande. The material and immaterial world must all be God's according to Mongwande philosophy. In that regard, it is somewhat similar to the Jewish understanding that body and soul are a unity (Gen 2:7). But, the Mongwande does not feel a sense of responsibility or guilt towards a God he has no conception of. His God is impersonal and requires no specific set of beliefs, or demands special codes of life. His understanding of good and evil is determined according to whether the conditions are to his favour or to his disadvantage. He might commit mistakes towards fellow men, but not against God. The closest we come in the Mongwande language according to Benjamin Lekens' *Ngbandi Dictionary* is *sia yè*, which means "to do wrong" or "make a mistake" or "be at fault" (Lekens 1952). Adding the word *li*, which has many meanings but in this context means "he", yields *li sia ye* and is the phrase most commonly used to denote someone having sinned. But this expression is really not that a person has committed sin. It is more that he has allowed himself or even been tricked into making a mistake. If a Mongwande does something wrong, it is not his fault. It is always other people, circumstances or outside forces that have been the real reason. As there is no concrete word for sin in the Mongwande language, there must be an approximate interpretation. It is more a behavioural and ethical matter rather than a spiritual one which will reflect upon one's soul. A Mongwande may wrong his fellow citizen, but never God. And of course, he cannot be judged by an impersonal force he knows nothing about. But does that necessarily lead to the conclusion that the Mongwande is a sinful person? No, absolutely not! In his view, he has not sinned against God and hence does not anticipate to be dragged before a divine judgement.

2.7.7 Animism

In his *Primitive Culture* (1871), Edward Burnet Tylor was the first who cohesively worked out the idea of animism (from Latin *anima*). He argues that religion began with the concept of the soul. However, his theories have been contested by later scholars. In his book *Animismus* (2004), Lothar Käser defines animism as a strategy of man to answer the questions and solve the problems of everyday life (2004:33). He contends that animism is not primarily a religion, but a worldview with its cultural system (2004:27). It is "a belief in the existence and efficacy of spiritual beings" (2004:21). These spiritual beings can be seen as "spiritual doubles" and as "seats of emotions, intellect and character" (SEIC) of the human body ("souls"), as well as "spiritual doubles" of objects ("spirits") (2004:107ff, 177ff). Another basic concept in animism is *mana*. It is "the unexpectedly efficient," a special explanation of the law of cause and effect. The term comes from Melanesia and was introduced into cultural anthropology by R. H. Codrington. When objects are filled with mana through rituals, they become particularly efficient and are called "fetishes" or plainly "medicine" (Käser 2004:71ff).

Is this general theory of animism applicable to the snake cult? The human "soul" which is called *tolo* (Molet 1979:40) or *toro* (Lekens 1952:326) has a very personal feature in that *toro* is among other things referred to in ancestor worship. When a Mongwande turns to his deceased grandfather, he believes he is actually communicating with his deceased personal grandfather's soul. Furthermore, the term *tolo / toro* is never applied to any other of the above mentioned "souls" or "spirits" such as *Banga*, *Ketua* or *Bekpa*. These latter are "nature spirits" wheras *tolo* or *toro* are "human souls." The only exception to this is when *tolo / toro* is applied to the "soul" of the snake *ngbo*. It is this *ngbo* aspect of *tolo* and the human aspect of *tolo* which unite and appear in the twins. As we have seen, "spirits" are everywhere, in the woods, in rivers and even particular trees. But, as I understand it, the human aspect of *tolo*, as discussed above, has a parallel in what Käser talks about regarding the "spiritual double" in humans. (Käser 2004:195).

The deceased play an important role among the Mongwande. They are objects of prayers and supplications. The living beings do whatever they can in order to obtain favours from the dead. They expect help from their ancestors whenever life gets too hard for them. For this reason, they build a little hut *nda-tolo* "house of the souls of the ancestors." Normally, the father performs the ceremony which takes place outside the hut. The ceremonies consist of prayers, singing and dancing. And when one desires rain, water is thrown on the ground. Waving a fish up in the air expresses a wish of good catch of fish. In the absence of a father, it is the eldest son in the family who conducts it. This little dwelling for the spirits was extremely important in the life of the Mongwande. All decisions are taken in front of it. Before going out hunting or fishing, they call upon their ancestors in front of the house to ensure a good result. In any case, it is important to be aware of the fact that the spirits of their ancestors are different from those of the forest and the fields in the eyes of the Mongwande. These observations lead me to the conclusion that the Mongwande religious system with its snake cult fulfills the conditions defining it as animism.

2.7.8   Good and Evil Spirits

The Mongwande had, as previously stated, a sort of distant relationship to the Supreme Being. Their observance of the many spirits around them, however, was more direct. Some of the spirits were of great importance, others of lesser significance. The nature of these spirits could be both good and evil. The *likundu* (m) were evil. They were quite receptive to all kinds of supplications and offerings which were given with the intention of getting them to yield to the person's mood and wishes. There were spirits that were bound to special topographical areas and named thereafter, such as spirits of the woods or forests, spirits of rivers, spirits of particular trees, spirits of hills, like *bagboli* in Monga. The second syllable, *mboli*, is also, strangely enough, a god in the Azande language, according to C. G. Seligman in the foreword to E. E. Evans-Pritchard's *Witchcraft, Oracles and Magic among the Azande* (1963). Evans-Pritchard also asserts that *mboli* most likely is a more recent intruder into the Azande language (Evans-Pritchard 1963:11). But the word *mboli* is also used in Mongwande. Halfway between Monga and Bondo there is a village named Mboli, "the village of God." The village is situated in the Azande territory. We, however, lived in Monga which is Mongwande territory. Yet, the hill we lived on is named Bagboli: "the hill of God." E. E. Evans-Pritchard describes *Mboli* as a Supreme God who has created the earth. In the translation of the Bible into the Mongwande and the Azande languages, both *Nzapa* and *Mboli* are used respectively as the name of God. The Mongwande and the Azande agreed that *Nzapa* (m) and *Nzambe* (li) were identical, having the same attributes, but different names.

In addition to the local spirits, there are spirits connected to persons, e.g. *motu na likundu* "a person with an evil spirit." The medicine man was often referred to as *motu na likundu* "a man with evil spirits." But ordinary people in the village might also be carriers of good or evil spirits, and with that also good and evil powers (Burssens 1958:135). One particularly great spirit was *Ketua*. This was the most popular spirit after the Supreme Being *Nzapa*. Then followed *Yayu* "heaven," *Sese* "earth," *Gegi* "atmosphere" and *Gogo, Mbongo* and *Banga* (1958:132). The spirits of the river were great in the eyes of the Mongwande. *Bomba* and *Sangu* were the spirits of the streams. *Bekpa* was the spirit of the waterfalls. He revealed himself from time to time as a rainbow and was also called *Congo*. There are also traces of two vengeful spirits *Yangba* and *Banda*. *Yangba* causes sickness in men and *Banda* poisons fish so they become inedible. With all these spirits the Mongwande religious system fulfills the criteria for being an animistic system.

Kilima (m) / *motu na mai* (li) was the real spirit of importance and the lord of the rivers. According to my informants Pierre Geru and Ernst Yanzere, *kaina* (m) was the spirit of the forest. If somebody drowned in the river, he was captured by *Kilima*, and if someone disappeared in the forest, he had been enticed by *Kaina* and just vanished. Other spirits were *Banga* (m) and *Gazoroma* (m) and *Yenda* (m). The Mongwande sometimes took their names after *Banga* spirits, as *Ge-banga*, *Ya-banga*, *Li-banga* and *Ke-banga*. Tanghe writes about the two words *mbongo* (m) and *banga* (li) as having their etymological origin from the rivers Mbomu and Uélé (Tanghe 1929:238). I never heard *mbongo* mentioned at Monga, but *banga* was a common name denoting fear and awe (Moen 2005).

Animal worship was well known among the Mongwande. There are traces of worship of both the leopard and the crocodile (Molet 1965:158). The common belief was that the soul of the chiefs and elders dwelt among these animals, especially in the leopards, *koi* (li) (Tanghe 1930:78-82). In a cult like the snake cult, the belief that the souls of deceased chiefs and elders dwelt in animals was not so prevalent. This cultic phenomenon was superseded by the greatness of the snake which was worshipped and venerated on all occasions. In the eyes of the Mongwande, the rainbow was identical to the twins, that is the snake children, and hence the snake, but not an ordinary snake, but rather as a sort of a sea serpent, almost like a dragon. This dragon or sea serpent had a red belly and a black back. And according to the Mongwande way of thinking, the colouring gives the rainbow-snake a two-pronged or dual appearance like the twins. Jean Leyder interprets this as a myth that has passed from generation to generation (Leyder 1935:39-44). He asserts, as I understand him, that there are a myriad of associations and ideas which govern the rites and the liturgy at the snake cult performances.

In figure 1, I have attempted to map out the general pantheon, myths and important elements of the Mongwande religious life. We see how a group of myths and spirits are coordinated within the Mongwande religious framework. First of all, we find a basic religious foundation A. Upon this foundation, the snake cult B-F raises its head and cuts through the tribe's various spiritual phenomena E-G, D-H, C-I. These spiritual forces are encroaching on the cult at the same time as they are exercising independent religious-spiritual activity.

Figure 1: Mongwande Religion

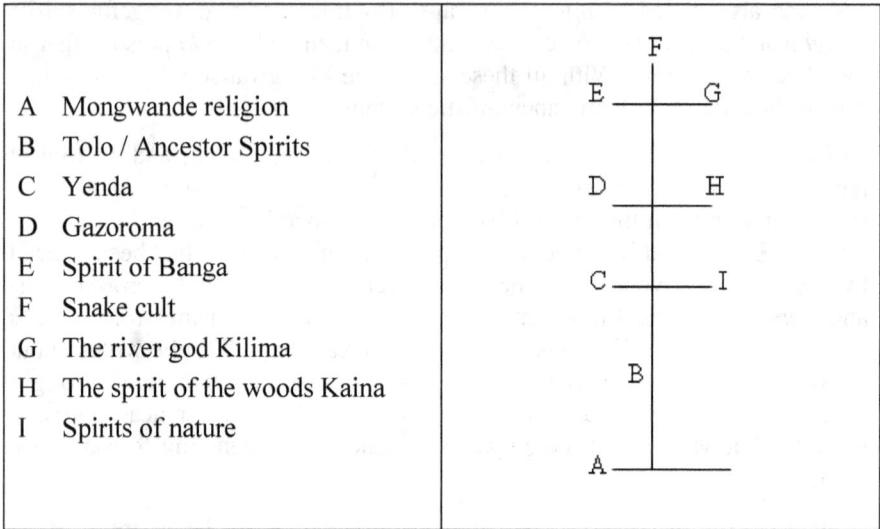

A Mongwande religion	
B Tolo / Ancestor Spirits	
C Yenda	
D Gazoroma	
E Spirit of Banga	
F Snake cult	
G The river god Kilima	
H The spirit of the woods Kaina	
I Spirits of nature	

(Diagram on right side showing vertical line with labels: F at top, E—G, D—H, C—I, B, A at bottom)

2.7.9 Mongwande Magic

There are normally three aspects of magic: the rite, the ritual condition of the performer and the incantation (Encyclopaedia Britannica 1988:25:88-91). These elements are believed to have supernatural power which causes super-natural forces or beings to produce or prevent a particular result such as rain, death or healing that cannot be obtained through natural means (Webster's Dictionary 1988:1:1358). Is magic religion? Is religion magic? Käser says that magic is the antithesis of religion: whereas in religion man submits to the invisible world, in magic man tries to manipulate the invisible world. In magic, objects are filled with mana and thus become very efficient, "unexpectedly efficient" (Käser 2004:79-83).

Käser is referring to the Bantu concept *ndoki* to show the typological similar-ity between *mana* and *ndoki* (Käser 2004:72). As far as I know, the expres-sions that signify almost the same functions in the Congo are *kindoki* (Sundberg 2000:46) and *likundu* (Moen 2005). According to Käser, the con-ception of *mana* is linked with magic in that both can manipulate and use a particular situation to its own advantage.

In his book *Religion og Kultus, Land og Kirke* (1971), Professor Sigmund Mow-inckel says: "The magic view is the most characteristic of primitive reality." This assertion is very often misused. Magic is understood partly as the initial stage of religion, and partly more or less identical with witchcraft and as a de-praved concurrent of religion. Both allegations are wrong. The magic view and its application in practice is not a religion, but it is a world and life view. It is a definite method to comprehend different objects and their coherence. It is a *Weltanschauung* or worldview that somehow corresponds with the reality view we try to formulate today based on laws of causality within physics, chemistry and psychology. Some researchers see magic as the primitives' attempt to create science. I am not sure if we should adopt the above mentioned assertions. But the point is that religion and magic are sometimes merging in a way that degenerate both religion and magic. Professor Mowinckel continues: "As each religion is determined in its expressions by its executers' reality view, it should be a matter of course that forms of old religions contain much of magic reality view and magic practice." But this isn't anything that has its root in the nature of magic. It is one thing however which magic has in common with religion, and specifically with religion as a cultic act, and that is that their objective is to produce effects which man cannot create himself. If magic means an action with intended supernatural effect, then every cultic act contains an element of magic. In this case we may talk about religious magic (Kristensen 1947). And Mowinckel supports this: "If magic also contains or even requires elements of a personal attitude to reality, then the same could be said about religion and religious act. At this point they are both expressions of a reality attitude that is far more in accordance with the laws of life than any spectator's attitude."

It seems to me that Professor Mowinckel is commuting between a scientific view and a biblical view as to the understanding of magic and religion. In some definite situations, he seems to assert that magic and religion have nothing in common. But then on the other side, he admits that there might be a common ground for them both, namely the intended effect which humans cannot bring about on their own. In their practice magic and religion have similarities, namely changing one substance into another, healing people, and exorcism. From this, we see it might be difficult to clearly differentiate between the two phenomena. Perhaps religious rites are just different ways of expressing one's beliefs, expressions of faith that concern the relationship between man and God, the relationship among humans and mankind's relationship with nature. In contrast, magic would then be an intended supernatural act towards a target, a target that exists out of reach for ordinary people. If we search a little further into magic and religion, we will find several points of resemblance between the two: They are both answers to many of the enigmas of life. They are means to helping people during times of difficulties, in sickness and death. They elevate, coordinate and enrich certain social values. When we study the functions of magic and religion we might from time to time make a distinction between them. This is the case for evangelicals who diffentiate an anthropocentric, animistic worldview which uses magic to manipulate its world to its own ends from a theocentric, biblical worldview which submits to God, creator and sustainer of the universe, who guides man to His ends.

The magical rites among the Mongwande are essentially concentrated around the superhuman forces such as the snake, *tolo*, *kilima* or astral bodies. The ceremonies are full of personal feelings with accompanying dances and ecstatic experiences. The vehicles or means of transference during the séances are both verbal oaths and concrete physical objects such as stone, wood artefacts and colours. It could be a matter of healing or a wish of full immersion in the supposed deity. According to Käser, the performer of the magic manipulates and takes power over the object of magic. This is clearly illustrated in the example of Yoyo.

Yoyo was a smith by profession and a very good one. Everything went well with Yoyo until his wife passed away. He got a new wife and life was good again. But all of a sudden he fell ill and word spread that no medicine, neither African nor European, could help him. He slowly withered away. I was asked to go and see him. Upon entering his house, I noticed that he was lying with his head in the wife's lap. I spoke with him and he told me that he was prepared to go to his ancestors. When I asked him if there was anything he regretted, he replied that he had no remorse whatsoever. Very shortly thereafter he died. The epicrisis stated: Cause of illness and death unknown. I felt that there was more to it than that and started investigating the case.

My inquiry was not in vain. The new wife he had acquired was in fact another man's wife. This man lived deep in the woods by a little lake named *mai na molimo* "the lake of spirits." The man had demanded his wife back but she wouldn't leave Yoyo. Yoyo came up with several solutions to the problem. But to no avail! In order to put an end to the matter once and for all, Yoyo bought a red piece of clothing, wrapped a certain amount of money in it and sent it to the woman's "first" husband. He, however, was infuriated and asked the elders in the town counsel for advice. They recommended that he go and throw the money and the cloth into the lake of spirits (*mai na molimo*) and then send the message to the perpetrator that "as the cloth is rotting in the water so shall you, Yoyo, rot to death." The man accepted the advice of the elders and did what they had told him to do. Yoyo received word of the curse and slowly but surely died.

How can we explain Yoyo's death? In this story, one might argue that the motif of revenge lay at the core. The original husband had been humiliated and hurt and was looking for a way to even the score. Looking back at Käser's assertion that the performer takes power over the victim, we can see how Yoyo succumbed to the will of the performer and the effect of the magic. In Western medicine, one might explain this in psychological terms, for example that Yoyo felt that he had done something wrong and felt so bad about it that he willed himself to death. However, from the Mongwande cosmological point of view, there were many reasons for his death, not just psychological or even medical or physical ones. Their belief, to my understanding, was that the curse had the desired effect, precisely as defined above in this section, a certain ritual was performed and a message conveyed, i.e. a spell was cast. The woman's real husband was vengeful and filled with rage. He had power to get supernatural forces (or beings) to bring death to Yoyo. Whenever I discussed Yoyo's death with his neighbours, they were all very insistent that spiritual powers were the sole reason for his death.

2.7.10 Symbolic World of the Mongwande

The word "symbol" is Greek and consists of the verb *ballo* "to throw" and the prefix *sym-* which means "together," forming the word *symballo* meaning "to throw together." The noun is *to symbolon* which means "a mark, token, sign." In the Greek world, for instance, a couple who was going to be separated for a long time could give each other particular signs of recognition. And a judge would receive a special sign when he entered the courthouse, and he got his payment when he returned it when leaving.

The word has its place in the science of religions as well as in the social sciences and linguistics. Today, it represents all kinds of signs, identifications and legitimizations which carry a common meaning independent of one concrete situation. Today, a whole world of symbols has emerged, particularly within religions. There are signs, marks, emblems, pictures, objects, items, even acts that have some connotative or denotative meaning. They have meanings beyond that which meets the eye. A symbol is abstract. The human being's ability to abstract and generalize is fully met in the function of the symbols. The church is full of symbols: the lamb is an image of the pious, patient and suffering Christ. The cross is an image of Christianity, baptism an image of death and resurrection, and communion is a symbol of fellowship with Christ and the congregation.

But there are symbolic signs and actions also in the profane world. For instance, the handshake between a seller and a buyer is a symbol of agreement. Human beings are surrounded by symbols and we may say that we live by symbols. This world of symbols is not unique for the western world. The Africans, and in our case the Mongwande, also live in a multitude of symbols. I have already touched on the concept of *ngbò*, but I feel that we need further research into the role of symbols in the life of the Mongwande generally and their religious life specifically. We know that symbols bring us knowledge about ourselves and open deeper dimensions of culture. We find language full of symbols. We know that some people cannot read but understand a simple sign. The sign carries the onlooker over into the wordless world, and the situation is understood.

The importance of symbols cannot be understated. Symbols can be more effective than the spoken or written word. This we can say as long as we are talking about the Western-European culture, but this cannot be said about

countries which do not have a written language. The Mongwande society is
such a culture. It was the traders and the missionaries who gathered and studies tribal languages in the Congo and presented them to the people. It was in
this way that the Mongwande language and other languages such as Sango,
Kikongo, Tshiluba, Kiswhaheli and Lingala, got a written form of expression.
The languages were transcribed into Latin characters and the Mongwande got
a complete new world of symbols which they had to learn. Before the introduction of the written language, the Mongwande were surrounded by a multitude of symbols, the meaning of which is deeply rooted in the Mongwande
people. These symbols never reached the stage of developing a literary form
as for example the Egyptian hieroglyphs or the Chinese characters. These
symbols and its message are mostly psycho-religious intended to help people
in time of difficulty. While working with the symbols that one doesn't know
the meaning of, one might get a feeling of distance, and what one might obtain
as information runs the risk of being superficial.

We usually interpret symbols according to what we see or read into them.
Observing an image or symbol in one context might yield a different meaning
than if it is seen in another context. Symbols have to be interpreted differently
according to the context they are in. But that is not all. Apart from the question
of context, there is another dimension to this problem which regards the item
or symbol itself on the one hand and the meaning or cognitive concept which
we attach to the item or symbol on the other hand. Figurative designs do not
have a meaning by themselves, whether geometric designs, visually depicted
letters or images. They are independent and self-representing as Emanuel
Kant's *Ding an sich* and not an intermediary of an irrevocable interpretation. It
is when we humans latch a meaning or a cognitive concept to them that they
have a meaning for us. If we are to go further with Kant's postulation, the
conclusion will be that we interpret the symbols according to our own understanding but that the *Ding an sich* is and will be impenetrable. What is important is to find the right code or the context at the time the figure was made.

It is just that which is making our interpretation of the petrographs from the
Stone Age or the stone carving in the Uélé area so difficult. One observes
carvings of men, trees, boats, depressions of feet and curly lines on the rock.
But what do they mean? We acknowledge that the figures might have their
own peculiarity. But we also know that the same figures or symbols might
mean something else placed in another setting. The context is decisive for the
right comprehension of the symbols. This is especially the case in the symbols
of language where the correspondence of sound (the spoken word), visual
representation (the written word) and concept yield meaning.

A good example of diversion into interpretation in the snake cult is the iron
cross which to a Mongwande is a representation of *ngbo* but to a European

could be construed as a Christian cross as is illustrated by André Scohy's dialogue with the Uélé people, i.e. the tribes who live between the Uélé river and the Mbomu river. The historians contend that the Mongwande and Azande have a common origin. Both wandered down south from the Sudan to the Ango district. In 1914, an engineer found strange engravings on some rock beds in this region. In 1949, André Scohy came to the area and found the same stone carvings. He wrote the book *L'Uélé secret*, dealing with this topic in a chapter he calls *Vers les signes mystérieux du mont Ngondu*, "Towards the mysterious carvings at the Ngondu Mountain" (Scohy 1955:86-100). The carvings had neither been described nor photographed before. Scohy asked the people: "Who made the carvings?" The answer they gave him was that God made them. "Isn't it your ancestors?" Scohy replied. "No, these figures were here long before our ancestors arrived." "Well, if that is the case, then it must be the people who were here before your forefathers?" "No, God made them at the time he created the earth." Scohy observed a cross among the engravings and asked: "Did they at that time know the cross?" "No, it is not the Christian cross. It is just a toy!" "What are all the different figures?" "They just indicate the articles for every day's use in olden days!" "What about all the depressions?" "These were used by the women when they were making bread." "There is a line there, what is that for?" "That is a river." We notice that the people in the area have rather straight forward answers to these questions. The text does not indicate that they do not attach any deeper understanding to the markings. Perhaps Scohy accepted their explanations at face value and did not search for a deeper meaning. I intended to interview these people but was unfortunately hindered by the war of independence (in the 1960s). If I had had the opportunity to go up there, I would have asked them about the curved lines. I would have asked them about the snake cult. Couldn't the curved lines be reflecting the snake cult? They told Scohy that they indicated rivers. It seems that Scohy didn't know anything about the snake cult. If he had known, he would certainly have asked the group. If he had asked them, they certainly would have refused any knowledge of it, because the snake cult in the Uélé area was a well kept secret.

To understand symbols and to interpret them correctly has been for me a recurrent theme. They appear in many different ways and can be interpreted in more than one way. Let us begin with the self-referential symbols or metaphors. Here we have the symbol as a picture or reflection for example of oneself. Basically, all symbols are reflections or references to what we wish and what we make of them. Above we have noticed that the people at Angou interpret the engravings according to what they think. The engravings are very old, no doubt, at least 3-4000 years, and were there when the Mongwande / Azande arrived in the 17-18th century. The figures appeal to our fantasy, but figuratively they are just *Ding an sich*: feet, circles, depressions, crosses, lines, needles, axes, etc. It seems difficult to reach any definitive interpretation concerning the symbols. We will have to give up all these speculations and rather launch into the question of how symbols relate to the Mongwande society. What role do the symbols play both individually and collectively? What is the meaning of the symbols for the village, socially, politically, and religiously? In order to answer a question of this kind, one will have to analyze the elements of the various symbolic phenomena.

I think that we should start with the symbolic meaning of colour. Red (*bengba* and *mbio*) was highly estimated among the Mongwande. Black was also used, but never to the degree as red and white. The colours were used in magico-religious situations, but also as decoration and as status symbol. My own research and observations strengthened my first impression that the colours were not only used with great pomp and ceremony, but were a symbol of the actual situation which could not be described with words. The two colours red and white were the main colours used in the symbolism identifying persons, roles or situations. It was not always easy to understand the colour's message. And one colour could have more than one meaning.

For example, the colour red clearly identified a woman as the chieftain's wife. If she put red on her body, all the participants could clearly see and understand that she was his wife. It was a sign of dignity. No one could touch these women. The message of the symbol could not be misinterpreted. A male who tried to excuse himself by saying that he did not understand the sign, would simply not be believed. In addition to being an identifier of the chieftain's wife, red signified also death and sometimes life. White was a symbol for life and good health. The colour black always meant death. So, in order to avoid conflict with the forces of life and death at the funeral, both colours were applied. The colour white was applied on pregnant women, signifying life and also signifying that the woman did not carry any evil spirit. White was also used as a colour during moon festivities.

The Mongwande are surrounded by a multitude of symbols in their daily life. Almost everything the Mongwande says or does is controlled by the invisible world. The Mongwande have many objects that have no power in themselves, but represent an invisible authority. The objects vary, such as the magic ash that is made every new moon, or relics from the ancestors, snake sticks, entangled plaits from skin or fibre or wooden sticks.

2.7.11 The Medicine Man and Healing Methods

I had a long interview with Kebanga, the medicine man. He came and put before me all his paraphernalia, fetishes, medicines, magic means, head dress, neck decoration and shoulder bandoleer. It was an unforgettable encounter. He agreed to demonstrate some of his instruments and answer my questions. The séance that Kebanga allowed me to watch turned out to be an experience of great value. Kebanga was a *wa kokoro* (m) or *motu na dawa* (li), a medicine man. He was also a former leader of the snake ceremonies. The medicine man who leads the worship, and the name giving ceremony in particular, was a very central figure. The position as the leader of the snake ceremonies was coveted by many medicine men. However, there were also many laymen and laywomen who claimed to be speaking on behalf of the snake, claiming the position as the spokesperson of the ceremony.

Though, I think Kebanga may have considered some of them irrelevant, I did take the opportunity to ask a number of questions while I participated as an observer at the séance to which he invited me. For instance, I asked him whether this was real or not. He didn't give a clear answer. But observing his rituals, I sensed that he believed that the borders between the real world and the unreal world faded. There was no point in asking him why he had become a medicine man or why people had believed in him and had been seeking his help. These questions were in his eyes irrelevant. But he did explain that it was the way of the world, the capriciousness of rivers and forests, sickness and death that prompted people to ask for help. That is why he became a medicine man. He had knowledge of good and evil spirits, about trees and herbs applicable as medicine. He was in control of forces that were out of reach for ordinary humans. His instruments, charms, amulets and tools were consecrated to give advice and allusion to success or misfortune, good health and illness, hunting and fishing, protection against sickness and crop failure, message about life and death. While my interest in his activity was merely theoretical, from his point of view it was practical. However, I found no reason to doubt his explanations. He was beyond a shadow of a doubt the religious centre of the Mongwande people. He represented good spirits and evil spirits and a formidable snake that ruled the world on the top of all these forces. Based on this authority he had an enormous influence. Kebanga used external stimuli, such as drugs or drums, in order to attain a state of ecstasy in which he could converse with the spirit world. And he communicated with spirits other than those of deceased people, i.e. nature spirits, power animals, etc. This last point sets him apart from what is classically attributed to the medium who normally does not talk to nature spirits as such, but rather to ancestor spirits (Käser 2004:277-296).

After having presented and discussed some elements of Mongwande culture in general, we will now turn our attention to the snake cult, a specific dimension of Mongwande culture.

2.8 The Snake Cult

2.8.1 The Concepts of Cult and Culture

The root-word of cult and culture is the Latin word *colo, colui, cultus* "to cultivate." The Latin word *culter* means "knife" or "plough share point" (Mørland 1990:143). The twofold meaning of knife (sacrificial knife) or plough share point for the cultivation of a field has given rise to two different concepts: cult and culture. The one meaning involves sacrifice and worship being the basic meaning of the term "cult," while the other denotes "cultivation" being at the basis of the concept of "culture." Today the word cult is used generally for ritual ceremonies that are associated with some form of worship of a deity or a spirit. The cult is an expression of worship, adoration and devotion. The characteristic of the cult is the devotion to a deity. This means also that the worshipper puts all his/her faith and obedience in the object for his veneration, meaning that the devotee feels that he stands in a specific cultic relationship with his deity. He experiences also that he has been a recipient of the Spirit and a participant in the holy goal, namely ecstasy, and has hence become part of the cult.

The word cult represents a rather small part of the cultural life of a society, and thus a small part of the semantic domain of the notion of "culture." There are many definitions of culture. In a literature survey up to 1950, Kroeber and Kluckhohn mention 164 definitions. According to Käser, culture can be defined as a comprehensive set of strategies developed by a people group to cope with everyday problems (Käser 1997:35).

In my opinion, the snake cult falls under both definitions I have briefly presented above: it is at the same time a cult (worship) and part of Mongwande culture. The Mongwande experience the snake cult séances as powerful and helpful. They feel that the cult gives them a feeling of fellowship. If it was not so, how could it be that the cult had been around for such a long time?

2.8.2 Mongwande Religious Expressions in the Snake Cult

Let us now take a look into the different elements of Mongwande religious expressions within the snake cult. The following list is not comprehensive and will be discussed in detail below: 1) ancestors' altar and worship of household gods (cf. Gen 31:19: Rachel stealing her father's household gods); 2) moon worship, the skin of the moon. The snake casts its skin and so does the moon; 3) worship of the ashes. The ashes are magic; they contain poison and kill; 4) the spirit of Banga is poisoning fish so it becomes inedible; 5) ancestor spirits; 6) worship of the rainbow; 7) *Yenda-Gazoroma*: the "snake god"; 8) the twins-birth's blood; 9) *Kilima*, the river god; 10) *Kaina*, god of the forest; 11) the spirit of a waterfall, of the wind, of the storm, etc.; 12) the snake sticks. The sticks are worshiped and used for property defence; 13) circumcision, a ritual of initiation; 14) *mbeti*, an instrument of divination; 15) amulets, protect against all kinds of evil; 16) roots of divination (Moen 2005:37).

2.8.3 Ngbò – The Snake

The word *ngbo* covers several concepts in the Mongwande language. In order to show these variations, I quote from Benjamin Lekens (1952:282).

Ngbò	snake, intestinal worms
Ngbò	twin(s), something which is glued together
Lala ngbò	young snake
Poso ngbò	empty snake-skin / cast-off skin
Kozo ngbò	the first born of twins
Ngambi ngbò	the second born of twins

Ngbò is the root-word and is translated respectively either as "snake" or "twin" providing that the accent is right. But *ngbò* may indicate a lot of other meanings, not only the meaning of twin and serpent. In some connections, it even refers to colours, like red, brown and yellow, or expressions as height, depth, width, enclosure or entrance, and outskirt of a village. The word is therefore open to interpretations. But, the word *ngbò* is mainly a collective word applied to all kinds of serpents in the Mongwande language. The meaning of *ngbò* as serpent is revealed by the accent. When we talk about the snake cult, we are referring to the *ngbò* concept which in the eyes of the Mongwande covers the whole cult in its entirety. *Ngbò* is a cultic word that can be compared with the Greek word *exousia* meaning "power" and "authority" in a religious context (Rom 13:1; Lk 23:7) (Foerster 1985:238-240). *Ngbò* is hence an ontological notion held by its believers to be a living, powerful sphere. It is characterized by its *ontos* "being" (pres. part. of the Greek verb *einai*) and can be summed up in the assertion "it is what it is." I have deliberately brought the verb *einai* into this discussion knowing full well of its theological nature, but it is the one word that clearly expresses what the Momgwande mean when they are talking about the character of the snake cult. The Mongwande snake cult is a folk religious element and as such has a deeper religious meaning that must be interpreted according to the methodology of the science of religions.

As I understand Paul G. Hiebert, in order to really grasp the idea of the host culture, missionaries will sometimes have to apply a wide variety of tools (Hiebert 1985). In relation to the snake cult, I reasoned that it would be useful to employ the concept of *exousia*, because I noticed that *ngbò* and *exousia* have similar functions. They both exercise their power within a certain framework: *ngbo* at the time of the birth of the twins and *exousia* at the time of conversion. These two great events are regarded as the foremost elements in these two religions, the snake cult and Christianity. The form of the snake cult is somewhat easy to discover but the real basic meaning of the said cult is not that easy to get hold of. The deeper meaning of the snake cult may be difficult to explain. There are several pivotal details one must consider. The snake cult does not offer salvation from sin. Neither does it promise heaven upon death. But clearly, it has served those who have come under its dominion in some way. The birth of twins is a testimony to its place in the Mongwande psyche. There is no doubt that the followers of the cult, according to their own testimonies, get answers to their prayers. However, it stands to reason that the basic meaning of the snake cult only concerns terrestrial desires. The twins are born in the name of the snake. They live and act within the sphere of *ngbò* as the Christian does within the sphere of the *exousia* of God. The twins remain there until the name giving celebration. Already when they are born, the twins are intertwined within a mystical magnetic power centre, and they are from the very beginning objects of an intense attention. The birth of twins is a biological mystery which cannot be explained by the Mongwande as anything other than an act of the snake. It is the snake that has brought these two snakes / twins into the world. From that angle, the cult gives identity to the father and the mother. It is interesting to note that even if it brings joy to the family, it also brings sorrow. The birth of twins signifies that the snake has been visiting the village.

The twins are identified according to their special status being two and not one as normally is the case for human children. Lekens suggests that they are called *ngbò* because they are born one after the other, or as he puts it in his vocabulary "entwined or bound together or double fruit" (Lekens 1952:282). The closed area around the house of the chief is also called *ngbò*. That area is usually thought of as sacred. Likewise, the cleared and orderly area of the village distinguishes it from the chaotic and hostile world outside. *Ngbò* also implies colour as mentioned above. Red is originally negative and bad, but may sometimes be appraised as positive. Blood is an integral part in ritual offerings as metaphor for cleansing. The word *ngbò* is therefore, put in the right context and tone, applied to a series of situations in the daily life of the Mongwande.

The ambiguous aspect of the theme at hand when using the word *ngbò* cannot be denied, says Molet, and refers as evidence to the following quotation: *Ya mbi adu angbò ose* "my wife has laid two snakes", instead of saying: "my wife has given birth to twins" (Molet 1970:49). In this case, the husband was so disappointed with his wife and the newly born twins that he did not call it a birth but rather laying eggs, an expression of contempt. This feeling of contempt is a recurrent theme in the snake songs.

The twins' name is automatically *ngbò* which means "snake children." This is affirmed by the fact that twins are considered as *ngbò* at the moment of their birth and they remain in the realm of *ngbò* until the name giving ceremony. At that feast they are intitiated into the community and given civilian names (Moen 1961). Molet writes:

> *Ngbò* "snake" and *ngbò* "twins" are anomalies. Snakes living in the forest are dangerous. Even though they have no wings and legs, their ability to move is formidable. They are poisonous creatures that strike their victims with great precision. They represent the powers of nature over which the inhabitants of the village have no control. Similarly, the twins are abnormal because they are two instead of one. They stand outside the normal order of the world. The birth of twins causes confusion and upsets the right order of inheritance. The right of the first born, being one of the basic elements in the history of man, is in jeopardy. The twins compromise the balance of society. The birth of twins is as great a danger inside the village as the menacing snake is outside. *Ngbò* is a monster, a materialization of disorder and concretisation of things abnormal (Molet 1970:51).

Therefore, when twins are born, the Mongwande react with repulsion and disdain, or is at least careful. The entire family into which the twins are born is included in the *ngbò* sphere and thus called "snake family." The mother (*ta*) and the father (*to*) are considered snakes and usually socialize with other snake families. None of the parents are particularly happy. Rather they feel sorrow which they try their best to ignore, or at best they try to console each other. The name giving festival, when the transformation from animal to human status takes place, will therefore be arranged as soon as possible.

2.8.4 Tolo Akotara and Tolo Ngbo: Ancestral Soul and Snake Soul

Tolo in Mongwande means "soul, force, shadow, picture or image." *Tolo* is the main feature in the Mongwande religious psychology. The Mongwande are undoubtedly animists. Everything is imbued with mystical forces that the Mongwande try to control by their magic. The whole world is animated by spirits, good and evil. The souls (*tolo*) of deceased persons might be helpful, but they can also be nasty and can hurt those who come under their power. Items belonging to the deceased are also powerful and could spiritually rule the village and the family through mediators like the sorcerers and sorceresses. The invisible powers of their forefathers also play an important role in nearly every situation of life and death (Molet 1956:36-41, 145-157). Ancestral worship was well known in Mongwande land. The forefathers provided all good things. The soul of the ancestors (*tolo akotara*) was the Mongwande denotation of the deceased's spirit. According to their belief, all of nature was animated by all kinds of spirits, but also the ancestors, the "living dead," existed in a mysterious way and conveyed messages for good or evil to their kin by dreams, hallucinations, imaginations, reflections and unexpected events.

Eventhough the term *tolo*, a "spirit double", appears in connection with humans, it is used also in reference to snakes. Consider the following expressions: *tolo akotara* "the soul of the ancestors" and *tolo ngbo* "the soul of the snake." But why snakes, when twins are born? Is it the double tongue of the snake or is it a mysterious inheritance from the Garden of Eden, as Tanghe purports? (1926). Whatever the reason, the birth of twins jeopardizes the entire power structure of the village. That is to say, because twins are snakes they assume supreme command in a village and surpass the chieftain in all matters regarding the execution of authority. Moreover, the father of the twins is called *tó ngbo* "snake father" and the mother is called *ta ngbo* "snake mother." I will say more below about various aspects of the snake cult and the twins, such as the relationship between nature and culture, the rites of passage, snake songs, the name giving ceremony, and the master of the snake cult ceremony.

2.8.5 Magic Ashes

The magic ashes serve both medicinal function (a poison for arrows) and as symbol of power. The person who has the magic ashes has power over the spirits. Let me recount a story which says something of the power of the ashes. One person had magic ashes in his possession and another had his twin snake children. They started a conflict one day. They both were strong believers in their own symbol. Most of the villagers though believed that the snake would win. To their surprise, the authority was pushed over from the snake to the *ndibere* "the ashes." How did they know that? They were able to know because one of the twins, a snake child, died. The snake had lost. The power of the ashes was greater than the power of the snake children.

The ashes were produced through a very intricate process during the New Moon. It is believed that the power of the regenerating moon imbues the ashes with spiritual power, rendering it capable of manipulating reality. The ashes have been filled with mana; they have become a "fetish" (Käser 2004:80-83). The ashes are a symbol of power and authority. They are used as a medicine, but can also cause bad luck as in this case. These magic ashes were renewed at full moon when the moon beams merged like snakes on the top of the trees. The Mongwande compared the moon with snakes: as the snake casts off its skin, so also did the moon. The moon-skin was actually *mica* and bestowed good fortune on anyone who found some lying on the ground. *Mica* contained *dawa makasi* "strong medicine" and could protect the owner from all kind of evil.

2.8.6 Snake Sticks

The most prominent symbol or fetish in the Mongwande society were undoubtedly the snake sticks. They are called *tolo ngbo* which as you might notice is the same name as the "soul of the snake." These sticks are put up at certain places. The bark is flaked off in such a pattern as to give the sticks the appearance of a snake. The symbolism of theses sticks is quite apparent. The communicative meaning is direct and cognitively easily understood by those who belong to the social and religious group of which this form and meaning is an integral part. In short, the snake cult worshippers see in the snake sticks snakes. This might raise the question about what role the snake plays in the human reproductive process when twins are born. Is it pure symbolism or has the snake been in direct physical contact with the parents, the father or the mother?

2.8.7 Name Giving Ceremony

The name giving ceremony of twins will be exemplified through the following story. A nice young couple had recently become Christians and joined the church. They had three children and she was pregnant and expected another one. When she delivered, she brought not just one child but twins to this world. They brought the twins to the church to be prayed for. But when this was done, they returned to their village where a big name giving festival took place! Why did they do that? Had the traditional snake cult still not lost its grip? And what happened at that ceremony? I was present to observe.

First of all, I noticed that the main focus of attention was on the twins. The next pivotal character was the medicine man. He was the head of the ceremony and supervised the entire performance, making sure that everything was executed according to the old traditions. He had all his paraphernalia with him. The people were considered guests. They were supposedly called upon in order to bring authority and dignity to the occasion. They brought with them gifts of all kinds: chickens, eggs, meat and fish. I could not avoid observing that whatever they presented to the twins was in pairs, like two hens, two eggs, two fish and two pieces of meat. I also noticed that the people were painted with red and white, signifying death and life respectively. Likewise, the eggs were cracked open and the white and the yolk was separated and given to the twins. The meaning here was that the twins had been declared pure and clean. The twins were no more snake children but humans. The rite of passage had been executed according to the medicine man's instructions. The snake children's status had changed, from that of snake to human.

I refer in this connection to Mary Douglas' *Purity and Danger* (1966). She argues that anything that is unclear and contradictory in a social setting is regarded as ritually unclean. This must be repaired as soon as possible. She refers to Leviticus 11-16 as the basis for her assertions. People do not like in-between situations, but require straight forward definitions. The indefinable according to Leviticus is not acceptable. What is unclear is impure. The status quo can only be rectified through rituals and ceremonies. I find that Douglas' thoughts along with the teachings in Leviticus are in accordance with my opinion after having observed these Mongwande ceremonies (Douglas 1966).

The question is: What is being done to transfer the twins from their status as animals (snakes) to the status of humans, from nature to culture? As mentioned above, the couple in question belonged to our church and had come to us in order to have the twins blessed and given names! But here they are in the midst of a crowd of people following the liturgies of the medicine man who was the master of the snake ceremony. The chieftain was announcing the civilian names of the twins thus transferring them from animal status to human status. When I asked the couple, "why they had done that," they showed no remorse. They merely did what their ancestors had done from time immemorial. They told me that they love the Christian God, but they could not ignore the old traditions. Of course, this moment in the life of the couple would not easily be forgotten. They were wedged in between the Christian God and the village religiosity.

Here we have not only been witness to what Hiebert calls split-level Christianity but also to a clash between two cultures. Not to mention the bi-cultural identity crisis which new converts may experience (Hiebert 1985:235-240). What did the church do to deal with these kinds of challenges? The answer is that the church did not do anything. At that time (that is in the 1950-1960s), concepts such as contextualization were not known to us in the Congo as means to cope with cultural clashes. The word contextualization was unheard of. And what about the couple, what did they do to cope with the situation? What should the couple do? The matter of fact was that the couple was also ignorant of how to tackle the situation.

Under the guidance of the medicine man, the chief pronounced the names of the twins in the form of an oath and the transference from animal to human took place. I had been witness to a ceremony that was undoubtedly one of the highest possible magical séances in the religious life of the Mongwande tribe. This also made painfully clear to me the reality and enormity of the challenges the missionary faced in terms of contextualizing the Gospel, avoiding split-level Christianity, or its kissing cousin Christopaganism, and helping new converts dealing with the transition between the snake cult and Christian faith.

2.8.8 Iron Snake

The iron snake cross *Yenda-Gazoroma* was presented to me in a village a few miles from Monga. It struck me as a unique piece of worship. It is about 50 cm long and has two pieces of iron like arms stretching out and up from each side of the stick forming almost a cross. The whole stick is formed as a snake. A necklace of iron and a little lump of gold was fastened to the necklace. The end of the stick was pointed, obviously made so in order to be put into earth.

My first question was what the purpose of it was and if it was still in use? I was well informed by the giver who was a new convert. "The use of it, he said, was to put it in earth and to pour oil over it, to hang meat, fish or other things on it, or just to address prayers or chant to its honour." A total worship took place around the stick. It was no doubt among the worshippers that their prayers would be answered and their faith would bear fruit. The new convert insisted quite strongly that the people believed in their worship. I asked him: "Do they really believe?" "Yes, they have faith in their old religious tradition." In the snake songs, we find *Yenda-Gazoroma*, the snake god. The snake sticks are holy and are worshipped. They have different functions within the cult, such as property defence. The iron stick seems important to the Mongwande. They pray to it. They worship it. They expect answers from it to daily questions, in times of sorrow and death.

2.8.9 Snake Songs

In my book *The Mongwande Snake Cult* (2005), I examined the snake songs from an anthropological point of view. In my opinion, the songs are not superficial folklore. They are carriers of rituals that follow their own ceremonial pattern with roots going far back into the past.

The songs, stanzas and strophes may be classified as poetry. They convey emotion akin to Blues. Above all, they express devotion and worship, primarily directed at *ngbò*. Oddly enough, the singing of the songs is done with a rather mocking tone and in an irreverent fashion. The choir leader leads in songs and the choir responds:

Leader:	*E wè ngbò, e wè ngbò!*	We mock the snake.
Choir:	O!	
Leader:	*Ngbò aga sio ló!*	The snake brings bad luck!
Choir:	O!	
Leader:	*Ngbò aga tèpere!*	The snake brings strife!
Choir:	O!	
Leader:	*Ngbò aga nzò lò!*	The snake brings beautiful things!
Choir:	O!	
Leader:	*Ngbò aga pàsa!*	The snake brings happiness!

We notice here that the song, and hence the singers, starts out by mocking the snake, but then turn around and pay homage to it. In other words, there is a certain kind of ambivalence connected with snake worship. As I mentioned, the Supreme Being is called *Nzapa* in Mongwande and *Nzambe* in Lingala. We do not find these names in this or in fact in any of the snake songs that I have researched. The object of the veneration is *ngbò*. As far as the snake cult devotees are concerned *ngbò* is the Supreme Being. He is their god. He provides everything the Mongwande need in life such as food to eat as expressed in the following song.

Tá ngbò kpworoko,	Snake mother,
mbi tá ngbò ló ge	I the snake mother am here.
Tá ngbò gbázin mbi na sa	The snake mother has denied me meat.
Tá ngbò gbázi mbi na kpmi	The snake mother has denied me fish.
Tá má sòngo yá mbi so má	Dear mother! Don't you understand I am starving?
Tá ngbò elé, elé, elé!	Snake mother elé, elé, elé!
Mbi tá ngbò lô ge	I the snake mother am here.
Yé kó mbi tá ngbò ká	Should I, the mother to the snake go over there and look for what?
Yé ko 'mbí tá ngbó, mbí gbà né	Should I the mother of the snake, search and search in vain for what?
Mbi kpwingo ngdano ti ndungu ngbò	I am dying from rheumatism, when I give birth.
Tá mo hê mbi kóndo mbi te má né	Why don't you give a hen to eat?
Yé kó mbi gbánzi na ngbò kó né	What, I am denying the snake! What is this then?
Tó ngbò so ya , tá ngbò so ya	Not so furious, snake father, not so furious, snake mother.

These are two of the 27 songs that I researched and treated in my book *The Mongwande Snake Cult* (2005). And again, there is no mention of the Supreme Being *Nzapa / Nzambe*) in any of them. They all refer to *ngbò* "the snake." Furthermore, the songs are concerned with the parents of the snake children as well as the snake children themselves. We see in the above song that the twins are asking their mother, the snake mother, for food, but she seems to be unwilling to give them any. In the next song, the mother is complaining that she is dying from rheumatism caused by her birth. She has difficulties in finding food. We observe also in this song that both the snake father and the snake mother are mentioned. The twins beg them not to be so furious towards them.

I conclude this section with a small strophe, or more a homage to *ngbo* as chieftain. I picked it up one night in the Lundu village, when I had the good fortune of being allowed to observe a ceremony.

Ngó, ngbó, ngbó, gbia te mbi ngbó, ngbó, ngbó
Snake, snake, snake, my chief, snake, snake, snake!

In these songs and dancing festivals, we are facing a dancing culture that both reveals and conceals its messages. The choir leader and other song leaders represent at times both the mother and the father, and even the twins. There are usually at least two groups respectively singing in unison or sometimes attacking each other. There is a constantly recurring theme like the one I have quoted above. To reiterate, in all these 27 songs, there is no mention of the Supreme God but *ngbò*. Besides, the songs express that the parents and dancers receive both miseries as well as happiness from their god *ngbò*. They are prone to scolding and the verbal fight has to be won by one of the parties. The scolding could be as follows: "You are of no value!" "You are snake children!" "You look like an elephant!" The answer from the other part of the camp would be: "You too are snake kids and should therefore honour the snake!"

2.8.10 Testimonies to the Influence of the Snake Cult

In the following section, I will present some interviews of individuals which show the influence that the snake cult has on the villagers and which display their fear of the snake.

2.8.10.1   Fighting Fire with Fire

Taking a walk not far from where I lived in Monga, I saw a man clearing the grass around an orange tree which was fenced in. I stopped and asked if I could take a picture of him, and the following conversation took place:

Question: "What are you doing?"

Reply: "I am cleaning around my tree."

Question: "Why do you block the path to the tree?"

Reply: "The items are set up in order to protect my tree."

Question: "The rods and sticks look like snakes."

Reply: "The snakes are watching my orange tree."

Question: "What are the baskets and the bunch of twigs doing?"

Reply: "It is powerful medicine that watches over my orange fruit."

Question: "In what manner are they watching?"

Reply: "The villagers are believers like me. They know the purpose of my rituals."

What he made clear was that he believed in the power of the snake and so did the villagers who were Christians, at least by name. The same power that the villagers feared, the same power protected his tree against any perpetrator.

The fact was that this man had seized control of an orange tree that otherwise every citizen had free access to. He had blocked the access to the tree with sticks and rods carved as snakes. He had yearned to grab a hold of that tree for himself, and in order to attain his goal he knew what he had to do. His claim on the tree had to be supported by supernatural forces and the only power to be reckoned with in the eyes of most people was the power of the snake. No one ventured too close to the tree because they knew of the power of the snake. The villagers were kept in check by their belief. The man was protected by his belief.

2.8.10.2   Ngbo from Nzama

Ngbo from Nzama was the one who initially introduced me to the secret of the snake cult. He was the leader of my workers. One day, while the workers were clearing the school ground, a snake suddenly appeared. When his fellow-workers tried to kill the snake, Ngbo started running away. I asked him to come to me and talk about it. He came and we had a very long and informative conversation about the impact of the cult on the Mongwande society. When I asked him why he didn't kill the snake, he replied: "I am born snake and cannot kill my own family. So I run away. I have now a civilian name received at the name giving ceremony. I no longer carry the name Ngbo, but people in the village know me as Ngbo, which means snake, and use this name all the time." "Why don't you join the church?" I asked him, "Are you afraid of the snake?" "Yes," he responded, "Somehow, I will never be eligible for the church." He left me without more ado.

2.8.10.3   Ngbo from Yakoma

Ngbo from Yakoma was a school boy who used to help my wife in the house. He had another name too, but was always called upon as Ngbo "snake." He was from a district 100 miles northwest of Monga called Yakoma. Tradition and local religious activities were quite strong in his district. So Ngbo was not in want of support and understanding in his home region. One day, he was called upon to come and kill a snake that had found its way into the house. He refused to come. When asked, "why?" he answered that he could not kill members of his own family. He too did not frequent the church. When asked, "why?" he said that he was not allowed to mingle with the Christians. When asked who forbade him to participate in the Christian meetings, he whispered: "the snake."

2.8.10.4   Fakula

Fakula was a chieftain and came to see me often. He did not belong to the church either but talked constantly about Christianity. One day, when he visited me, I showed him a piece of iron formed like a snake. The name of that piece was *Yenda Gazoroma*. The moment when he got sight of the piece of iron, he yelled out that I should remove it immediately! He turned away his face and looked anywhere but at the iron object. "Are you afraid?" I asked him. "Yes", he said. "This is *Yenda Gazoroma*, the gods of our ancestors." And added gravely: "These gods were of tremendous help to our forefathers." Shortly before Fakula passed away, he gave me a couple of old knives, "animated," as he said, "with the spirits of his ancestors."

2.8.10.5 Yoyo

Yoyo is the last person I will mention in this list. He belonged to the church. His wife had died and he was looking for another. He found one but she was already married. Yoyo overlooked that fact and brought the woman into his house. After a while the wife's real husband threw a spell on Yoyo and he fell ill. No medicine, neither Western nor African, helped and before long he was gone to his ancestors. People said that he died because of an evil spell cast upon him by the wife's husband. Others said that he died from the spell of the snake.

2.8.11 Age of the Snake Cult

How old is the snake cult? I was amazed when the villagers replied that the snake cult was *biroko na kala-kala* meaning "centuries of age." I read later in the catholic missionary Tanghe's work on the Ngbandi that the Mongwande originate from the Darfur area in Sudan and that they got the snake cult from the Jews. Tanghe argues that the Jewish settlements were scattered over a great part of central and northern Africa. He insists on having evidence for his assertion. As the Jews moved southward the Mongwande fled from the eastern Sudan and brought the story about the snake in the Garden of Eden with them. His statement that the snake is the first created animal and it revealed great wisdom in the biblical story caused the Mongwande to use the story to explain the mystery of the birth of twins. Tanghe (1925:II3.435-438) suggsests that all this originated in the biblical Garden of Eden. Further, he asserts the following: "A capuchin missionary [a branch of the Franciscans] writes from French Guinea, West Africa, in the years 1681-1682 to his superiors and informs them that people in Guinea are honouring the devil in the form of a snake: The devil tortured them and spoke to them through the snake they worshipped." This testifies to the age of the snake cult.

Important historical discoveries have brought to light new evidences on probable Jewish settlements around in the middle part of Africa. The ancestors of the Ngbandi seem to have fled the eastern Sudan in order to get away from the Jews. Moreover, the narratives of the Bible were common knowledge among peoples because of the Jewish captivity in Babylon, and later among the Christians, for instance the Copts, who still live in Egypt. There is no reason to be surprised that the Mongwande knew about the stories of the Bible in olden days.

The snake is especially mentioned. In the myths and orphical cosmology, the snake is even the beginning and the end of the universe. Since the snake is particularly mentioned, it gives to the Mongwande reason to believe that the snake really was the first born among the animals. Therefore, as the oldest and first created animal, the snake was declared to be the chief (*gbia*) of all other animals. The name chief (*gbia*) carries a two-fold meaning: it denotes the personal and official functions of the chief (*gbia*). The qualities of the chief (*gbia*) are metaphorically transferred to the twins; so the twins represented both the chief and the realm of animals (Moen 2005). The deacon Yanzere and pastor Kembi told me that an evil spirit has surely proclaimed that the twins are the snake and as such ought to be honoured.

If we ignore all the philosophical view points, it seems easy to explain that the evil spirit in the snake drama had taken place in the earthly paradise, the Garden of Eden. The story has been inherited by the Mongwande who practiced it in the snake cult (Tanghe 1925a:246f).

There are some points we should pay attention to in the above. Firstly, there have been several ideas about the movements in and out of Africa. The last and more modern one is that people of today have originated in Africa and started their wanderings from there over the globe. Secondly, we have no scientific evidence, as of today, that the Mongwande ever met the Jews in the Sudan and got the knowledge about the snake from them. Thirdly, it is no doubt that the Mongwande insist and believe that they have come from the Darfur area (probably in the beginning of the 18th century). It is nevertheless possible that they have encountered the Jews there and adopted their story about the snake and brought it with them to the area of the southern part of the Central African Republic and the northern part of the Democratic Republic of the Congo where they live today.

2.8.12 General Evaluation of the Snake Cult

Why is it that the Mongwande religious life took the form of a snake cult? In all my field research during almost ten years, it was very difficult to find the roots of the snake cult. According to the Mongwande themselves, the cult came with them when they departed from the Darfur or Kordan territory in Sudan in the 18th century. The Mongwande had no doubt about their origin. They proclaimed with pride that they were Sudanese. This is also supported by Tanghe (1926; 1929), Burssens (1921; 1958) and Molet (1970).

Tanghe who was a catholic missionary argued that the Mongwande had got the snake worship from the Jews in Sudan. They had quite simply adopted the Garden of Eden narrative and brought it with them when they arrived in the northern part of the Congo. There must have been something that thrilled the

Mongwande to the extent that they maintained this practice up until modern times. The biblical narrative of the snake tells us that the snake was the most "crafty" (meaning "cunning, sly, wily") of the animals the Lord God had made (Gen 3:1). The snake seems to be an object of awe in many cultures, and for some hitherto unexplained reason, many people are wary of them. Rightfully so, perhaps, they can after all inflict excruciating pain and horrific deaths to any unfortunate person who gets bitten by a snake. They are very difficult to defend oneself against, particularly with their quick strikes and effective camouflage. The reverence of the snake is to be found in several religions and myths all over the globe and the Mongwande are no exception. In fact, the oldest and most traditional religious exercise among the Mongwande tribe seems to be the snake cult. Somehow the above mentioned characteristics of villainous and cunning also allude to wisdom, which for the Mongwande is very important. And in the form of the snake, the Mongwande find deep meaning and manifestation of these traits. Furthermore, the cult is in a way a family oriented cult. When a wife delivers not one baby but two at a time, the family is immediately absorbed into the snake family. As I have already mentioned, the wife becomes a snake mother and the father likewise a snake father. The snake families stick together in joy as well as in sorrow. These snake families become related to the snake and to other snake families as well, and they can never hurt or kill a snake nor kill or hurt related snake families. In form, one might acknowledge the fact that the snake cult reveres real snakes, however in meaning their veneration is directed towards the character of the animal.

Does the snake cult play any role among the Mongwande as of today? As my interview with Kumbowo in chapter 6 will show, it does. It is not in the forefront of the society today, but in the background, in the forest. Will it survive? In my opinion, it will. There has been quite a shift towards old traditions and many religious groups have popped up after the struggle for independence, which are, if nothing else, cloaked in old religious traditions. We should still be mindful of the impact the birth of twins has in the village. After all, it overturns the order and power structure in a village completely. The chieftain is dethroned and the people who claim to take their orders from the snake assume leadership of the village, a situation which is rectified and restored at the name giving festival.

The first thing the Mongwande did following the birth of twins was to fence in an area in which they built a little shelter for the infants. The twins stayed there until they were presented to the village and given identities and names at the name giving ceremony. But, what was this space? The enclosure was a symbol that those inside the fence were outside the human social life of the village. As domestic animals were fenced in, so were the twins too. What was done for the cattle was now done for the twins because they belonged to the same category, namely animal. The twins were isolated from humans and humans were not allowed to keep in touch with the twins except for the parents. Everybody understood the language of the symbols. The parents had to admit that they accepted the claim from the village that their children were not like other kids; they were animals. On the other hand, I think the enclosure protected the children from possible attacks by both people and animals. The enclosure was a symbol of nature. In fact, what we are witnessing here is the most important meaning of the snake cult: the doubleness of the snake worship, nature and culture.

The parents didn't understand what had happened to them and wanted to disassociate themselves from the fact that their children were snakes, but as parents they could not. Instead of disclaiming responsibility, they accepted this freak of nature with humbleness. Here, we see the ambiguity in the cult: the parents' hate and love relationship with their children which they loved, and the serpent which they feared. And now, their very own children were snakes. It cannot have been an easy predicament for them. On one side, they wanted to remove themselves from the responsibility, on the other side they identified themselves with their children and the forces that these monsters had bestowed on them.[2] Therefore, as the children were not humans but animals, the parents too had to take upon themselves the status of animals for a short period of time.

The visible sign of this status was the clothing. The clothing code became a ritual act that was one of the most impressive symbolic happenings in the snake cult. After having observed this kind of attire in Nzeret, my conclusion is that it constitutes some sort of identification with nature. The parents followed instructions that demanded a visible token of obedience, subjugation and identification. They covered themselves with twigs and leaves in order to show that they are one with nature which has visited them and given them *ngbò* "twins." I notice that Molet also asks questions regarding a series of issues as to clothing, village, field, rain forest and enclosure / isolation, *tolo ngbò* "snake sticks," and snake mother and father and mother sticks (Molet 1970). On an abstract level, all these symbols indicate probably the comprehension a Mongwande possesses of the world around him. It seems that the Mongwande don't have a cosmogony, and in their philosophy there is no distinction between the material and immaterial world. They are one and the same and hence the Mongwande belong to both worlds. However, the individual Mongwande is facing a constant struggle for life and the results of this battle for daily living have become for him sanctities like houses, corn fields, roads and so on.

---

[2] See snake songs No. 2 and 24.

One thing seems clear, and that is the battle between the controllable and the uncontrollable world, the workable field and the village in contrast to the impenetrable rain forest, the tilled field as opposed to the forces of nature. The Mongwande have conceptualized the world around them in terms they understand and which is expressed through the snake cult. The ambiguity of the snake cult might perhaps have been based on the physical appearance, the forked tongue of the snake, but in the course of time, has developed into a sophisticated religious-psychological system with a visible form but not so visible meaning or content.

After having discussed some elements of Mongwande culture with a special focus on the snake cult, in the next chapter we will look into the concept of contextualization. This will imply the discussion of some foundational, epistemological questions. We do this because of the inherent missiological question of how Bible and culture, theology and the other sciences, how belief and knowledge relate to each other.

Chapter 3
The Method of Contextualization

3.1 Introduction

In this chapter, I intend to give an account of what the word "contextualization" stands for. I will do so by referring to the World Council of Churches' Theological Education Fund (TEF), and to the models of Stephen Bevans (1992/2008) and the reflections on contextualization by Paul G. Hiebert (1985/2006) and Charles Kraft (1997/2005). Then I will look for the need for contextualization and the methods to be used in the contextualization process of Christianity into the Mongwande culture in the Northern Congo.

The interesting thing about contextualization, as I understand, is that the idea springs out of the sphere of pedagogy. If that is clear, it is easy to see that contextualization is primarily about education, communication, mediation, etc. It is a method or a series of initiatives one might follow in order to teach and spread the Gospel. It is not the Gospel itself that passes through a process of contextualization. No, the message, the word of God, is divine and cannot change, even though the comprehensions and expressions might vary in the different cultures, even from person to person.

The word first appeared in 1972 in a publication of the Theological Education Fund entitled *Ministry in Context* (Coe 1972). It appeared at a time when many new churches in the southern hemisphere struggled for their life. They struggled against colonialism, against the varieties of local religions, against mission boards whose decisions were not always wise. They also struggled towards political and religious independence. In the midst of all these problems, Scripture fell subject to question. Was it the Holy Word of God? Should it be followed? And if so how, according to whose understanding, the Europeans' or the indigenous peoples' understanding? The methodological principles of interpretation (hermeneutics) became more of a problem than a help. Then, out of the secular worldview, came the word contextualization. It refers to the manner how a given culture can use its own mentality and codes to understand and express any new body of knowledge. In our case, the new body of knowledge is the Gospel. Contextualization expresses what the church can do in a more effective and respectful way in order to make the Gospel comprehensible and relevant to the local people. The Lausanne Conference in 1974 discussed the theme "Gospel and Culture," which is, as I understand it, the core of the question (Lausanne Covenant, § 10, Stott 1975). Christian thought does not only concern religion but also culture. Michael Frost and Allan Hirsch provide a definition of contextualization (2003:83). According to them, contextualization is:

a dynamic process by which the eternal God's message is contextualized within particular time and socio-cultural aspects. This implies a thorough research of the Gospel in the light of the receiver's worldview in order to accommodate the message, putting together a code of symbols comprehensible and meaningful to the recipient. Contextualization means to communicate and contextualize the Gospel through word and work and planting churches in a way that is understandable for a host population within their local cultural context (Frost & Hirsch 2003:83).

Contextualization is mainly concerned with the presentation of Christianity in a way that meets the deepest needs and longings of people and penetrates their worldview so that they may follow Christ but all the same remain deeply rooted in their own culture. So far, the definition is quite satisfactory. Even so it is necessary to pursue further some relevant factors of the subject. Contextualization is functioning only as long as one is subscribing to certain presuppositions. First and foremost, the authority of the Scriptures must incontestably be accepted and held as the highest instance regarding all matters, as the Word of God. The Gospel is supracultural in the fact that it not only concerns all the cultures, but that it is above all human cultures, and even precedes all others. The Word of God is eternal and unchangeable. Secondly, we have to acknowledge that this eternal message can be and must be expressed in a specific time and wrapped in a cultural mould so it might be conveyed and comprehended (Frost & Hirsch 2003:83, 86).

The most outstanding example of someone who stepped into another culture and became a part of it, keeping at the same time his own identity and integrity, was Jesus Christ himself (Ph 2:5-11). He stepped down into humanity: "The word became flesh and made his dwelling among us" (Jn 1:14). He participated in the human experience by being true human but at the same time remaining true God. He did not loose his identity (Kraft 2005:84). The texts of the Bible show how the early Christians contextualized when they first spread the glad tidings among the Jews and later among the Greeks (Kraft 1979:64; 2005:85).

3.2 Contextualization and Scripture

3.2.1 The Authoritative Position of Scripture

Hiebert says: "The Bible is the fully authoritative record of God's self-revelation to humans. It is God's Word and we turn to it not only to hear God's message of salvation but also to see how he works in and through human history in accomplishing his purposes. Scripture is the standard against which we measure all truth and righteousness, all theologies and moralities" (Hiebert 1985:17). And Nancy Murphy makes a similar assertion in her workbook on "Epistemological Holism and Theological Method" (2006). I agree with them in viewing the Bible as the Word of God and that our central task is to bring the Gospel to a lost world. We may think that we have a lot of tools to carry out this work. The solutions might be more or less presumptuous. If these are not rooted in the Word of God, they will not serve as effective remedies. As Christians however we know that God has revealed the Bible. However, we know that the revelation of God has been given us in historical and cultural contexts. This means that if we want to understand the Bible we will have to relate it to the time and the setting under which it was bestowed upon us. We must look at the moving history of the people of Israel and the specific characters and personalities like Abraham, Isaac, Jacob and the greatest and most important of them all, Jesus. It is in Him that Scripture must be understood. The whole revelation points at Him as the focal point in the Old Testament and as the centre in the New Testament (Lk 24:44-46). He is the Son of God "who, being in very nature God, did not consider equality with God something to be grasped, but made himself nothing, taking the very nature of a servant, being made in human likeness" (Ph 2:6).

In John 20:22, Jesus is empowering his disciples with the Holy Spirit to preach the Gospel of forgiveness of sins. The importance of the Holy Spirit is repeated again and again in the NT. It is the Holy Spirit that guides the apostles throughout the Middle-East. The Holy Spirit accompanied the preaching and prepared the hearts of the listeners to accept Christ. The Holy Spirit is also working with today's missionaries in their effort to bring salvation to the peoples of the nations.

The very centre of the message of Christ was at the time of the apostles the kingdom of God. It still is the kingdom of God that is the ultimate goal of our preaching. By the kingdom of God we mean a divine kingdom that encompasses both heaven and earth. And on earth we are dealing with the kingdom of God in the shape of the church. The church consists of individuals who have met Jesus Christ through the Holy Spirit and their experiences have brought them together in communion with one another in local congregations. These groupings of people stand answerable to the Lord for the proclamation of the kingdom of God.

The members of the church have been given gifts to be used according to the needs of the church (1Cor 12:28-31). According to Revelation 1:6, the members of the church are priests. And since all members are priests, we have the priesthood of all believers. This means that they all have the right and privilege to approach God whenever they want. This means also that all the converts in developing countries (or the West for that matter) have the same right and responsibility to read and interpret Scripture as missionnaries do. The missionaries are the models for the new converts. We must teach them to read the Bible and to discern God's message within it.

Here we have a great task ahead of us because we will have to differentiate between the Bible and various theologies. When we talk about the Bible, we mean the pure, uncensored text of the Bible. But when we talk about theologies, we are talking about human comprehension in historical and cultural contexts about biblical teaching. Thus, we speak of one Bible but of many theologies: that of Luther, Calvin, the Anabaptists, and others. We may say that Christian theology, as Hiebert states, "has one foot in biblical revelation and the other in the historical and cultural context of the people hearing the message" (Hiebert 1985:19).

We read and interpret Scripture as all other writings. But we may read and interpret all other writings with a bit of scepticism. We cannot do that with the Holy Bible. Our duty toward the Holy Scripture is to remain faithful to the biblical truth in it. Our first task in this matter will be the exegetical one, meaning that the Bible is understood in its original cultural and historical context. The second task is to discover what the meaning of the biblical message is for us today in our particular context. We call this hermeneutics.

3.2.2 Why Theology Must Be Contextual Today

In his book *Models of Contextual Theology* (1992/2008), Stephen B. Bevans is asking the question: "Why must theology be contextual today?" (2008:9-15). He is answering by pointing at several factors that ought to be taken into consideration: the historical events, the intellectual currents, the cultural shifts and the political forces. Additionally to these external factors, there are internal factors within the Christian faith which indicate the necessity of practicing contextualization. Actually, these internal factors are more important than the external ones, since they point to a contextual imperative within Christianity itself. In the earlier days of the church, the internal factors were not regarded as important. But due to historical circumstances expressed in the external factors, they have shown themselves to be essential to Christian faith and theologizing.

Bevans mentions as the first of these external factors "a general dissatisfaction with the classical approaches to theology in both the First and the Third Worlds" (Bevans 2008:9). I do not intend to go through all the details. However, behind it all there has been the understanding that the Holy Scripture is unchangeable, a so called *theologia perennis*, meaning more or less an everlasting, unchanging hermeneutic. This view has been challenged in the First World and the Third Worlds in the name of relevance, Bevans argues (Bevans 2008:9). In Asia, Africa, Latin America and Oceania, voices have arisen insisting that the traditional approaches to theology really do not make sense. Having been a missionary in South-Korea for eleven years, I often heard insinuations about the interpretation of the Bible, especially in the light of the

Yin-yang philosophy. Yin is earth, female, dark and passive, while yang is conceived of as heaven, light, white, male. The Yin-yang philosophy is in short representing the duality of the world: dark-light, death-life, male-female, good-evil and so on. I must admit that I found the Koreans and even the Korean Christians quite indulged in this old traditional thought. I found however several native symbols, beliefs, witchcraft and miracles that were difficult to explain away. That be as it may, in facing these kinds of things, it is understandable that both missionaries and local people find theology to be a cause of dissatisfaction and frustration in the sense that if theology cannot satisfy the host culture neither can the host culture satisfy Christian theology. Bevans discusses several models which can be used, but none of them is fully applicable to all situations.[3] To me it seems that the only way out of difficult situations is dialogue. The persons and the groups involved will have to dig deeply into their own particular cultures and join in a serious dialogue. By doing so, they might have a chance to attain a common workable contextual theological platform.

The second external reason why theology should be understood contextually is the oppressive nature of older approaches. Theologians in Latin America discovered that traditional theology marginalizes the poor and that the church actually justified the domination of the poor by the rich and powerful. The same thing seems to take place anywhere in this world. To point at special churches in this regard is futile. Churches old or new, catholic or protestant, all have a tendency to be dominant in their contextual setting.

Thirdly, the churches of the Global South are demanding the development of contextual theologies as part of their development of identity. There is no doubt that colonialism fostered a feeling of subservience and that all good things originated in the land of the colonizers. Slowly but surely, African, Asian and Latin American countries woke up, particularly in the aftermath of the Second World War. They became aware of their own values, and that their culture is as valuable as that of the Western people. A sense of expressing this new consciousness of independence grew forth.

In the Democratic Republic of Congo, a tentative effort started in 1921 through the renowned church of Simon Kimbangu. They grew quickly to become quite a big church with great influence. The Belgians feared their claim for independence and started to relocate some of the leaders to various places around the Congo, even up to the Monga region, the area of the Norwegian Baptist Mission. In 1957, an organized group emerged that was legally recognized in 1959 and accepted into the World Council of Churches in 1969 under

---

[3] See the discussion in the section 3.5. "Models of Contextualization."

the name of *L'Église de Jésus-Christ sur la terre par le prophète Simon Kimbangu*. It is an African Initiated Church (AIC). Though mostly uncritical, we find tentative traces of contextualization in the Kimbanguist Church, such as in the question of magic and witchcraft, songs and dancing, services of healing, education and youth work.

A fourth external factor concerns the way the contemporary social sciences view culture. Some researchers distinguish between a classical conception of culture, while others have pointed towards an empiricist notion of culture. The latter defines culture as a set of meanings and values, while the classical notion conceives of culture in a restricted sense, namely as higher civilization in terms of music, art and architecture. If we work from a strictly classical conception of culture, there can be only one type of theology: one that is valid for all times, all places and all cultures. But if we follow the empirical notion of culture, there cannot be a theology for every culture and period of history: "Theology ... functions precisely as the way that religion makes sense within a particular culture" (Bevans 2008:11).

As we have noted above, these various external factors, though important, bring out some internal factors that also point to contextualization as a theological imperative. These factors were brought to light by the forces of history and the movements within Christianity itself. They are actually strong arguments for a theology that takes culture and cultural change seriously.

The first among the internal factors is the incarnational nature of Christianity. God so loved (*agape*) the world that He wanted to share himself with men and women (Jn 3:16). But in order to carry out his loving wish, he had to do it in such a way that all of humanity could grasp it. So we read in John 1:14 that God became flesh, a human being, in the person of Jesus. Incarnation is the process in which divinity became humanity. If that message is to be understood by people, through our agency, we ourselves would have to continue the process of incarnating the message in our lives. We humans are already incarnated, already flesh. So the "incarnation process" to which we refer would consist of incarnating ourselves as missionaries in and within any given local culture, take on their manners, learn their language, ways of thinking and values, while submitting ourselves to the authority of Scripture. The message of the Gospel must become authentically African, Asian, and Latin American through us.

The second internal factor is the sacramental nature of reality. By using the word reality, it means that God is revealed not only as an idea but in concrete reality through Jesus Christ. It would perhaps make more sense to a Protestant to use the term "embodied spirituality" rather than "sacramental reality." This is grounded in the fact that God rendered us living creatures in that He blew the breath of life into our nostrils (Gen 2:7). This would suggest that God uses concrete things to help us to appreciate the depth of our relationship with Him in Jesus Christ. Catholics for example encounter Jesus in the poured water of baptism and the gathering around the table of bread and wine, in oil given for healing or as a sign of vocation in gestures of forgiveness or commissioning. But these sacraments are only concentrated ritual elements that point beyond themselves to the whole of life. Persons, history and things can become transparent and reveal the creator as lovingly present in creation. The Bible is interpreting the ordinary, the secular, in terms of religious symbolism. This is also the task of theology today: to reveal God's presence in his world.

Thirdly, we can speak of a shift in the understanding of the nature of divine revelation as being an internal factor determining the contextual nature of theology. In the Catholic Church, revelation was conceived before the Second Vatican Council in terms of propositional truth. Researchers like José de Mesa and Lode Wostyn argue that revelation was presented in form of eternal truths handed down to us from Christ and the apostles (Bevans 2008:13). Faith was understood to be the intellectual assent to those truths. All these were systematically arranged and presented as the Catholic faith. As God's revelation of these truths had ceased with the death of the last apostle, nothing was to be done but to communicate the message of salvation from generation to generation.

Theological thought leading up to Vatican II began to shift its emphasis from the above mentioned comprehension and to started to speak of revelation in more interpersonal terms. Revelation was from now on conceived as the offer of God's very self-communication to men and women. The giver, God, is also the gift. The faith of the receiver is understood as a personal response as well as a gift of a person to God. As I understand it, the shift is rather radical and very delicate for an evangelical. Revelation was shifted from being an unchangeable and eternal truth to being comprehended in terms of a self-sacrifice of God to men and women. God's offer had to be made in terms that could be understood by humankind. He did it in relation to Israel, to the Jews at the time of Jesus, to the Hellenists, to the Europeans, and subsequently to all the peoples of the earth. The traces of God's contextualization can be followed all the way through history.

The fourth internal factor is the catholicity of the church. The word stems from two Greek words: *kata* and *holos* giving *katholikos* meaning "whole, undivided and universal." According to ecclesiastical writers, since the 2nd century the "catholic church" was distinguished from local communities and from heretical and schismatic sects. According to St. Cyril of Jerusalem (348), the church is called catholic on the ground of its worldwide extension, its doctrinal completeness, its adaptation to the needs of men of every kind and its moral and spiritual perfection. These characteristics, which are found in many history books, are enough to describe the church's activity, dynamic and dimension. As to the universality or catholicity, it stands for an appeal to engage all kinds of people and to enter into serious dialogue with every culture in order to bring them the fullness (*plerôma*) of Christ. As this is the real meaning of the word catholicism it calls for a contextual approach to theology by its very nature. This is the task of the *ek-klesia* "community," in common English "the church." With this scope in view, we need a new approach to theology and contextualization.

In this section on external and internal factors, we also ought to pay attention to what we find at the heart of Christianity: the Trinity. Lately, there has been a renewal of trinitarian thought in theology and missiology. Contemporary theologians speak of God as triune. We need to take a deeper look into the mystery of trinity: the trinity in unity and diversity. Through the presence of the Spirit and the concrete flesh and humanity of the Logos, God is working for salvation in the midst of a human context, its culture, its events, its sufferings and its joys. We need to theologize contextually because God is present and acts contextually. God is not only present but he is the very essence of the contextualization process. Jesus says: "For this is the will of him that sent me" (Jn 6:40). Jesus is here speaking of a divine commission. God the Father has sent the Son, the Father and the Son send the Spirit, and the triune God sends the Church. Recent missiology speaks of the *missio Dei* and the *missiones ecclesiae* (Newbigin 1963/1999; Kraft 2005:38-56). The latter is expressed in the different versions of the Great Commission (e.g. Mt 28:16-20).

Christ came into the world as an outsider, sent by God. Likewise, Jesus sent the missionaries, from the apostle Paul on to the missionaries of today, as outsiders into foreign cultures. This encounter requires another tactic, another education. The question is: "What kind of education? What kind of theological training might lead to a fruitful encounter between the Gospel and the host culture?" This investigation leads to a series of thoughts and words. Words like contextuality and contextualization have entered the scene covering topics such as indigenization and inculturation. There has been an explosion of writing and thinking since the word contextualization emerged in the 1970s. There are three main functions in contextualization: 1) the relevant communication of the Gospel, 2) the critique of the host culture and 3) the creation of a community of faith relevant to the socio-cultural context. I do not find particular difficulties either with points 1 and 3, but would question point 2 which entails critical engagement. Are we here speaking about the host culture and criticism of this culture or are we concerned about our own culture? In this regard, how far may we go? In my estimate, we cannot uncritically criticize without some sort of checks and balances.

3.2.3 Contextualization Is Appropriate Christianity

The above title sounds like a mathematic equation, and actually it is. After my strenuous "pilgrimage in the desert" of these studies of contextualization, I could not avoid drawing the conclusion that the content and meaning of contextualization was equivalent to the content and meaning of of the term "appropriateness". In my search for the best wording, it seems that Charles H. Kraft's work, *Appropriate Christianity* (2005), offers some fitting insights. I his closing discussion on proper terminology, Kraft remarks:

> The word we use when defining what we mean by contextualization, as we did above, is the word appropriate. When people ask us what our word means, we say, appropriate to the cultural context and we may and may not remember to say, and also to the Bible. Since what we all seek is appropriate Christianity, a Christian expression that is appropriate both to a given social context and to the Scriptures, why not just say that our ideals are appropriateness in both directions (Kraft 2005:4).

Kraft does not hesitate to define the concept of contextualization in terms of the idea of "appropriateness". These two terms overlap each other or blend together into one main thought: appropriate Christianity. That being said, I feel that we need to have a look at what Bevans perspective in his *Models of Contextual Theology* where he declares quite forcefully:

> There is no such thing as "theology," there is only contextual theology: feminist theology, black theology, liberation theology, Filipino theology, Asian-American theology and so forth. Doing theology contextually is not an option, nor is it something that should only interest people from the Third World, missionaries who work there, or ethnic communities within dominant cultures. The contextualization of theology, the attempt to understand Christian faith in terms of a particular context, is really a theological imperative" (Bevans 2008:3).

Contextualization is a process that takes place whenever Christianity encounters a local culture. A contextual approach to theology is somehow a radical departure from traditional theology. At the same time it is very much in continuity with it. In other words, in order to understand theology as contextual, we will have to accept the fact that it is something both new and traditional. Yes, this is true, but it is not only both new and old or traditional, it is also appropriate, meaning that the result of the research on the biblical text, agreed upon by the host culture and the western culture, contains the truth.

There has been a great deal of discussion in the past about what kind of Christianity one should present to new converts. What would be maximally meaningful within the host cultural context and maximally faithful to the Scriptures? A lot of expressions emerged to enlighten the understanding of the new concept, such as incarnation, adaptation, accommodation, indigenization, inculturation, and finally contextualization. At this post-modern time, there has been great activity for this new angle of approach to the problem of a meaningful comprehension of a particular text for the two parties in question. I am sure there is today and there will certainly emerge in the future, problems indicating that contextualization is not done once and for all. The verb "to contextualize" and the substantive "contextualization" are products of development and will surely not stop here. We are after all talking about language and language changes as time passes by. There will surely be many variations of understanding of any of the terms we use. What does contextualization mean? Contextualization means to do what is necessary in order to make sure that Christianity is expressed in ways that are faithful to the Scriptures and appropriate to the context of the receiving group.

In his *Appropriate Christianity*, Charles H. Kraft relates his encounter with a professor of theology who asked him what the difference between systematic theology and contextual theology was. When the professor heard Kraft's answer, he had a hard time to understand it. It had never occurred to him that contextualization was God's way of dealing with theological truth in relation to human culture and language and that therefore it should be a part of the teaching of theology (2005:4).

The word to be used for the process of contextualization, according to Kraft, is the word "appropriate." This is in complete accordance with my own understanding of our topic. To contextualize is to be appropriate to the cultural context and, of course, to the Bible as well. We seek appropriate Christianity, i.e. a Christian expression that is appropriate both to a particular context and to the Scriptures. In order to repeat myself, we are actually seeking appropriateness in both directions. The term contextualization helps us with regards to the inculturation of Christianity at the receptor's end, while assuming that we know what we are doing at the Scripture's end. With the term appropriate we seek to be alert to the fact that we need a measure on either side of the equation as I have indicated above. We have noted above the need of an appropriate approach to the host culture, but we need also an appropriate approach to the Scripture.

As I see it, we are dealing with contextualization and talk primarily about contextual theology. This is of course true, but any appropriate contextualization ought to be aware of and treat Christianity as a whole. If we would like to be considered biblical, we will have to deal with a series of issues and dimensions like relationship, understanding and freedom. These items proceed mostly from encounters, such as allegiance, truth and power. Kraft suggests that an appropriate approach to Scripture should be understood to involve appropriateness in all three of these above mentioned dimensions (Kraft 2005:6,99-116). Kraft is pointing to an appropriate approach to truth. He asks:

Have we held God's truth enough up against cultural truths? Have we adequately worked out a program by which means we can attain our goals? Have we done enough with what might be termed how to move appropriately toward God's ideals? Appropriate approaches to the truth and knowledge dimension of Christianity need to include biblically-based treatments of the process of theologizing that can be taught in Western and non-Western institutions. We should also be attentive to the fact that appropriateness is not only a form, but an inner meaning or content. The question will then be: are these meanings scripturally appropriate? And here we are right into the problems of interpretation. The next question will emerge: who shall interpret the text, the villagers or the missionaries? Here again, another problem pops up whose interpretation should be recognized as the word of God? The only solution is a cross-cultural approach to that problem. The result of that hermeneutic exercise must be accepted by cultural insiders as well as outsiders. The receivers are the people who will interpret the forms and attach meanings to them. The missionaries' task should be concerned mostly with the question of whether the meanings in their minds are scriptural or not.

With regards to appropriate relationship, I find it proper to ask with Kraft: what does a biblical and socio-cultural appropriate expression of commitment (allegiance) to and relationship with God through Christ look like for any given society? Kraft points out that even when Israel broke the covenant with God, God did not exercise his right to be free from the covenant. Kraft recommends as culturally appropriate an idealistic level, and for Christians an appropriate biblical level (Kraft 2005:6).

Kraft's conclusion is convincing when he states that the two words "contextualization" and "appropriateness" end up in a sort of arrowhead, namely "appropriate constellation" and "contextualized appropriation" (Kraft 2005:5-6).

3.4 Contextualization on the Worldview Level

In addition to the above considerations, we have to observe on what level we seek to influence the local community. The rites and religious practices we see in a society are often just visible expressions of a deep-rooted worldview. As leaves and flowers are only visible parts or consequences of plant breeding, it would be superficial to limit ourselves to working only with the surface level culture. We pick the leaves or the flowers but we have done very little with the root itself. That's why, in a contextualization project, we have to pay attention to the deep-level culture. It is the only way to create lasting changes in the host community. In order to be able to say something about the surface and the deeper levels of culture, we will have to take a closer look at worldview.

Culture denotes the structural customs, the underlying worldview and the immanent values that control the life of human beings. The cultures are the pattern of life of humans and their way of handling their biological, physical and social environment. By culture we understand a collection of acquired knowledge, a world of thoughts, which might be called worldviews, ideas, concepts and behaviours, together with objects being created by this worldview (Kraft 2005:33).

The concept of worldview has been mentioned. This is the deepest level of culture. It is about cultural structured assumptions and values (including allegiances and commitments). It is the foundation of what people perceive, and how they react to reality. Worldview is part of culture and makes up the deepest presumptions on which people base their lives (Kraft 1979:53-57; Kraft in Bevans 2008:37-39; Hiebert et al. 1999:18-20, 168f).

On the surface level, we find behaviour pattern. But this behaviour is nevertheless the least significant of culture. What takes place on the surface is not only a response to the outer phenomena and influences, but also an expression of what is happening on the deepest level of culture and in the psyche of the human being. And it is on the deepest level that we find what philosophers and cultural anthropologists call worldview, that is, the assumptions that control our behaviour on the surface. If something affects the surface of the culture, it might also affect other cultures on the same level. And the effect thereof will surely be influenced by the worldview structure that is to be found on the deepest level of culture (Kraft 2005:86-87).

Culture is in itself neutral. It is like a framework that a person is acting on. It is a pattern or structure. The higher level is manifold: you will find within western culture German, French or Norwegian culture. The culture has no power in itself. The power that always seems to compel people to follow this culture-manuscript and keep them conformed is inside human beings and is called habit. Habit is strong, even though it can change from time to time and modify old traditions. It is important to acknowledge the power and position of habit in cross-cultural work, also the possibility of habit change.

As mentioned, culture is about acquired patterns of behaviour. But these elements are meaningless without human beings. It is people who create society (Kraft 2005:10-11). It means that if somebody is under pressure to conform to the rules, the pressure is from our fellow men not from culture. I am charting this fact in the table below.

Table 1: Personality and Culture

Personality	Culture
Surface Behaviour What we are doing, thinking, saying or feeling, whether conscious or unconscious, for the most part thinking in grooves, but also in creative ways.	**Surface Structure** Cultural pattern related to what we do, think, say and feel, as habit.
Deep-rooted Behaviour To suppose, evaluate and engage or undertake something out of habit, but also based on creativity. To choose, to feel, to reason, to interpret and to evaluate. Additional meaning. To explain, to relate to other, to commit oneself to other persons as well as to oneself. To adjust oneself or try to change the circumstances around us.	**Deep-rooted Structure** Pattern that has to do with the doer or put the suppositions, evaluations and the obligations that belong to the deep-rooted level, into practice. Pattern that concerns emotions, reasoning, interpretation, estimation and explanation plus relation to other, commit oneself, adapt oneself or decide to change things happening around us.

Both cultural structure and worldview structure are functioning inside as well as outside human beings. We are sometimes so overloaded with it, that we do not notice our own culture and worldview, except when we visit foreign cultures. We very often look at our own culture as the only right way to think and to do things. And we might fall into the trap of connecting our culture to Christianity in a way that we believe that in order to become real Christians, the converts must culturally follow our way of doing things. Jesus was clear on the point and tackled the problem quite differently. He left his divine abode and came to our earth. He became a human being without loosing his identity and integrity. He is the most outstanding example of contextualization.

For the missionary, contextualization begins with a critical analysis of the host culture in the light of Biblical teachings. It concerns the deep-rooted level with its assumptions and opinions. It touches not only the cultural superficial level.

In this way, Christian work is very much occupied with subsystems, for instance, family, friends, education, language, religion, economy, etc. In the same way, if one deals with seed in a particular way, the fruit and leaves might burst out differently. If we can reach the worldview of humans, we may be able to make some impact on their culture. Jesus did that. He sought to enter into contact with the people's worldview in order to bring about change. Through narratives he made the people reconsider their basic values. And changes at the deep level can put the structure of society out of balance (Kraft 2005:86). For example, the church demands that a polygamist shall keep only one wife and get rid of the others. This is not only difficult for the new convert, but it is even more delicate for the church as divorce also is frowned upon by the church itself. On one side, polygamy is unbiblical; on the other side, divorce is also unbiblical. As a solution to this dilemma Kraft suggests that changes at the deep level, that will take a long time to come to fruition, ought to be dealt with accordingly. A long term perspective might be needed. In cases like polygamy, the process may go on for generations (Kraft 2005:133).

The point is that in implementing lasting changes it is not enough to carry out superficial changes, but one must go for far-reaching restructuring on the deep-rooted level where the values, assumptions and meanings are located, that is at the worldview level.

3.5 Models of Contextualization

In dealing with the concept of context, it soon became quite clear that the approaches to the contextualization process called for a variety of methods. As this area of research developed, several models presented themselves as being necessary in different situations. In order to show how diverse approaches to contextualization might look, the Catholic theologian Stephen Bevans presents a typology of models in his book *Models of Contextual Theology* (1992/2008).

Another slightly different typology of models is presented by Dean S. Gilliland, an evangelical missiologist, in his book *The Word Among Us* (1989:313-318) and in his article in the *Evangelical Dictionary of World Missions* (2000). There Gilliland mentions Paul G. Hiebert's critical model which was presented first in an article in *Missiology* (1984).

In this section, we will first present the different models, and then particularly Hiebert's critical model. In a next step, we will evaluate the models in relation to our purposes.

3.5.1 Introduction to Bevans' Typology of Models

The liberal Catholic theologian Stephen B. Bevans begins his book *Models of Contextual Theology* (1992/2008) by stating that contextual theology is a "theological imperative" (Bevans 2008:3). Contextual theology understands the nature of theology in a new way. The enterprise of contextualization is a departure from the traditional way of doing theology. It is something new doing theology by taking culture and social change in culture into account.

Because contextualization is a new way of doing theology, the contextual theologian faces a number of issues and questions that were seldom dealt with in classical theology. What contextual theology has realized is that theology has not always been done discursively. The discursive form was mostly used since the Middle-Ages. Theology today, we can conclude, must be contextual theology. Contextualization is not something on the fringes of the theological enterprise. Bevans concludes that it is the very centre of what it means to do theology in today's world.

Among several possible basic orientations in theology, two seem to have particular relevance for contextual theology: one can work out a theology that is basically creation-centred or one can do theology from a fundamentally redemption-centred perspective. A creation-centred orientation sees creation, the world, as sacramental: the world is the place where God reveals himself; it expresses itself in daily life, in ordinary words, through ordinary people. A redemption-centred theology, in contrast, is characterized by the conviction that culture and human experience are either in need of a radical transformation or in need of total replacement. There might be many basic theological orientations, not only these two. But these two are relevant for contextual theology and we will have to choose from them in determining what kind of model or method we see fit.

After having dealt with the issues of criteria for orthodoxy, Bevans launches out on the issues of cultural identity, popular religiosity, and social change. He argues that all three aspects have to be taken into consideration when one develops a truly contextual theology. This needs to include and balance each of these elements along with the elements of Scripture, tradition and other aspects of context, such as social location and particular experience (Bevans 2008:17).

In his book, Bevans is proposing various models of contextual theology. He wishes to speak of theoretical models of the inclusive or descriptive type. The various models, he says, emerge out of the various ways that theologians combine the above mentioned elements that make a theology contextual (see the following diagram adapted from Bevans 2008:32).

After having characterized each model on a diagram, Bevans will follow up on each one of them. The countercultural model is the most conservative. Recognizing the importance of the context, it radically distrusts its revelational power. The translation model is one that puts emphasis on fidelity to what it considers the essential content of scripture and tradition, while certainly taking into account experience, culture, social location, and social change. The most radical of the six models, the anthropological one, will emphasize cultural identity and its relevance for theology more than scripture or tradition. While considering scripture and tradition important, they are themselves a product of contextual relative theologies that have been hammered out in very particular contexts. The practitioner of the praxis model will focus on the importance or need for social change as she or he articulates her or his faith. The one who prefers the synthetic model will attempt the extremely difficult task of keeping all of the elements in perfect balance. Finally, the view of the transcendental model focuses not on a content to be articulated but on the subject who is articulating. The hope here is that one will be able to express one's faith in an authentic contextual manner, if one is personally authentic in one's faith and in one's being-in-the-world (Bevans 2008:32).

Figure 2: Models of Contextual Theology

Transcendental
Model

Anthropological Model	Praxis Model	Synthetic Model	Translation Model	Countercultural Model
.	.	.	.	.
.	.	.	.	.
.	.	.	.	.

Experience of the present (Context)	Experience of the Past
Human experience (personal, communal)	Scripture
Culture (secular, religious)	Tradition
Social location	
Social change	

3.5.2 The Translation Model

The translation model of contextualization is probably the most employed and usually the one that most people think of when they think of doing theology in context, and it is probably the oldest model. Any translation has to be a translation of meaning, not just of words and grammar. Translation has to be idiomatic. It must be done by functional or dynamic equivalence. The translation must be informative and relevant so people can respond to it in action.

Bevans uses Cyril and Methodius and David Hesselgrave as examples for the translation model (2008:45-49). As I understand Hesselgrave, his emphasis is on communication (1980; 1989). He is pointing to the fact that a message is always encoded or contextualized in terms of culture, history and context. He maintains that God is using human symbols and these symbols take on a su-pra-cultural and universal meaning. The Gospel kernel we find in 1Corinthians 15:1-4 was determined by the Holy Spirit and not by a particular socio-cultural context. There are many principles and authoritative sentences in the Scripture that cannot be changed by translation because they are universal and carry an eternal essence. They are what we can call axioms. In this case, it seems that Hesselgrave does not separate between form and meaning, and that the likelihood of contextualization taking place is rather slim. Still, these ex-pressions are axiomatic, meaning that they are self-evident and obvious. They stand firm in their own power. They need no proof of their divinity or eternal power. Even though these expressions are unchangeable they might be trans-lated into meaningful forms. It might be that in order to achieve the goal of contextualization, one must take two steps backwards and one forward by decontextualizing the Gospel in terms of one's own understanding of the scriptural text. And, according to Hesselgrave, decontexutalization would work something like this:

> Decontextualization is needed in order to arrive at the supracultural message which is conveyed in cultural meaningful forms. The cultural wrappings must be folded back in order to get the gift of truth, the Western wrappings of the mission-ary's culture (where the missionary is a Westerner) and also the wrappings of bib-lical culture itself. When one comes to the Scriptures, one must be especially cau-tious, for in the Bible God Himself chose the language and form by which the truth came to be unfolded. The words are God's as well as the truths ... As for contextualization it is needed to make the message meaningful, relevant, persua-sive, and effective within the respondent culture (Hesselgrave & Rommen 1989:222 in Bevans 2008:46).

It seems quite clear that we are here engaged in the work of translation and contextualization in a dialogue situation. How does one actually communicate the Gospel within a varying, radically differing world? Hesselgrave asks the question and answers by saying that one must pay attention to oneself as source of the message and to the Gospel as substance of the message, and to style as the means of communication. We should keep in mind, he insists, that contextualization is never a once-and-for-all accomplishment and that it is best done by the insiders of a culture. Hesselgrave is giving advice to the mission-aries as to how to behave and how to translate. He is emphasizing that the missionaries ought to be well educated and that his/her style should be open, respectful and thoughtful. The Gospel must be presented in terms of forgive-ness and a peaceful mind. I find Hesselgrave's work well sustained and his suggestions regarding how to work out a contextualization program worth-while to follow. It is certain that if we want to win others to Christ, we must approach them in their own language. Then we can quite naturally have a dialogue between faith and culture. This is not a novel idea but has been the tactic as long as mission has existed. Hesselgrave is an example of the evangelical approach to the translation model (Bevans 2008:45).

The Catholics have also had a major exponent for a certain strand of this model in the person of Pope John Paul II (Bevans 2008:49-53). Even though he represents a catholic interpretation of the model, I choose to include him in this section to show the span and various elements that can be emphasized in one and the same model. His approach emphasizes inculturation (2008:50). This expression was introduced into the Catholic Church by Pope John Paul II in 1979. The process of inculturation is described as starting from the top down. One can find a "top-down" definition in *Redemptoris Missio* in a quotation from the final document of the 1985 Extraordinary Synod: "Inculturation means the intimate transformation of authentic cultural values through their integration in Christianity and insertion of Christianity in the various cultures" (2008:50). In the eyes of a Protestant, this approach might be construed as an accommodation, which is an uncritical exchange of symbols. This is not a formal-correspondence mode, but rather a creative dynamic equivalent translation of the unchanging supracultural Gospel by means of symbols and thoughts from another culture. The church itself may be enriched through this process. The pope is referring to the Pentecost experience by saying that the church came into being as a universal church not merely as a particular church, that of Jerusalem. He continues by saying that Christian universalism was inaugurated in the beginning in the diversity of cultures. The methodological effect on the process of inculturation is subtle but profound. We start with a universal (supracultural) message which can be expressed or translated into particular cultural forms. It is obvious that the aim of contextualization is to translate the message of faith in terms understandable to the culture in question.

When we speak of translation in this chapter, we do not have in mind a literal word-for-word translation, but in Charles Kraft's terminology "formal equivalence translation." Any translation has to be a translation of meaning, not just of words and grammar. A good translation is one that captures the meaning of the text. Then it has to be idiomatic or as Kraft says, it must be "dynamic equivalence translation." The aim of this dynamic equivalence translation is to elicit the same reaction in contemporary hearers or readers as in the original hearers or readers.

If there is a key presupposition of the translation model, it is that the essential message of Christianity is supracultural or supracontextual. Practitioners of this model speak of a "Gospel core." Another basic metaphor that reveals this presupposition is that of the kernel and the husk: there is the kernel of the Gospel, which is clothed in a cultural, non-essential husk.

What exactly this essence consists of, however, is a matter of debate among the advocates of the translation model. In any case, what is clear in the minds of the practitioners of this model is that the essential, supracontextual message can be separated from a contextually bound mode of expression. The first step in contextualizing a particular Christian doctrine or practice is to strip off its wrappings, the contextual husk, in order to find the Gospel kernel. Methodologically, it is important to note that the starting point in this process is always the supracultural-supracontextual essential doctrine. The message must be clothed in a language and pattern that people can understand.

At this point, we want to insert an example of translation. We choose to translate Genesis 1:1-2 from English into Bangala-Lingala.

Bangala (Bangala révisé 2000): "[1] Na ebandeli Njambe ajalisaki lora mpe mokili. [2] Mokili ezalaki mpamba, ata eloko moko te azalaki na kati. Molili ejipaki bojindo na mai. Molimo na Nzambe azalaki kotambola na likolo na mai."

Bangala (Version 1960): "[1] LIBOSU libosu Nzambe ajalisaki lora an mokili. [2] Nasima mokili azalaki sika pamba; biroko azalaki na ye te. Butu azalaki na misu na mai, nasima molimo na Nzambe atambulaki na misu na mai."

English (NIV): "[1] In the beginning, God created the heavens and the earth. [2] Now the earth was formless and empty, darkness was over the surface of the deep, and the Spirit of God was hovering over the waters."

Lingala is one of the four *lingua franca* languages used in DRC Congo. The others are Swahili, Kikongo and French. Lingala was orginally a tribe language belonging to a riparian group (Ngala-Bangala) at the Congo River. It was picked up by the colonialists as a very handy means of communication with its few words and simple grammar. In the beginning, it was just called Bangala, but has lately been elaborated into what it is today, a commercial language after the model of Swahili. The Bangala 2000 Bible version is not very different from the 1960 version.

Now let us examine a few words and the placement of the different words. I take it for granted that Bible readers have a certain knowledge of the general principles of hermeneutics such as the literal interpretation, the moral interpretation, the allegorical interpretation and the anagogical or mystical interpretation. So I am not treating these principles one by one, but rather use the principles when matters demand single treatment. I notice that Bevans and also Hesselgrave somehow regard the word for word method negatively. My experience is that we are operating at two stages when translating. The first one is to find the identity of the word and the second is to find the logical place of the word in a sentence or in a context. When identifying a word, there is a word for word consideration. In order to get a meaningful sentence or context one ought to know the meaning of that single word. In order to translate, one should know the language, the verbs, nouns and the grammar quite thoroughly. When one is translating, one begins by reading the sentence word for word, then one arranges the words in one's mind and pronounces the sentence in meaningful and comprehensible language.

If we compare the two translations above, we find that they are more a paraphrase than a word for word translation. We are here presented a fully meaningful context. Some word's identity fit right into the foreign word's identity like *Njambe/Nzambe* "God." *Molimo* is the translation for Spirit. The Lingala vocabulary is too poor to cover all the ideas of the Bible. The phrase "the surface of the deep" and the phrase "over the waters" must somehow be tranlated from words that actually are carrying other connotations, namely *misu na mai* which means "eye and water." We have a metaphoric constellation in the Lingala language. By interpreting the text this way, it has become understandable to the Lingala reader, and just as the English context is meaningful to the English speaking people, so has the Lingala translation become meaningful to the Lingala speaking people. But before it has reached that stage, the words have been transformed and placed into comprehensible and logical sentences in the mind of the interpreter.

In evaluation of the translation model, we can put forward the following reflections: there is no other model that takes as seriously the message of Christianity as recorded in the Scriptures and handed down in tradition as the translation model. It recognizes the ambivalence of contextual reality, whether that be a person's or a society's experience, a culture's or religion's system of values, a person's social location or the movements of change in the world. Nevertheless, there are some questions related to an exclusive or even a preferred use of the translation model. One criticism focuses on the idea of culture that underlies the model's theological method. The presupposition is that every culture is roughly similar to every other culture and what is important in one will be important in another. Questions are rarely asked as to whether there really are such parallels. Criticism can also focus on what is perhaps the key idea of the translation model: the supracultural or the supracontextual nature of the Christian message. It it highly improbable that there can be such a thing as a "naked Gospel." The present debate on this issue suggests for instance that the message of Christianity is always inculturated. And rather than seeking to locate an essential core, one must find a way of discerning cultural patterns that incarnate Christian existence and meaning into new cultural settings. This is called the "onion" model, as opposed to the "kernel and husk" model.

3.5.3 The Anthropological Model

The anthropological model is located at the opposite end of the spectrum from the translation model. If the primary concern of the translation model is the preservation of Biblical revelation while attempting to take culture, social change, and history seriously, the primary concern of the anthropological model is the establishment or preservation of cultural identity by a person of Christian faith. In the context of the anthropological model, therefore, the answer to the question as to whether one is aiming to become a Christian Filipino or a Filipino Christian is very definitely the former option. What is important in this model is the understanding that Christianity is about human persons and their fulfilment. This does not mean that the Gospel cannot challenge a particular context, but such a challenge is always viewed with the suspicion that the challenge is not coming from God as such, but from a tendency of one contextual perspective (Western, Mediterranean) to impose its value on others.

The anthropological model is "anthropological" in two senses. In the first place, this model centres on the value and goodness of the human person (*anthropos*). Human experience, as it is limited and yet realized in culture, social change, and geographical and historical circumstances, are considered the basic criterion of judgment as to whether a particular contextual expression is genuine or not. It is within every person and every society and social location and every culture that God manifests himself. Second, this model is anthropological in the sense that it makes use of the insights of the science of cultural anthropology. By means of this particular discipline, the practitioner of the anthropological model tries to understand more clearly the web of human relationships and meanings that make up the human culture and in which God is offering life, healing and wholeness. This second significance of the anthropological model points to the fact that the main emphasis of this approach to contextual theology is on culture.

The starting point of the anthropological model is, broadly speaking, to present human experience, with a particular focus on human culture, secular or religious. When applied to the question of inculturation, there are many ways to realize this process and no one way can to be considerered as definite. The translation model, on the contrary, works largely out of the presupposition that revelation is contained in a supracontextual and unchanging message. The anthropological model, however, understands revelation in terms of a personal and communal encounter with the divine presence. Compared to the praxis model, which understands revelation as the presence of God in history, the anthropological model would, however, emphasize that it is within human culture that we find God's revelation. The anthropological model sees a mutual benefit for both the particular culture and a wider Christianity. By applying the techniques of cultural anthropology and sociology, the practitioner of the anthropological model attempts to listen to a particular context in order to hear within its structure the very word of God, hidden there like a dormant seed since the beginning of time and ready for sprouting and full growth.

The strength of the anthropological model comes from the fact that it regards human reality with utmost seriousness. It attests to the goodness of all creation and to the lovability of the world into which God sent His only Son (Jn 3:16). Its idea of revelation goes beyond that of the translation model in that it recognizes revelation to be not essentially a message, but the result of an encounter with God's loving and healing power in the midst of the ordinariness of life. And it allows men and women to see Christianity in a fresh light. Another positive aspect is that the anthropological model starts where people are, with people's real questions and interests, rather than imposing questions asked from other contexts.

But a major danger is, however, that this model falls easily prey to a cultural romanticism. On the one hand, this romanticism is evidenced by what is often a lack of critical thinking about the particular culture in question. On the other hand, such cultural romanticism is blind to the fact that the idyllic picture of a culture that the practitioners of the anthropological model paint, does not really exist. Researchers point out that acculturation, or encounter of one culture with another, is happening all the time, even despite efforts of some societies to seal a culture off. The particular insight of the anthropological model is that the theologian must start where the faith lives, and that is in the midst of people (Bevans 2008:59-61).

Bevans presents two examples of the anthropological model: Robert E. Hood and Vincent J. Donovan (Bevans 2008:61-69). Having been a missionary in Africa in the northern part of the Democratic Republic of Congo for about 10 years, I am sympathetic to Hood in many aspects of his views on theology in the African context. His project seeks to demythologize what he considers to be an all-too-Graeco-Roman Eurocentric tradition in non-western Christianity. He does this so that the values and cultural expressions of other non-western non-Greek-influenced cultures can find expression in Christian theology and worship. One reason for this is the assumed superiority of western culture coupled with an assumed inferiority of the African and Asian races. Hood has employed his method to reflect particularly on the doctrines of God, Christ and the Spirit. Perhaps the best example of how the method might help change theological and doctrinal content is his reflection on the doctrine of the Spirit. Hood attempts to make a link between the traditional notion of God the Holy Spirit and the various good spirits whose existence and role are so crucial for understanding the African and Caribbean worldview. The biblical worldview regarding the Spirit of God, Hood argues, is very similar to the African worldview regarding the spirits. In the end, Hood proposes a new alternate theology of the Holy Spirit, based on the African worldview and his reading of Scripture and tradition in light this worldview. Hood's ultimate point is that African-American religion could be made more relevant to black people by admitting its ideas into the mainstream of theology (Bevans 2008:61-64).

In the final analysis, I think that while emphasizing the continuity between the Bible and various cultures, Hood forgets about the enormous discontinuities existing between them. Vincent J. Donovan in his *Christianity Rediscovered* (1978) does likewise. I think many missionaries would recognize his statement about the "naked Gospel". Many missionaries in Africa will also resonate with his experience and description of the meeting with the Masai and the Eucharist. Despite my critical comment above, I think that the anthropological model with its emphasis on continuity is very worthwhile for missionaries to ponder upon.

3.5.4 The Praxis Model

If the translation model focuses on Christian identity within a particular context and seeks to preserve continuity with the older and wider tradition, and if the anthropological model focuses on the cultural identity of Christians within a particular context and seeks to develop their unique way of articulating the faith, the praxis model of contextual theology focuses on the identity of Christians within a context particularly as that context is understood in terms of social change. The praxis model is a model that has come to be the basis of the theologies of liberation, but has also come to be used in the emerging discipline of "practical theology" (Fabella 1979). The praxis model is a way of doing theology that is formed by knowledge at its most intense level, the level of reflective action.

All too often the term "praxis" is used as a trendy alternative to the word practice or action. For example, one might declare somebody a "practical type" as opposed to a more "professorial type." That is well, but how will it work out in praxis? This use of the word, however, is wrong. Praxis is a technical term that has its roots in Marxism, in the Frankfurt school. It is a term that denotes a method or model of thinking in general, and a method or model of theology in particular. Modernity characterized by the thought of Descartes and especially Kant introduced the idea of rationality and subjective responsibility. This modern focus on the subject was deeply revolutionary. From that time on, it became clear that nothing is either true faith or right morality which is not our own. In consequence, external authority is, in principle, an unsound basis, and individual judgement, not merely a right but a duty.

This was a revolution in the whole thinking world, in particular in theology. The method had to be changed. What became necessary was, first, a rigorous use of the historical-critical method to find out what the church truly did be-lieve, why it believed it, and whether such belief was still necessary (positive theology). Then in a second reflection, theology sought to probe the meaning of what was to be believed (speculative theology). When we speak of the praxis model of contextual theology, we are speaking about a model which suggests as its central insight the idea that theology is done not simply by providing relevant expressions of Christian faith, but also by commitment to Christian action. The praxis model employs a method that in its most profound sense is understood as the unity of knowledge as activity and knowledge as content. It works on the conviction that truth is at the level of history, not in the realm of ideas. The praxis model implies the liberation model of theology (Bevans 2008:71-73).

As should be evident from the preceding section, the key presupposition of the praxis model is the insight that the highest level of knowing is intelligent and responsible action. Another key assumption of the praxis model is its notion of God's revelation. The practitioner of the praxis model presupposes the impor-tance of the cultural aspect of the context in developing an understanding of faith. God's presence and invitation to work beside God are available to all women and men equally (2008:73-76).

The great strengths of the praxis model are its method and its undergirding epistemology. It seems that Marxist analysis has broken radically from a pre-occupation with rationality and meaning, and that the Marxist perspective on the primacy of praxis is a much more comprehensive way of knowing than that of a mere intellectual affirmation. That this praxis perspective is not nar-rowly Marxistic is evidenced by similar perspectives being proposed by other thinkers quite different from Marxism in many ways.

I believe that the praxis model as such is basically sound. It is based on an excellent epistemology, its understanding of revelation is very fresh and excit-ing, and it has deep roots in theological tradition. The model has come under some criticism, however, in its concrete form of liberation theology. Some feel uncomfortable with liberation theology's use of Marxism. Others point out its selectivity and even naïveté in terms of its reading of the Bible; still others criticize liberation theologians' concentration on what is negative in society and their "inability to see intermediate manifestations of grace" in society, meaning expressions of popular religiosity. While some of the critiques are valid and some a misunderstanding of liberation theologies' deepest concerns, this is not the place for an extended evaluation (Bevans 2008:77-78).

Bevans is presents two writers as representatives of the praxis model: Douglas John Hall and Virginia Fabella. Both these writers have a great deal to offer in their contributions. Douglas' concern is to present a theology that is "indigenous to the North American experience". In so doing, he wants to construct a "practical theology" that could be incorporated into the living structure and program of the church (2008:79-83).

The catholic Filipina Virginia Fabella has shown herself as a defender for the Asian women and their place in the Christian community as theologians. Fabella's Christology is fundamentally shaped by her basic commitment to the liberation of Asian women. Faith in Jesus today is not about believing Nicean or Chalcedonian formulas (though it does not exclude them), but about being transformed and empowered by Jesus' vision of equality and liberation (2008: 83-87).

3.5.5 The Synthetic Model

The conception of the way Filipino thought is to be developed is a perfect example of the fourth model operative in the construction of contextual theology, the synthetic model. The synthetic model is a middle of the road model. For scriptural justification, it might rely on the process of the formation of the Bible: the Bible came about gradually through a collection of individual books, each of which was formed within the context of present concerns interacting with contemporary culture, neighbouring cultures, and ancient traditions.

We do not speak about an artificial model when we talk about a synthetic model. In the first place, this way of doing contextual theology seeks to be a synthesis of all the other models described by Bevans. It tries to preserve the importance of the Gospel message and the heritage of the traditional doctrinal formulations while at the same time acknowledging the vital role that context has played and can play in theology, even to the setting of the theological agenda. In addition, the synthesis model will include the importance of the reflective and intelligent action for the development of a theology that does not ignore the complexities of social and cultural change. Furthermore, this approach seeks to include other resources and other contexts. In sum, the model is synthetic in the Hegelian sense of not just attempting to put things together in a kind of compromise but developing, in a creative dialectic, something that is acceptable to all standpoints (Bevans 2008:89-90).

A fundamental presupposition of the synthetic model is the composite nature of a human context as the situation in which men and women live. Practitioners of the synthetic model would hold that every context has both elements that are unique to it and elements that are held in common with others. Practitioners of the anthropological model might admit these common grounds in theory, however their emphasis is much more on the uniqueness of a particular culture or situation. What is important for the synthetic model is to emphasize both uniqueness and universality, since one's identity emerges in a dialogue that includes both.

In the synthetic model one starts with listening to culture for basic patterns and structures, analyzing culture in order to discover its basic system of symbols. Out of such a "thick description" will emerge basic themes for a local theology. At the same time, however, these themes need to be in dialogue with the basic themes in Gospel tradition. This dialogue between culture and tradition has a mutually transforming effect on both conversation partners. Schreiter's expression of the synthetic model, which has also been described as the "semiotic model," can be pictured as two parallel columns in constant interaction and dialogue with one another (Bevans 2008:90-93; Schreiter 1985:22-38).

Perhaps the strongest aspect of the synthetic model is its basic methodological attitude of openness and dialogue. In our contemporary, postmodern world so filled with what David Tracy refers to as plurality and ambiguity, truth will not be reached by one point of view, trying to convince all others that it alone is correct. That is neither possible nor, as the situation has revealed, even desirable. Truth in this scheme of things is understood not so much as something "out there" but as a reality that emerges in true conversation between authentic women and men when they "allow questioning to take over." The synthetic model makes a real effort to make theologizing an exercise in true conversation and dialogue with others so that one's own and one's cultural identity can emerge in the process. Perhaps more than any other model, the synthetic model witnesses to the universality of Christian faith.

But there is another aspect to this last positive trait of the synthetic model: it is always in danger of "selling out" to the other culture, tradition, or social location and so always needs to be appropriated with some suspicion. Openness is a good thing, and it cannot be discarded, but the theologian must always be aware of the power and subtle manipulations of a dominant culture (such as Roman, U.S. American or French) as well (2008:93-95).

Bevans presents Kosuke Koyama as one representative of the synthetic model (2008:95-99). He is one of the most imaginative and widely-read Asian theologians. In an address to the American Society of Missiology in 1984, Koyama spoke of "the Asian approach to Christ." To speak of Christ in Asia today, he said, God has to be understood in four ways. First, God must be imaged as impassioned over against the basic Asian idea of salvation as non-involvement. Second, God must be imaged as discontinuous, again over against the Asian idea of salvation as blending harmoniously with the cycles of nature. Third, God needs to be seen as embracing reality in divine involvement rather than simply as transcendent of it. And fourth, God must be understood as on the periphery of life, for the periphery is revealed as the true centre. These four images, Koyama says, are triggered by a study of the spiritual life of the East. As far as I am concerned, it seems to be very questionable whether the biblical God can be conceived of as impassioned and non involving as Koyama suggests.

Bevans presents José de Mesa as a second representative of the synthetic model (2008:99-102). He is a lay theologian born in the Philippines. His theological observations seem a little different from our way of thinking. De Mesa and his friend, Lode Wostyn, seek to construct the following three hermeneutical principles: (1) revelation happens in and through human experiences; (2) experience is always interpreted experience; and (3) experience and its interpretation in the past has to be critically correlated with the present-day experience in a particular local and cultural context. Bevans says that Koyama's and de Mesa's reflections represent a strong exercise of what he calls the synthetic model. Both examples seem to us examples of non-critical contextualization.

3.5.6 The Transcendental Model

In the Gospel of Mark, Jesus says that a new patch cannot be put on an old garment and a new wine cannot be put into old wineskins (Mk 2:21-22). This parable illustrates very clearly the key insight for understanding the transcendental model of contextual theology: there are some things that we cannot understand without a complete change of mind. Some things demand a radical shift in perspective, a change in horizon, a conversion, before they begin to make sense. Without this shift or conversion, we are struggling to find an answer to what amounts to an inadequate question.

The transcendental model proposes that the task of constructing a contextualized theology is not about producing a particular body of any kind of texts; it is about attending to the affective and cognitive operations in the self-transcending subject. What is important is not so much that a particular theology is produced but that the theologian who is producing it operates as an authentic, converted subject. A contextual theology will not appear primarily in the books, but in the mind of men and women (Bevans 2008:103f).

The term "transcendental" is meant to refer to the transcendental method that was pioneered by Emanuel Kant in the eighteenth century and developed later by other philosophers, who attempted to interpret what they discovered to be genuine "intellectualism" in Thomas Aquinas' term of subjectivity and historical consciousness. The transcendental model proposes a basic switch in the process of coming to know reality. Instead of beginning with the world of objects, one begins with the world of the subject, the interior world of the human person. Lonergan writes: "Objective knowledge, knowledge of the real, can only be achieved by attaining authentic subjectivity. It is in attending to one's transcendental subjectivity therefore as it reaches out naturally toward truth that one finds oneself doing an authentic contextual theology" (1972:92).

A fundamental presupposition of the transcendental model is that one begins to theologize contextually not by focussing on the essence of the Gospel message or the content of tradition as such, nor even by trying to thematize or analyse a particular context or expression of language in that context. Rather, the starting point is transcendental, concerned with one's own religious experience and one's own experience of oneself. When one starts with oneself, however, it is important to understand that one does not and cannot start in a vacuum. Very much to the contrary, one realizes that as an individual, as a subject, one is determined at every turn by one's context: I am precisely who I am because I exist at this particular point in time, I am a recipient of a particular national and cultural heritage, and so forth.

The first presupposition leads naturally to the second: that which might seem private and personal is really something that can articulate the experience of others. The third assumption of the model is in regard to the notion of divine revelation. God's revelation is not "out there." The only place where God can truly and effectively reveal himself is within human experience, as a human person is open to the words of Scripture as read or proclaimed, open to events in daily life, and open to the values embodied in a cultural tradition. Revelation, in other words, is only revelation revealing God's self and offering friendship to men and women. Revelation is understood as an event not contents. It is something that happens when a person opens himself or herself to reality.

The fourth foundation stone on which this model rests is the conviction that while every person is truly historically and culturally conditioned in terms of the content of thought, the human mind nevertheless operates in identical ways in all cultures and at all periods of history. This means, as I understand, that the basic cognitive operations for Asians and Africans will be the same even though their cultures are different. This means that not only professional or trained theologians are capable of doing theology. The transcendental model easily admits the fact that any Christian who authentically tries to appropriate his or her faith is participating in the theologizing process and is doing genuine contextual theology. Like both the anthropological and the praxis models, the transcendental model insists that the ordinary Christian believer is a theologian, perhaps even of primary importance (Bevans 2008:104-107).

The transcendental model points to a new way of doing theology. With its emphasis on theology as activity and process rather than theology as particular content, it rightly insists that theology is not about finding out right answers that exist in some transcultural realm, but about a careful but passionate search for authenticity of expression of one's religious and cultural identity. A second advantage of this model is that it clearly recognizes the contextual determination of the person who theologizes. Thirdly, the universal structure of human knowing and consciousness provides a common ground for mutual conversation and interaction.

However, there is reaction to this model that it is too abstract and too hard to grasp and to put into practice. It seems difficult to be thinking of theology, studying it, writing about it or lecturing on and, at the same time, to think of it as the actual activity of seeking understanding as an authentic believer and cultural subject. A more serious objection, however, is that the very universality that is one of the model's advantages is not really universal at all, but seems to be more the product of western, male-dominated cultural thought forms. Do people really come to understand in the same way, or are there really different ways of knowing? Is the transcendental model of contextual theology just another subtle way that western (and perhaps patriarchal) thought attempts to domesticate endeavours to think in alternative ways? If subjective authenticity is the criterion for authentic theology, what or who provides the criterion of subjective authenticity? Finally, since it is so hard to be an authentic believer and an authentic human, it might seem that a theology that depends on these criteria would never get started. The transcendental model might simply be too ideal or at best only a "meta-model" that lays down the condition for the possibility of any theological thinking (2008:108).

Precisely because of its character as a meta-model, every authentic theologian might be cited as an example of the transcendental model of work. No genuine theology has ever been developed outside some specific context; and so, from the writers of the Scriptures (Luke, Paul) to various Christian writers (Augustine and so forth), Christian tradition has been the product of men and women who were both true subjects and people of living faith. Among the many that could be mentioned, Bevans mentions Salliee McFague and Justo L. Gonzalez. They both have a large list of publications dealing with different topics. McFague talks mainly about "the purpose of theology." Bevans believes that of all the works of Gonzalez his *Manana* is the most self-consciously contextual theology (coming out of his cultural roots and social location). *Manana* attempts to articulate a Christian theology from a Hispanic perspective. It is in fact a brief summa of a systematic theology (2008:109-116).

3.5.7 The Countercultural Model

The sixth and last model Bevans presents is the countercultural model. This model takes context, experience, culture, social location, and social change with utmost seriousness. It recognizes that human beings and all theological expressions only exist in historically and culturally conditioned situations. On the other hand, however, it warns that context always needs to be treated with a good deal of suspicion. If the Gospel is truly to take root within a people's context, it needs to challenge and purify that context.

> If it is truly the communication of the Gospel, writes Lesslie Newbigin, it will call radically into question that way of understanding embodied in the language it uses. If it is truly revelation, it will involve contradiction and call for conversion, for a radical *metanoia*, a U-turn of the mind (Newbigin 1986:5f in Bevans 2008:117).

What this model realizes more than other models is how some contexts are simply anti-ethical to the Gospel and need to be challenged by the Gospel's liberating and healing power. The native soil of a particular context needs to be weeded and fertilized in order that the seeds can be planted. The counter-cultural model draws on rich and ample sources in Scripture and tradition (Bevans 2008:117f).

One thing that can be said about the term "countercultural model" is that it is not anti-cultural. Some researchers have tried to use it that way. But the term, however, is intended to express the strong critical function that the model plays over against human context. In no way, it regards the human context as something to be replaced with a purer religious one. We might speak of this model as one of encounter and engagement, engaging in the context through respectful yet critical analysis and authentic Gospel proclamation in word and deed. Bevans has in mind a notion of culture in the broadest sense, one that includes everything: human experience, whether personal or social or in its secular or religious dimensions (2008:119).

A first presupposition of the countercultural model is the radical ambiguity and insufficiency of human context. True contextualization accords the Gospel its rightful place of primacy, recognizes its power to penetrate every culture and to speak within each culture, in its own speech and symbol, the word which is both No and Yes, both judgement and grace. This model presupposes a U-turn or a conversion. Once more, it is Newbigin who expresses it most seminally: Revelation, the heart of which is the Gospel, is not essentially the "disclosure of eternal truths" but the "total fact of Christ" (Newbigin in Bevans 2008:121). This notion of "total fact" needs developing. In the first place, revelation, the Gospel fact in the sense of the Latin *factum*, is something that has been done. What has first been done is that God in Jesus of Nazareth has become incarnate in human history. Second, as human being, Jesus preached the reign of God, died a horrendous death on the cross, and was raised again by God to live among us. Third, these deeds (facts) point to the truth about salvation. The model certainly has a more universal relevance. The model, as Bevans argues, takes its origin from the realization that Christianity in the West exists in a context that is very un-Christian in its basic spirit. According to the practitioners of the countercultural model, the Gospel encounters or engages the human context through its concretization or incarnation in the Christian community, the church. The countercultural emphasizes the importance of Christian "practices": reading the Bible, communal activity, etc. Some critics accuse those who participate in these activities of "sectarianism." These formed and transformed Christians' life and work in the world, testifying by their lifestyle and choices that they live according to the Gospel and not according to the surrounding cultural atmosphere. Christianity is not only historical in that it is based on historical facts; it is an interpretation of history and committed to involvement in history. It is precisely because the Gospel is the clue to history – the *lens* through which history can be viewed rightly – that we can say that faith in the Gospel calls Christians to a genuine encounter or engagement with the human context (2008:120-124).

This model finds its strength from its rootedness in Scripture and Christian tradition. With the possible exception of the translation model, no other model discussed by Bevans, wants to be as engaging of and relevant to the context while at the same time remaining faithful to the Gospel. It recognizes that the genius of Christianity lies neither in its endorsement of the status quo nor in its cultivation of "the new and the next," but in its challenging and transforming power. With the possible exception of the praxis model, no other model discussed here recognizes the deep ambiguity and even anti-Gospel character of context. Particularly, regarding to so much western culture, with its emphasis on individualism, unlimited choice, school violence and so on.

Bevans points to four areas of caution that need to be mentioned in relation to this model. First, although most practitioners of the model recognize the need to be countercultural rather than anti-cultural, the danger persists. This was certainly a danger for missionaries in times past, and while many accusations of missionaries destroying cultures in their efforts to preach Christ are surely exaggerated, such destruction did indeed take place.

A second caution is related to the first. The missionaries should not isolate themselves. One of the marks of the church remains in its catholicity which calls the church to engagement with the whole world. The danger of sectarianism is always present.

A third caution regarding the countercultural model is in its relatively temporary make up, at least in terms of the practitioners in the context of the contemporary West. The practitioners tend to be white and for the most part middle-class. This, however, may be changing. This social location may point to a particular point of view that is served in their critique of contemporary western culture.

Finally, there is a danger of Christian exclusivism over against other religious ways. However, one of the great strengths of the countercultural model is its clear courageous stand in the midst of what is often a lazy pluralism of religious belief, one that reduces religious faith to mere opinion or taste (2008: 124-126).

As examples of the countercultural model, Bevans mentions the "Gospel and Our Culture Network" (GOCN), which has come into existence as the fruit of the ministry of Lesslie Newbigin, and the Catholic theologian Michael J. Baxter (2008:127-137).

3.5.8 The Critical Model

Having surveyed the various models that Bevans presents, in this section, we will focus in more detail on Paul Hiebert's critical model as it suits our purposes particularly well (Hiebert 1984; 1985:183-192).

The idea with contextualization, as previously mentioned, is to perceive the culture as a receiver culture with respect and efficiency, for the sole purpose of teaching them the word of God. That does not mean uncritically accepting everything that a culture contains. No, that might open the road for syncretism which is a blend of Christian traditions and rituals and traditions of the receiver culture. On the other hand, an absolute rejection of local customs and practices is no ideal method either. The reason is that an intolerant attitude may cause conflicts between Christians and new converts. Besides, an attitude of intolerance may lead the receiver to go underground and conceal his beliefs and practices. The result of this manoeuvre could be a so called "split-level Christianity" or "double Christianity." There are a lot of examples for this kind of development. In chapter 2 I have written about a young couple who came to my church to get their twins blessed. After the blessing they went straight back to their village and joined the villagers in a big name giving festival.

The way I see it, contextualization is about two main subjects. Firstly, it is about how the missionaries and their culture relate to the culture they shall work in. Secondly, it is about how the converts in the receiver culture evaluate their own culture in the light of the Bible and the newly acquired knowledge which the Gospel brings.

Let us take a look at the missionary and his/her culture. Hiebert proposes that the sender-culture first of all investigate the receptor-culture (Hiebert 1985; cf. Frost & Hirsch 2003:89). This act will have to be carried out with dignity and respect. The objective for this kind of operation is to learn the language, values, customs, and traditions of the receptor culture. The reason for getting thoroughly into these items is to be able to present Christianity in a manner that makes the message comprehensible and meaningful to the receptor people.

Moreover, Hiebert is recommending a strong commitment to the Bible, its superiority and unalterable, eternal authority (1985:89). This last point concerns the new converts as well, which brings us to the second aspect which I have previously mentioned, namely how the local people evaluate their own culture in the light of the Bible. I shall return to this subject later on.

We shall now take a closer look at earlier examples of contextualization or lack of it. There was no talk about contextualization in "the olden days." The local culture was either refused or denied all together (Moen 2005). The reason for this lays in the fact that the right comprehension of Christianity was linked to western culture. For instance, the drums that were used at the Mongwande rituals were understood as they were from "the devil" and could therefore not be used in the church. Local musical instruments were replaced by the western organ. However, in many societies, there is no specific division between right or wrong instruments. In our opinion, it seems difficult to conceive of a secular world, existing independently from God. All belongs to God and happens in accordance with God's will, and one may try to influence this worldly reality by turning to the spiritual sphere. Religion is part of this reality by all means. This was the reason why customs and practices were very often rejected. This "rejection of customs" could produce some heavy consequences. Primarily, it could lead to alienation from Christianity (Hiebert 1985:184; cf. Frost & Hirsch 2003:184).

When the old host culture is rejected, it leaves a void (vacuum) that must be filled. If this gap gets filled with western customs and practices like songs, instruments, etc., this might be something artificial and forced upon the local people, though we have examples to the contrary. For instance, when the African Americans accepted the Gospel, with western music and its development, this could be characterized as a successful project regardless of the fact that these people could complain that their cultural heritage was taken away from them or forbidden and replaced by western rites and instruments. It could have created in the African Americans a bitter and negative attitude toward Christianity, giving place to feelings of hostility. However, when this success story does not happen, it might be that the local people simply go underground and conceal their religious secrets. This could then lead to a problem of so called "Christo-paganism" or "heathen-Christianity," a hidden syncretism. An example of this is when white children are brought up with African gods and customs and later carry these ideas with them to the Catholic Church. This results in turn to a split-level or double Christianity (Hiebert et al. 1999:392). This means that the local population while holding to their old practices and traditions confess at the same time their faith in Christ. This old fashion way of relating to a receptor culture is not only a refusal of the local culture but also a refusal of contextualization as concept and practice (Hiebert 1984:9).

On the other hand, we have cases where the missionaries have responded quite differently to the local culture. In some cases, some have uncritically accepted everything that belongs to the host culture. The problem with this point of approach is that it can lead to an open syncretism which may result in turn in neo-paganism. Syncretism and its expressions like neo-paganism are a kind of mixture of Christianity and local culture. We know that every person has some sort of mental baggage and as new converts they will have to consider and reconsider their lives in the light of the standards and teachings of the Bible. It is at this point that the missionary's role will be central, because he must, to the best of his ability, teach them the truth of the Bible and guide them through misconceptions and confusions. Besides, uncritical contextualization is overlooking the fact that there are common cultural sins which are found in the institutions of every society (Hiebert 1985:185; cf. Frost & Hirsch 2003: 185).

We can summize then that these two first ways of relating to culture, either rejection or uncritical acceptance of the host-culture's beliefs and traditions, eventually produce syncretism. The one leads to a void (vacuum), bitterness and finally goes underground (a hidden syncretism), while the other leads to open syncretism and Christo-paganism. Therefore, with the passage of time, researchers have come to acknowledge the necessity of a third method. Missionaries and leaders will have to be educated and well equipped to cope with new cultural situations according to the basic idea of contextualization described in the TEF document of 1972 as mentioned above (Coe 1972).

This third way of relating to and handling a local culture is called "critical contextualization." Critical contextualization neither rejects nor accepts uncritically the different customs and traditions in any given host-culture, but takes all the elements into consideration in the light of the Bible and its truths (Hiebert 1985:186-190). Again, Paul Hiebert will serve as our point of departure and his model as the scarlet thread in our example. Here is how the process of critical contextualization could be pursued in practice.

Having analyzed his culture and the local culture and having committed himself to the authority of the Bible, the missionnary and the new converts will have to reconsider the local culture in the light of the Bible. The church acknowledges the need of behaving according to the Bible in all aspects of life. The Gospel has full claims on the lives of believers. With that in mind, it is all up to a Christian to acknowledge all the rites and practices that she/he is surrounded by, from rituals relating to birth, wedding and death, popular music and the economical system in society.

After that is done, the local church leaders have a responsibility to guide the new converts in collecting and uncritical analyzing their proper traditions and practices. It may be fruitful to look closely at the rituals in connection with funeral and analyze each item (like songs, dances, recitations), and try to find out their meaning and function within the framework of the place that burial rites hold within the community. The purpose is to understand the old pattern, not to evaluate or to judge them. At this stage of the process, critizing local practices would not be helpful in allowing the local population to speak openly about their customs: locals may stay silent in fear of being condemned by the missionary (Hiebert 1985:186).

The pastor or the missionary should then guide the church in Bible studies on themes relating to the practice in focus, for instance, traditions connected with marriage. The leader can teach a Christian view in this matter (1985:186f). This point is usually very important, because if the host population does not understand and accept the Biblical view, they will not be able to make up their minds concerning their cultural practices. It is right here that the role of the missionary/pastor is important because it is here he can offer exegetical keys to help the new converts get a true comprehension of the Bible. I am not talking about a true perception or a true interpretation which is a question of creed. But it is very important that the local church participates actively in the process so it may grow in its faith and ability to discern between what is truth and what is not truth.

In the third step the church evaluates critically its earlier traditions and practices in the light of the newly acquired Biblical teachings and understanding and takes a decision concerning the use of these in its life. The leader can share his view on the matter and guide the church to see what the Bible says about the themes. But it is important that the people take the decision and thus show that the question is their question and not somebody else's. It is not something that has been forced upon them. They must feel free and sure of the result if they are to change. In this manner the missionary and the pastor will avoid becoming religious police. In addition, the chance to go underground has diminished considerably. It is the local people who shall carry the plan into effect. It is important that the people feel that the decisions made and the conclusions reached are their own (1985:186f).

The reaction of missionaries to local customs, the fourth step, may vary: some customs and traditions may be kept because they are not in conflict with the Bible. They are not unbiblical like things that are neither condemned nor ordered in the Bible, such as men wearing dark suits, popular songs that are not improper for Christians, etc. (Frost & Hirsch 2003:90).

Some customs will obviously be rejected, as they are clearly irreconcilable with a Christian life-style. It might be that the missionary must help the local people to watch out for things that are inappropriate for the Christians, but the host church has overlooked. On the other hand, the locals may point at certain things that in their eyes or "ears" might be indecent, even though they are not perceived like that by the missionary (Hiebert 1985:187).

The church may some times modify some old customs and give them a Christian meaning. In this regard, Christmas is a good example. Christmas is an ancient heathen festival, but has been given a Christian meaning, marking the birth of Jesus Christ (Frost & Hirsch 2003:90).

The church now and then substitutes rejected customs with Christian customs that are borrowed from other cultures. Substitutes of the kind are often functional because they minimise the cultural vacuum emerging when old local customs are rejected.

Sometimes the local church is simply adding foreign, Christian rituals like baptism and the Lord's Supper in order to foster continuity with the common heritage. Christians live in two traditions: cultural and Christian. It gives the new convert a way of expressing the new faith. It also shows the link that ties together the new converts to the international and historical church. The host culture can also create new symbols and rites with intent to communicate or pass on the Christian faith in form and meaning that is native and meaningful in the culture. It might be songs, ceremonies, rites or even objects.

After guiding a host congregation through a process of analyzing its own culture in the light of biblical teachings, the missionary or the pastor must help them organize new practices, customs or rituals. In so doing, the receiving church and the sending church have reached new "rituals" together which express more fully Christian meaning as a whole. The rituals are Christian because they are expressing biblical doctrines. They belong also to the local culture in which they have been composed, created by a cross-cultural communication between the host congregation and the missionaries in forms which are easily understandable by those in the local community (Hiebert 1985:186-190).

In summary, Hiebert, Shaw and Tienou (1999:21-29) formulate the four major steps of the critical contextualization process particularly well (cf. also Hiebert 1984; 1985:183-190):

1) Cultural analysis: Before anything can be done the missionary/researcher must study the local culture or a particular phenomenon. This might be difficult depending on time and place or personalities involved. Secular objects are usually easy, but religious items and rituals may be kept very much secret. Christians must go beyond phenomenology to ontological evaluation at the worldview level.

2) Biblical analysis: In order to test the claim of truth of different beliefs and values the Christians must study the Bible in relation to the themes in question.

3) Evaluation of culture in the light of Scripture: The congregation must critically evaluate their beliefs and customs in the light of the Scriptures.

4) By this step we have arrived at the final process according to Hiebert, which he calls the passage for transformative ministries. Meaning that minis-

try helps people to move from where they are to where God wants them to be. One cannot expect people to abandon all at once the old ways and adopt new ones. People can only move through a process of transformation. This step will include the proper contextualization faithful to Scripture and relevant for culture by accepting, rejecting, modifying, tolerating or creating cultural elements.

By offering a very clear framework for a contextualization process, the critical model becomes something like a "meta-model" for the other models of contextualization.

3.5.9   Evaluation of the Models

In this section, I have dealt with the theoretical part of the models of contextual theology. It is time to come to their evaluation. Together with the critical model, I found the translation model and the anthropological model most fit for my use in this work. Although the four other models have their qualities and points of importance, I found what I was looking for, however, mainly in these three models. I will only make a few comments about the translation and anthropological models, as the critical model is found at the heart of my work in what follows.

First, the translation model is in my opinion the model that comes naturally as the first thing we have to do when we encounter a new culture with its language and customs. We have to learn that particular language and to a certain degree accept the customs. Since the primary concern of the translation model is to preserve the biblical text and at the same time to take the host culture seriously, for me, the translation model presents itself as a first choice and most applicable method. Preserving the biblical text in the new context means some form of translation, which may imply maintaining a one to one equivalence. However, I notice that there is some reluctance to a word to word translation. As a translator myself throughout almost 30 years of missionary service, I most humbly state that to ignore the necessity of a word to word translation is to throw away the basis of a language. One has to know what the words mean, and it seems natural to begin here. Only then can one put the words in an orderly sequence with the intent of conveying meaning. We must remember that we are facing a completely new world within the host culture. The practices and forms of worship may be radically different from that of our own but the meaning and emotions may not be so far from ours.

Second, the anthropological model has also its values and to a certain degree is concerned about the establishment or preservation of cultural identity. In this connection, the question will emerge whether we talk about a Christian Mongwande or Mongwande Christian. The difference in nuance is important, as in one case individuals belong to a church but are not believers by heart; that is, they are nominal Christians only. It is the reason why I refer to the human institutions in Monga. We see that the list is quite long and could be much longer, if we had taken into account all the human, social, religious and political institutions. This calendar delves into marriages and divorces or dissolution of marriages, initiation, association sealed by magico-religious rites, blood relationship and funeral associations. The question will be: How far can a Mongwande retain certain pratices and still call himself a Christian? Could there be something in these institutions which we, as foreigners, do not comprehend and therefore say "no" or "yes" for that matter? According to Hiebert, we should let the local Christians decide themselves.

3.6 Contextualization of Social and Religious Life

In this section, we will demonstrate the need and emphasize the importance of contextualizing Christian life to the whole of culture by presenting some elements of Mongwande social and religious life in their relationship to biblical and Christian concepts.

3.6.1 Individual and Collective Worship

While the worship of the household gods is just a personal exercise of religion, the snake cult embraces the whole family, other families that have twins, and the whole Mongwande village. Twins are the sign of the snake's presence in the family and the village. How are we to deal with this kind of religious practices? Revelation 20:2 describes how the old serpent was cast out. But it turned out that it was not that easy to get the snake out of the mind of a person. To read the Bible over the head of the culprit was no magic formula either. The challenge of living life in the context of one's cultural setting has caused the downfall of one of God's faithful servants more than once. It is for this reason that I would like to add love and patience to the list of qualities that are important in the work of contextualization. A contextualization program is not accomplished in a few weeks time. It might take months or years. One might even say that it is a never-ending process.

3.6.2 Family Life

Of all the complicated questions we meet in foreign cultures, I think polygamy is one of the most difficult to deal with. Questions asked about polygamy and the answers given have most of the time been ambiguous. Systematic theology is limited in helping us to find satisfactory answers, since systematic theology is about constructing a single systematic understanding of ultimate truth that is logically consistent and conceptually coherent. But it difficult to rely on such a

system when working in cross-cultural settings; that is, in constructing systematic theology, one does not take into account the outward circumstances
and changes that have taken place to form the situations and customs of a
people group. The approach of biblical theology seems more promising. This
theology has its advantages, using questions, methods and assumptions of
modern historiography. It is advantageous because it gives us the diachronic
dimension of the biblical worldview. It is focusing on biblical history, not so
much on present events.

An even newer concept has entered the theological scene, missional theology,
which stands for a way of thinking biblically about God's mission in the world
here and now. For many missionaries, the question, when facing polygamy out
in the village was: "What does the word of God say to those who live in polygamy?" Well, we do have a word about marriage both in Matthew 19:1 and
in Mark 10:1. But none of these passages from the Bible were actually applicable to polygamy. Out of this ambiguous situation arose a specific way of
coping with polygamy through the methods of missional theology. Missional
theology is well suited for this problem because it seeks to build bridges between biblical revelation and human contexts. And here we are dealing with
men and women, people with flesh and blood, body and soul.

Through centuries, polygamous marriages have been regarded as from Satan
and had to be rejected. Polygamous marriages have been forced apart by the
missionaries, and many families have been destroyed. However, by studying
the facts, listening to arguments from various points of view and using a little
theological reflection, it is quite possible to reach an acceptable solution. We
should not forget that entering into a polygamous marriage is in most cases a
situation of privilege for an African woman, even life maintainance. When I
read Kraft's argumentations concerning the chief Amadu and his fate I am
convinced that missional theology has a sure future place within contextual
theology. According to Kraft, systematic theology is not applicable in this case
of Amadu, but only missional theology. In order to clarify this issue, I quote
the case of Amadu:

> Amadu is the chief of the village. When missionaries came, they asked him for
> permission to stay, and, out of hospitality, he allowed them to do so. After three
> years of ministry a small church of believers was formed, made up of two singles
> and five young couples, all monogamous. Having heard of the Gospel and seen its
> effects on new believers, Amadu, came and wanted to be baptized into the church,
> along with his five wives. What should the missionaries do? (Kraft 2005:131-130).

Our church in Monga experienced the same thing early in its history: the chief
of the Monga territory, Bela, had about 30 wives. He came and asked the missionaries to be baptized. The missionaries told him to get rid of all of his
wives but one of them. He did so but kept the youngest one. He then joined

the church and became a very faithful member, still alive and active when I left the Monga area in the early sixties. As I see it, the missionaries did right in the question of polygamy but wrong in the question of divorce. If we consider polygamy and divorce as cultural issues, which they really are (not religious ones), they should not be dealt with as biblical sins. In this regard, I agree with Kraft in his efforts to illustrate the methods of missional theology (2005:125, 130-133). There are situations where we may be forced to abandon the systematic theology approach to the benefit of missional theology, meaning we will have to formulate new principles in accordance with the biblical teachings for the new converts.

3.6.3 Songs, Dances and Music

Songs, dances, music and just real, pure joy stream out of Africa. No people I know have the capability to celebrate and to express thoughts and emotions as Africans. It is through the songs and music we come to learn about what is deep down within people. We know that Africa consists of hundreds of different people groups with their particular languages and customs. Even up in the Monga territory, there are quite a few different tribes. It is a strange thing though that very little of the Mongwande cultural heritage has found its way into the church. In the church song book *Lembo na Sasaipi* with its 133 songs, no song composed by a Mongwande has been found worthy to be incorporated into this book. As to the snake songs, none of them either has been sung or copied for using elsewhere. The reason is that they are being judged to contain words from the devil. I have just learned that this missionary attitude has been changed and that a new songbook has been introduced. It is difficult to accept snake songs outside of the circle of snake worshippers. However, it is not easier with the other cultural artistic expressions such as dancing. If there is a difference in perception and tone between the African and Western styles of songs, there are even greater differences between the African and the Western way of dancing. Does God have something to say about dancing? Doesn't the Bible say a great deal about dance? David, for example, is dancing before the Lord (2Sam 6:14). He was happy because the ark of the Lord was brought up to Jerusalem. Why is dancing forbidden in Christian worship in the Mongwande context? I do not know, but only guess that it is considered to be the devil's work as the Christian church seems to have always has claimed. It is sometimes a real suffering during the morning services in the church to watch how the churchgoers struggle as they try to sing Western religious songs. This area of art cries for contextualization.

Western music, even up to this day, is dominant in Monga. In the church, you have a cabinet organ, or a bigger organ, a piano and a guitar. Seldom, do you see Mongwande music instruments like drums, flutes and stringed instruments.

I know that the Mongwande use these types of instruments in the snake cult worship. But why couldn't they be incorporated into the ordinary worship services in the church? Furthermore, why aren't song, dance and music used in the propagation of the Gospel? Nothing is so penetrating as song and music, and this is especially so in the African context. The art of music serves to powerfully communicate the Gospel and its content (faith, hope and love) in the most pleasant way to the people.

3.6.4 Healing and Prophecy

We have noticed that in the encounter between Christianity and the African cultures new churches are populating the scene. These groups, the so called African Initiated Churches (AIC), remain mainly faithful to their Christian foundations, but are mostly outside the other ordinary church organizations. This is because they have preserved some African elements in their midst. One of the more distinctive marks is healing. This is not foreign to the more established churches either. But what is unusual is that they use methods of traditional medicine. The medicine man is appearing within these circles embodied as a Christian prophet. Prayers, dreams, visions and divine guidance characterize their lives. The ordinary churches have usually refused these phenomena on the grounds that it causes trouble in the church and may create disagreement with the missionaries.

Some prominent figures have come out, like Simon Kimbangu, founder of the Kimbanguist church, and Kimpa Vita and André Matswa in Ngunzism (Sundberg 2000:105-127). They insist that they have been sent by God to their people, and that they have received authority from him to preach the Gospel and heal people. Swarms of healers and prophets have emerged and proclaimed to be called by God. What is interesting is that if we investigate that call a little closer, we find that it is surprisingly similar to the old traditional pattern. It starts with sickness of some kind, not an unknown pattern within the Judeo-Christian world (Ps 30; Lk 17:15). These prophets in question are healed by the Holy Spirit and ordered to go and preach the Gospel of salvation and heal others. They experience this with great intensity. They often testify that Satan tempted them, but by the power of God they were able to overcome. They consider theyselves to be prophets (*nebi* in Lingala and *nabi* in Hebrew) or men of God (*motu na Nzambe* in Lingala and *nyi te Nzapa* in Mongwande). What they are doing is combining the new Christian culture with the old Mongwande culture and the snake cult. In fact, Simon Kimbangu, who was deported with some believers up to the Monga area, is an example of this phenomenon. Villagers still speak of him with great reverence because of his strong influence. What we are observing here is actually some sort of syncretism. I wonder what would Kraft do in the case of these healers and prophets practicing both Christianity and local religion? What kind of method would Kraft employ here?

I had ample time to investigate both the Kimbangu church and two other churches near Monga. One of these was the *Kulinga na Kundima,* "Love and Faith" church. They received the name because they swapped wives. That action was the sign that the members in the church loved and trusted each other: "You say you love me, show me your love by letting me have your wife." Another group was the so called *Kitiwala* church. I was told that these churches incorporated traditional rites as part of their cult exercises, blood offerings, offerings of lambs and socially they lived in polygamy. It appears to me that the above mentioned churches have gone beyond the borders of Christian morality. In my view, the question whether we should pass a final judgement or not, would depend upon whether certain cultural practises within the framework of the church leads to the rejection of faith in Jesus Christ or not (Jn 16:9).

As it stands, the Christian church has been contextualizing throughout its history under the notions of adaptation, accommodation, indigenization, inculturation and contextualization. The aim has been to adapt or appropriate Christianity within the local culture without losing the very centrepiece of the Gospel, Jesus Christ our Saviour, out of sight.

3.7 Conclusion

Going through Bevans' magnificent work, I join him in his conclusion that each one of these models has a certain validity in its proper setting. Each has its advantages and problems. I draw the conclusion that Bevans gives a set of tools that are very helpful for engaging in the contextualization process.

However, the critical model, which Bevans has not considered and which respects the authority of Scripture, seems particularly suited for our purposes. With Hiebert's critical model of contextualization, evangelicals have a valuable tool with which to work out the meanings of Scripture in the varieties of mission contexts. Hiebert's critical model seems to be a kind of a "metamodel" also to be applied when using the other models. Gilliland maintains that contextualization cannot take place unless Scripture is read and obeyed by believers. The strength of contextualization is that if carried out properly, that means critically, it brings ordinary Christian believers into what is often called the "theological process" (Gilliland 2000:227).

The objective of contextualization is to bring data from the whole of life of real people into critical dialogue with Scripture with the intent of finding meaningful application of the Word which "dwelt among us" (Jn 1:14).

Chapter 4
The Snake in Scripture

4.1 Introduction

In this chapter, I will investigate the concept of the snake, as it appears in the Bible, in order to see whether there might be a relevant link between the biblical snake concept and the concept of the snake as it appears in the Mongwande snake cult. I will start with a lexical study of key words, followed by an analysis of biblical passages containing the term "snake" or its cognates. I thereafter present a concept study. My method consists of lexical and exegetical work using the NIV version of the Bible. The main lexical sources in this chapter are Kittel's *Theological Dictionary of the New Testament* (TDNT), the *New International Dictionary of Old Testament Theology and Exegesis* (NIDOTTE) and the *New International Dictionary of New Testament* (NIDNT).

4.2 Lexical Studies

4.2.1 Terms in the Semantic Domain

The Hebrew word for snake is *nahash*. It occurs over forty times in the OT (see list of passages below). It appears in parallel with *shᵉpipon* "viper" (Gen 49:17), *peten* "cobra" (Ps 58:4), *'akshub* "viper" (Ps 140:3), *sip'oni* "viper" (Prov 23:32; Jer 8:17), *sepa'* "viper" (Isa 14:29), and also refers to Leviathan (*tannin*), the sea monster (Isa 27:1). The adjective *sarap* modifies *nahash* to indicate either its reddish colour or inflammatory bite (Num 21:6; Deut 8:15). Moses cast a bronze or copper (*nᵉhoshet*) snake, which was later named Nehushtan (Num 21:9; 2Kgs 18:4). When *sarap* appears as a nominative, it indicates either seraphs (Isa 6:2, 6), the snakes in the wilderness (Num 21:8), or some other kind of snake characterized as *me'opep* (lit. flying; Isa 14:29; 30:6). The understanding of this last type as "flying serpents" rests on a report by Herodotus (3:107, 109), but the biblical description could also indicate a jab or prick, thus NIV "darting." The word *sarap* refers to literal and figurative snakes (Num 21:6, 8; Isa 14:29). The seraphs we see in Isaiah's vision (Isa 6:2) need not to be understood as winged serpents. The word *tannin* however designates a range of creatures from sea snakes (Gen 1:21) to land snakes (Ex 7:9, 10-12) and the mythological sea monster (Job 7:12). Psalm 58:4f associates the act of charming with *peten*, which is likely the Egyptian cobra (also called *uraeus*), rearing up from the Pharaoh's headgear. It appears in parallel with *tannin* "serpent" (Deut 32:33; Ps 91:13), *'ep'eh* "adder" (Job 20:16, NIV), and *sip'oni* "viper" (Isa 11:8). The *'ep'eh* (NIV adder) may be the deadly sand viper (*Echis colorata*). Palestine today is home to over thirty species of snakes of which only six are poisonous. These species are presumed in nearly all biblical references to snakes. The "f" sound in many of the Hebrew terms is likely onomatopoeic for the snake's puffing noise (Stallman 1996a:84-88; 1996b:1129-1132).

The LXX translates the different Hebrew terms usually with *ophis* or *aspis*. The LXX translators were apparently uncomfortable with the figures Rahab and Leviathan, twice omitting reference to these sea monsters (Job 9:13 and Isa 51:9; Ps 74:14). In Isaiah 27:1, they construed "Leviathan the gliding serpent" as "the dragon, the fleeing serpent" (cf. Job 26:13 and Ps 89:10 for similar interpretive moves).

Following this line of thought, the NT uses *ophis* and *aspis*, the terms for "snake," and additionally the term "dragon" (*drakon*) in a synonymic way. In the NT, "dragon" (*drakon*) is mostly used as a synonym for Satan. The term snake is also paralleled with the term "scorpion" (*skorpios*) with his sting (*kentron*). Additionally, a generic term *therion* is used meaning "wild animal" or "beast" (Bietenhard & Budd 1986:507-511).

4.2.2 Occurrences of the Term in the Bible

I found the term snake in the Old Testament around twenty five times. The passages are as follows:

Gen 3:1-4: *Now, the serpent was more crafty than any of the wild animals* the Lord God had made. He said to the woman, "Did God really say, 'You must not eat from any tree in the garden'?"

Gen 3:13-14: Then the the Lord said to the woman "What is this you have done?" The woman said, *"The* serpent *deceived me and I ate." So the Lord God said to the ser*pent: "Because you have done this, *cursed are you above all the livestock and all the wild animals! You will crawl on your belly and you will eat dust all the days of your life.*

Gen 49:17: *Dan shall be a serpent by the roadside, a viper along the path* that bites the horse's heels so that its rider tumbles backwards.

Ex 4:3: The Lord said, "Throw it on the ground." Moses threw it on the ground and it became a snake, and he ran from it.

Ex 7:9-10, 15: When Pharaoh says to you, "Perform a miracle," then say to Aaron, "Take your staff and throw it down before Pharaoh *and it will become a snake.*"

Num 21:6-9: The the lord s*ent venomous serpents among them*; they bit the people and many Israelites died.The people came to Moses and said, "We sinned when we spoke against the Lord and against you. Pray that the

Lord will take the snakes away from us." So Moses prayed for the people. The Lord said to Moses, *"Make a snake and put it up on a pole; anyone who is bitten can look at it and live." So Moses made a bronze snake and put it up on a pole. Then when anyone was bitten by a snake and looked at the bronze snake, that person lived*

Deut 8:15b: He led you through the vast and dreadful desert, that thirsty and waterless land, *with its venomous snakes and scorpions.*

Deut 32:33: Their wine is the venom of serpents, the deadly poison of cobras..."

2Kgs 18:4: He removed the high places, smashed the sacred stones and cut down the Asherah poles. He broke into pieces the bronze snake Moses had made, for up to that time the Israelites had been burning incense to it.

Job 20:16: He will suck the poison of serpents; the fangs of an adder will kill him.

Job 26:13: By his breath the skies became fair; his hand pierced the gliding serpent.

Psalm 58:4-5: Their venom is like the venom of the snake, like that of a cobra that has stopped its ears that will not heed the tune of the charmer, however skilful the enchanter may be.

Psalm 91:13b: You will trample the great lion and the serpent.

Psalm 140:3: They make their tongues as sharp as a serpent's, the poison of vipers is on their lips.

Proverbs 23:32: In the end it bites like a snake and poisons like a viper.

Ecc 10:8-11: Whoever digs a pit may falll into it; whoever breaks through a wall may be bitten by a snake. Whoever quarries stones may be injured by them; whoever splits logs may be endangered by them. If the axe is dull and its edge unsharpened, more strength is needed but skill will bring success. If a snake bites before it is charmed, there is no profit for the charmer.

Isa 14:29: Do not rejoice, all you Philistines, that the rod that struck you is broken; from the root of that snake will spring up up a viper, its fruit will be a darting, venoumous serpent.

Isa 27:1: In that day, the Lord will punish with his sword, his fierce, great and powerful sword, Leviathan the gliding serpent, Leviathan the coiling serpent; he will slay the monster of the sea.

Isa 59:5: They hatch the eggs of vipers and spin a spider's web. Whoever eats their eggs will die, and when one is broken, an adder is hatched.

Isa 65:25: The wolf and lamb will feed together, and the lion will eat straw like the ox, *but dust will be the serpent's food.* They will neither harm nor destroy on all my holy mountain, says the Lord.

Jer 46:22: Egypt will hiss like a fleeing serpent as the enemy advances in force; they will come against her with axes; like those who cut down trees.

Am 5:19: It will be as though a man fled from a lion only to meet a bear, as though he entered his house and rested his hand on the wall *only to have a snake bite him.*

Am 9:3: Though they hide themselves on the top of Carmel, there they will hunt them and seize them. Though they hide from me at the bottom of the sea, *there I will command the serpent to bite tem.*

In the New Testament I found the term snake around fourteen times. The passages are as follows:

Mt 7:10: Or if they ask for a fish, will I give them a snake?

Mt 10:16b: Therefore be as shrewd as snakes

Mt 23:33a: *You snakes! You brood of wipers*! How will you escape being condemned to hell?

Mk 16:18a: *They will pick up snakes with their hands;* and when they drink deadly poison, it will not hurt them at all; they will place their hands on sick people, and they will get well.

Lk 10:19a: I have given you authority to trample on snakes and scorpions and to overcome all power of the enemy; nothing will harm you.

Lk 11:11: Which of you fathers, if your children ask for fish, will give them a snake instead?

Jn 3:14: Just as Moses lifted up the snake in the desert, so the son of man must be lifted up, that everyone who believes in hi, may have eternal life.

Act 28:3: Paul gathered a pile of brushwood and as he put it on the fire, a viper, driven out by the heat, fastened itself on his hand.

1Cor 10:9c: We should not test the Lord, as some of them did *and were killed by snakes.*

2Cor 11:3: *Just as Eve was deceived by the serpent's cunning,* your minds may be led astray from your sincere and pure devotion to Christ.

Rev 9:19: The power of the horses was in their mouths and in their tails *for their tails were like snakes.*

Rev 12:9: The great dragon was hurled down, that ancient serpent called the devil or Satan, who leads the whole world astray. He was hurled to the earth, and his angels with him.

Rev 12:14-15: The woman was given the two wings of a great eagle, so that she might fly to the place prepared for her in the desert, where she would be taken care of for a time, times and half a time, out of the serpent's reach. Then from his mouth the serpent spewed water like a river, to overtake the woman and sweep her away with the torrent.

Rev 20:2: He seized the Dragon, that ancient serpent, who is the devil, or Satan and bound him for a thousand years.

4.2.3 Basic Meanings

When the OT talks of serpents and vipers (Ps 140:3), the most dangerous creature in Palestine seems to be the *Vipera xanthina* (Gen 49:17). Researchers assume it is the deadly horned viper. The snake stands for death and annihilation because it kills. It was feared throughout the OT.

The notion of snake has been used metaphorically very often, particularly by the prophets. Micah warns the neighbours of Israel that they will eat dust like a snake if they don't believe in God (Mic 7:17). Egypt is compared to the sea monster Rahab. From the king's root, Isaiah says, vipers and serpents will spring forth (Isa 14:29). Amos speaks rather cynically about those who are waiting for the day of the Lord. Their experience of that day will be as if they were bitten by a snake (Stallman 1996a:85, 87).

Intertestamentary literature mentions the snake often and uses it as a metaphor for temptation and deceit. The earlier pseudepigraphic literature does not connect the snake in Eden to the devil. And the Jewish interpreters gave the credit for healing in the wilderness to God. The Qumran community seems to have understood the snakes of Deuteronomy 32:33 as metaphors for pagan rule (Stallman 1996b:87, 88).

In the NT, the snake is used in positive and negative ways. In his dialogue with Nicodemus, Jesus compares his crucifixion with the elevation of the bronze snake in the wilderness (Jn 3:14-15). Jesus urges the people to pray and insists that the Heavenly Father will not give them a snake when they ask for fish (Mt 7:10). Taking the snake as a model, Jesus encourages his disciples to be shrewd as snakes and innocent as doves (Matt 10:16).

In the NT, the snake has also been regarded as a strange and menacing animal, dangerous to life and full of devilry and deceit. Because of its closeness to the earth and waters, the snake has been linked to the subterranean gods and their powers to give and take life. Both Jesus and John the Baptist are use figurative language when they address the Pharisees. They call them "a brood of vipers" (Matt 3:17; 23:33). The condemnations of the scribes and Pharisees by Jesus and John the Baptist most likely came about because they did not repent and therefore were seen as linked with Satan, and certainly with the "viper." In their mission, the disciples obtain authority to tread upon snakes as a consequence of the downfall of Satan (Lk 10:18-19). Snakes can be picked up without danger by God's people in mission (Mk 16:18; Acts 28:1-6). In Romans 16:20, Paul figuratively talks about the snake in the Garden being crushed under the feet of his readers. When Paul warns against apostasy, he draws a comparison to the situation with the snake in the Garden of Eden (2Cor 11:3). And the horses of the demonic cavalry have tails like the snake (Rev 9:19). We see the snake in Revelation appearing in different variations as an enemy of God. We meet him on the first pages in the OT and we meet him on the last pages in the NT. The church warns against listening to Satan and be led astray from devotion to Christ.

In the NT, the dragon (*drakon*) is most frequently associated to the snake. It is mostly used as a synonym for Satan (Rev 12:9). Associated to him is the scorpion. The scorpion is well known in the Middle East and Africa. It has an elongated body and a segmented tail that is tipped with a venomous stinger. The sting can be fatal to young children. In contrast to the snakes, the scorpions are always demonic. The king Rehoboam speaks sarcastically of his father who scourged his people with whips, whereas he himself will scourge them with scorpions (1Kgs 12:11). The notion of scorpion is very often used figuratively in the NT to convey the idea of harm and scorn. In Luke, we see that Jesus is emphasizing the heavenly Father's eagerness to come up with the right answer to his son's request (Lk 10:19; 11:12) (Bietenhard & Budd 1986: 507-511).

The snake stands therefore for death and annihilation because it kills. It casts off its skin, and by doing so, can represent life and resurrection. Furthermore, the snake represents sun and moon, life and death, light and darkness, cunning and malevolent, wisdom and blind passion, as well as keeper and destroyer.

4.3   Exegetical Studies

4.3.1   The Narrative of the Fall (Gen 3)

We meet the snake (*nahash*) for the first time in the Garden of Eden (Gen 3:1, 2, 4, 13, 14). The snake was one of God's creatures. This animal distinguished itself from the other animals by its way of acting. He could speak and carry out a shrewd conversation with Eve. The snake had no feet but could move faster than most of the animals. He had no wings but still he was seemingly able to fly in the crown canopy. And coiled up circling around itself, it became a symbol of the world. Once almost a chief, he was cursed to the ground (Gen

3:14). There is no mention in Genesis of what, precisely, the seed of the woman is, but it must be the Christ to come. He renders conflict into conquest and emerges victorious in the war between Him and Satan (Rev 20:1-10). The enmity between the woman and the snake comes to full expression in Revelation 12 (Rev 12:17; cf. 13:4; 16:13-14).

When the snake makes his entry in Genesis 3, it appears theologically well informed and starts with a probing, almost scientific question: "Is it true that God...?" This question leads man into disobedience. The presence of the serpent in the garden raises many questions. Genesis 2:9 tells us that the Lord God made "the tree of life ... in the midst of the garden, and the tree of knowledge of good and evil." God looked at his creation and saw that it was good (Gen 1:31). However, he also created the serpent. Does this mean that God also thereby created evil? What seems to be clear is that God created the possibility for evil, in creating the "tree of knowledge of good and evil". Yet there are some texts that leave us perplexed. For instance, we are told in the book of Job (1:6) that Satan (the snake) appears among the "sons of God." The Lord himself also states in Isaiah 45:7: "I form the light and create darkness, I bring prosperity and create disaster". The first chapters of the Bible reveal that already at an early period God's people were struggling with the reality of good and evil. What is certain is that God's creation was unassailably perfect. It was all there to be used by man. The Lord God even warned Adam and Eve not to eat of the fruit of the tree of knowledge which stood in the midst of the garden. Man was created in the image of God, meaning that he was given God's own characteristics, namely the ability of love, faith, hope and will. That last capacity was to become the doom of mankind. Man's own decision led him astray. But it was not all together his own choosing.

We read in Genesis 3:1a the following: "Now the serpent was more crafty than any of the wild animals the Lord God had made." This scenario is as it were quoted from old Egyptian philosophy and literature where men are changed into animals and vice versa (Grimberg 1978:288f). We encounter many of the same components: a woman, a tree, an animal, there is a conversation going on, there is fruit to be eaten, knowledge to be acquired, and last but not least, there was a ban on eating fruit from a certain tree. The story gives the impression that neither Adam nor Eve were especially tempted to eat until the snake appeared on the scene. The text indicates that the snake was craftier than any of the wild animals the Lord God had made. (Gen 3:1a). An animal that speaks is unheard of in ancient Egypt and is exceptional in biblical time, and that it is speaking to a woman and not to the husband is also strange. It was not customary in those days that women spoke on behalf of the family.

The seems to indicate that the snake gets all the blame, or most of it. It is subtle. It is most wise and it can speak. It is different from all other animals: it is abnormal because it has no limbs and no feet, but runs faster than many other animals or humans (cf. Douglas 1966). Regarding Mongwande culture, Molet writes: it has no wings but flies from one tree to another. It crawls around on low-land plains as well as in the forest or in the rivers or mountain, even in the trees and on the branches (Molet 1970:55). It used to be worshipped in classical times imbued with the same characteristics all over the world (Cooper 1978/1993).

Let us take a closer look at the exchange between the woman and the snake. She says that God has forbidden them to eat the fruit from the tree of life and the tree of knowledge. The snake replies with the following words: "You will not surely die, for God knows that when you eat of it your eyes will be opened, and you will be like God, knowing good and evil" (Gen 3:4-5). He twisted the mind of the woman to believe that God did this for his own sake, not for them, that God was afraid of competition and therefore banned the eating of the fruit. The fruit looked good and was pleasant to the eyes. Besides, they might become like gods. She ate and gave her husband to eat; and he did eat. They did not obey the law of God and the fall of man was complete. Yes indeed, God created the possibility for both good and evil. But he gave humanity the ability to choose between them both. The first humans did not obey the word of God and fell. The snake launched into the first example of hermeneutics ever and his interpretation misled mankind to a total catastrophe. We can conclude from this passage of the Bible that disobedience and disbelief in the Lord God became the cause of evil in the world.

4.3.2   The Bronze Snake among the Israelites (Num 21:6-9)

After leading the Israelites out of Egypt, Moses faced complaints from his people. This resulted in God sending venomous snakes among them. Upon Moses' prayers, God asked him to make a bronze snake and hang it on an elevated pole in the midst of the people. It was known at that time that snake charms could help avoid snake bites, but to heal snake bites was not known. There has been quite a debate among scholars about this matter. Is Nehushtan identical with the Mosaic snake? Is the snake pole a Jebusite fertility symbol? Does it have anything to do with the Zadokite priesthood? Was it something Moses constructed? Were the Israelites thinking of returning to Egypt through snake-infested territory? I will not attempt to answer these questions, but only mention them to illustrate some of the elements of the debate.

Is this reason to believe that the Israelites at one time in their history worshipped the snake? One of the theories is that they had some sort of snake cult conception. We ought to delve into the matter and investigate what might have taken place. We know that ethnic groups in the olden days around the globe venerated the snake, for instance Uroboros in Egyptian and Greek mythology

(Cooper 1978/1993). As we are dealing with human beings and their religious-cultural life, we should not be surprised if we should find some kind of zoola-try, even among the Israelites.

When Moses was called to bring the Israelites out of Egypt, God transformed Moses' staff into a snake. God had two purposes for doing this: firstly, to weaken Moses so he would obey God (Ex 4:1-5), and secondly, to strengthen Pharaoh's determination to oppress God's people (Ex 7:8-13). In Numbers 21, we read that the people had been wandering in the desert for quite some time and started to complain that they were getting tired. They had no more bread or water, and felt they lived on the edge of subsistence. They spoke up against God and Moses, and God answered by sending "venomous serpents among them, and they bit the people; and many Israelites died" (Num 21:6). Instead of being rescued by their God and his prophet, they were punished. Snakes invaded their compound and many of the people died.

Again they turned to their leader Moses. But this time, the attitude of the people was quite different. They confessed that they had been obstinate: "We have sinned against the Lord and you; pray to the Lord that he takes away the serpents from us. And Moses prayed for the people" (Num 21:7). Without any hesitation or contradiction, Moses turned to Yahweh and his supplications were heard by God who said to Moses that he should make a bronze snake and put it up on a pole. Then when anyone was bitten by a snake and looked at the bronze snake, that person lived (Num 21:8). Does this statement reveal a sort of "fight fire with fire" attitude? Or does it reveal a snake cult? The image of the snake carved on canes is not unusual, even in Mongwande society in today's Africa. I have a sample of the same in my office, and the story goes that it carries the legacy of Moses. When Moses was forced to identify himself before Pharaoh, he cast down his rod and it became a serpent (Ex 7:10). But he was not alone in this exercise. The Pharaoh's magicians did the same. Knowing what we do about magic and the snake's role as deity at this time of early civilisation, it would not amaze me if the image of the snake was carved on the cane at the time of this performance in the presence of Pharaoh. In fact, the story suggests this probability.

Furthermore, Scripture informs us that Moses made a serpent of brass and he put it on a pole and it came to pass that if a serpent had bitten any man "when he looked up to the serpent of bronze, he lived" (Num 21:9). Reading this narrative over and over again, it seems to me that a main intention of the story is to point out the struggle of the people of Israel in the desert under the lead-ership of God. Here we follow the formation of a theocratic state, a state sys-tem that they were forced to give up in the 9th century B.C.

In conclusion, I have a couple of questions I would like to ask. First, Moses was ordered by God to make a "fiery serpent." Why? Was this some kind of divine retribution? Fighting fire with fire? The term "fiery" usually stands for burning and consuming fire, destructiveness and aggressiveness. As Israel had been quite aggressive towards God and Moses, did God repay this by applying some sort of retributive principle? No, it was not a retaliation for the people's sin, but rather a lesson reminding the people not to react in this manner again.

Secondly, I started by asking if the nation of Israel practiced a snake cult in a certain period of their history. As far as we can see, the Bible doesn't reveal anything of the sort. But Numbers 21 raises the question of whether this was an isolated incident in the history of the Israelites or not. In addition, there is a dubious expression in verse 9: "... anyone who is bitten can *look* at the bronze snake. And when he *looked* at the serpent of bronze, he lived" (Num 21:9b). Does the term "looked at it" indicate a situation of worship? Do we see here any suggestion of a devoted, believing, person looking up to the snake hanging on a pole and having her supplications and prayers answered? The text is not explicit on this point. However, in my collection of snake gods, amulets, artifacts, and relics, I have the *yenda-gazoroma*, a piece of iron formed like a snake. The lower part of the stick is sharpened in order to be able to stand upright in the ground. It reminds me of the pole with the snake hanging on it. Do we have a legacy from the time in the Garden here? In old Egypt and elsewhere in the world, zoolatry was not unknown. Almost all kinds of animals were venerated and special attention was paid to the snake (Rom 1:23, 25). I assume therefore that the Jews coming out of Egypt brought with them some of the Egyptian religious-cultural heritage (cf. Ex 32). The Bible reflects such an assumption, as we read that Yahweh's fight against all kinds of idolatry was a reality among Israelites.

4.3.3 Jesus Christ – Antitype of the Snake in the New Testament? (Jn 3:14-16)

In the midst of the nation of Israel, about 1200 years after the incident in the desert, something strange happened. We read in John 1:14: "The word became flesh and made his dwelling among us. We have seen his glory, the glory of the One and Only, who came from the Father, full of grace and truth." In the above verse, the evangelist is describing in a few words the most important event in the world. The Word of God (*logos*) is incarnated in the man Jesus Christ. Here we are reading about the incarnation. Jesus is the living Word and gives "those who believe in him authority to become children of God; not by the blood nor by the will of flesh nor by the will of man, but of God" (Jn 1:12f). Alan Richardson is writing in his book *An Introduction to the Theology of the New Testament* the following:

> The paradox of revelation, as the Bible understands it, is that God can reveal himself to sinful man only by veiling the brightness of his true glory. This veiling of

> his brightness is a gracious act of the divine condescension: the true light, appearing amongst men, was veiled in order that they might see. Otherwise, they would have been blinded by excess of light. Thus, the incarnation itself was necessarily a veiling as well as a revealing of the light; if it had not been the former, it could not have been the latter (Richardson 1958:60).

According to Richardson, the divine truth must veil its brightness in the robe of human nature. So God reveals himself by the paradoxical act of hiding himself in the humanity of Jesus Christ. We see that God reveals himself and he veils himself in the flesh which Christ got from Mary his mother. The noun "incarnation" stems from the Latin verb *carnis* meaning "in flesh." This word reflects one of the deepest theological meanings in the Bible, if not the most profound: "to make known the secret of the glad tidings" (Eph 6:19b). The glad tiding is that the Word (*logos*) became flesh and dwelt among us (Jn 1:14). The essence of the doctrine of the Incarnation is in other words that the pre-existent Word has been embodied in the man Jesus of Nazareth.

Jesus humbled himself, becoming obedient unto death, even the death of the cross (Phil 2:6-8). Right here we are at the centre of the Gospel, namely that Jesus was hung on a tree and we read from John 3:14: "And as Moses lifted up the serpent in the wilderness, even so must the Son of man be lifted up." Even though the Old Testament and the New Testament are products of different times and even though the cultural, not to speak about their political life, has changed a great deal, we meet again the serpent. But this time the serpent does not appear as a subtle destroyer but as a metaphor for a saviour.

A new era (*aion*) has begun on earth as the Son of Man was born, lived and died for all humankind. As the serpent had been lifted up above the people in the desert to bring healing, likewise Jesus has been lifted up on the cross to bring salvation. And he declared with a loud voice: "It is finished" (*tetélestai*) (Jn 19:30). There is no doubt that John held Jesus to be the antitype of the bronze snake that Moses lifted up in the desert. It was one of the many metaphors that Jesus used in speaking to Isralites to describe the saving benefits of his death on the Cross.

4.3.4 Christ's Victory over the Great Snake (Rev 12:7-11)

In turning to Revelation, we find that the figure of the snake emerges under many names: Satan, devil, snake and dragon. The passage in question begins by telling us that Michael and his angels fought against the dragon. The text designates heaven as the place of the battle, possibly in the future. Given that there are three major streams of interpretation of the book of Revelation – the preterist, the futurist and the eclectic interpretation – it seems difficult to specify the time for that particular war.

Searching around in the text, we will find a number of actors: Michael the archangel, as well as the great dragon called the Devil and Satan which deceived the whole world. We find also God, the Lamb, and an announcer who shouts out that a war is going on and that the Snake and his angels were cast out. The war against Satan and his collaborators is the main drama in this cataclysmic battle. The war culminates in victory for those who believe in the blood of the Lamb. They overcome Satan by the blood of the Lamb and by the word of their testimony.

If in Genesis 3, we read about the expulsion of Adam and Eve from the Garden of Eden, caused by the deceiving Snake, here in Revelation 12, we read that the old serpent was cast out and that salvation has come. The text shows that salvation is for all mankind, surely also for the Mongwande, who finally can get rid of the snake cult. Humanity has passed from utter despair to utter happiness!

In the NT, the term "dragon" (*drakon*) is mostly used as a synonym for Satan (Rev 12:9). In this passage, we find the fourfold denotation as dragon, serpent, devil and Satan. The dragon has seven heads, ten horns and its tail sweeps down a third of the stars. When the woman gives birth to the man child, the dragon stands by so that it may devour him. But Michael with his forces defeats the dragon and casts him down. The dragon is ruling through the beast and causes the inhabitants of the world to worship it. Those who worship the state, personified in its ruler, worship the devil (Rev 13:2, 4). Finally, the dragon is thrown by God's angel into the abyss, for a thousand years (Rev 20:2). In Revelation 11:15, we read that the kingdom of the world has become the kingdom of our Lord. Satan and his forces are finally eliminated.

The dragon is the animal with the bewitching and crippling look. The dragon and the serpent are known in the old myths as ugly destroyers that create chaos. Likewise, the Egyptian Pharaoh is called a dragon, an enemy of God's people (Ezek 29:3; 32:2). According to the book of Job, monsters and dragons live in the sea (Job 7:12), but God kills the dragon (Job 26:12f). God is the only one who can defeat the serpent and the dragon and create cosmos out of chaos.

4.4 Ambiguity of the Snake Concept

In the Bible, the snake is not only portrayed as evil, but represents partly wisdom (Gen 3:1; Mt 10:16) and is partly symbolic of that which gives life (Num 21:9; Jn 3:14). Jesus tells the people who might be persecuted because of their belief in him, to be on guard against their persecutors and be "shrewd as snakes and innocent as doves" (Mt 10:16). The snake that was lifted up on a pole by Moses in the wilderness is a type of Christ, who was hung on the tree so that the world should be saved by him (Gen 3:24; Num 21:9; Rev 2:7). The

Church Father Tertullian (c.160-c.220) tells us that the Christians in his time called Jesus "the good snake" (Bergmann 1947:6-8; Cooper 1993:193-198). But at the same time, as we have seen, the snake is also the enemy of Christ. The evil snake is Satan and the dragon (Rev 12:9). In some places snakes are worshipped as gods, for example in Egypt. In contrast to other animals, the serpent possesses some characteristics that make it unique in the animal world. In the Bible it can talk and it is cunning. Kittel and Friedrich (1985) describe the snake as both divine and demonic.

There seems to have been a development in the understanding of the snake. The picture of the snake in antiquity and in the OT is an animal fitted with both good and evil character. But it gradually looses the good elements and becomes more and more malignant until we meet in the NT a full scale malicious animal that is used for metaphorical purposes. For instance, as we see Jesus cry out to the Pharisees: "You snakes. You brood of vipers" (Mt 23:33). The snake is malicious and so are the Pharisees. In this way the NT talks about the malignancy of people through comparison with snakes.

4.5 Conclusion

In this chapter, I have briefly analyzed some biblical concepts that are related to the Mongwande snake cult. I started with lexical studies and went on to exegetical considerations. The word studies in the NT turned out to be more comprehensive and useful, despite the great differences of opinion among specialists. However, I have kept my examination of the words within a certain logical limitation. There is no doubt that the most dominating view in the Bible is that the snake, the dragon, and the scorpion are given names that correspond to their negative characteristics. The words are mostly used figuratively and metaphorically to characterize evil. There is no real zoolatry to be observed, at least not in the NT, despite hints in the OT literature.

Moreover, we find that during Israelite history a form of conceptualization has taken place. We have observed a certain dominance of the snake concept in the Israelite society. We have equally noted the ambiguous nature of the snake in Scripture in that it is associated with good and evil, it heals and it kills. It is for this reason that I proposed the notion of "the double meaning of the snake concept," which naturally leads, in my opinion, to the narrative of the Fall of man. We have asked: Is Jesus Christ the antitype of the snake in the NT? Yes, it seems like it, but Scripture ends with Christ's victory over the great snake (Rev 12:7-11).

Chapter 5
Evaluation of the Snake Cult in the
Light of Scripture

5.1 Introduction

This chapter is an attempt to assess the Mongwande snake cult in the broader context of the Mongwande culture in the light of Scripture. Seeing that it would be difficult to measure the entire culture of a people within the scope of this chapter, I will therefore seek to measure and evaluate indicators for the theoretical concepts proposed. These indicators may again be divided into different categories or variables. I recognize that any evaluation will always be subjective. My views are not necessarily shared by others. Still, I venture to present in this chapter some of what I have understood of the subject matter. There are good and evil characteristics in all cultural life. Some attitudes, characteristics, religious and social customs which I hold to be good may be judged by others to be evil. To evaluate the Mongwande culture in the light of Scripture will certainly be a demanding task.

5.2 Continuity and Discontinuity between Scripture and Culture

5.2.1 Continuity and Discontinuity

What kind of reaction would we expect from the evangelical church if an evaluation of the snake cult were to take place? First of all, the message of the Gospel is non-negotiable. Trying to change the word of God according to the culture one is working in, is impossible. The great commission is a God given mandate. This may seem to indicate that any evaluation of culture in the light of the Bible will fail. But there are indications of the contrary. There are similarities and there are differences between the Gospel message and the cultures it encounters. God created man in his image (Gen 1:27). A multitude of peoples live on the planet. And so as a result we find numerous different cultures and religions. The Christian Mission encounters these sociological and anthropological phenomena and does its best to bridge the differences. My opinion is that the differences between Christianity and various religions seem more visible, while the similarities are more hidden. The Biblical concept is taken for granted by Christians, but the cultural concept is often condemned even before any serious discussion has taken place.

Which are some commonalities between the biblical practices and the Mong-wande snake cult? Prayer is as common a phenomenon within the snake cult as it is within Christianity. Worshipping the snake includes supplications and venerations. The emotions with which both the Christians and the snake wor-shippers present their prayers were, as far as I could observe, the same. They prayed directly to the snake. Some made a snake figure from a piece of iron. The figure was placed standing in the earth.[4] Offerings like meat, fruit and rice in small bags were hung upon the figurine.

Other common features are fellowship structures and ethics. Tradition should not be forgotten when talking about ethics. It is one of the forces that unite the people around the snake worship. In that it binds together the different snake families, it plays the same role as the church in the Christian world. These socio-religious gatherings have become traditions that have roots going way back in time. What should also be noticed is the respect the Mongwande have for their religious practices and the obligations to the snake. Their subservi-ence to the cult is noticeable. In my book *The Mongwande Snake Cult*, I have described a case against a preacher, where obedience towards the civilian laws based on reverence for the snake is astonishing (Moen 2005:132-140).

What are the differences? Let me just cite a few elements: The Christian God is transcendent, holy, eternal, almighty, unchangeable, loving and forgiver of sin. The snake cult does not possess any of these attributes.

The Christian concept of sin does not exist among the Mongwande. There is no need for a mediator between God and the human being. Committing sin against God is unheard of. One might commit a crime or sin towards the soci-ety or individuals, but never towards God. Man is neither good nor evil. He is just human. The snake cult offers no salvation from sin and guilt. No promise is made for a better after-life. There is nothing redeemable for the human be-ing in the Mongwande snake cult. Preaching about salvation and redemption is more or less incomprehensible for the Mongwande.

We have to know and accept these similarities and differences if we are to put Christian theology and the Mongwande culture in a proper context (Rom 7:7). But in fact, there seems to be no immediate basis for contextualization. Sup-pressing local religious practices and replacing them with Christian ones would eliminate any need to struggle with contextualization. But do we really want suppression? No! In what follows, I juxtapose, in tabular form, similari-ties and difference between the two religions and as we can see, there are quite a few points of connections. In my understanding, this opens the way towards a more contextual theology. One element that would be helpful in this process

---

[4] The author has such an item.

is to discontinue with mission agency style leadership and focus more on developing local leadership and theologies. As I understand the situation in mission today, it is totally different from shortly after the Second World War. Most of the mission churches enjoy independence. We should probably have started the process of contextualization a long time ago and not waited until the national movements forced the missionary leadership to surrender more or less involuntarily.

5.2.2 Comparative Evaluation

We notice in Table 2 below that there are a lot of concepts that show some similarity between the snake cult and Christianity. As with other cultures, the snake cult can be conceptualized. I have compared these Mongwande snake cult concepts with Christian concepts in a comparative research.

The leading character in the cult is the snake, playing the role of God and Christ (Moen 2005:120). He is an animal but he may modify his form and enter the village in the guise of twins (Molet 1970). When this happens and twins are born, it creates domestic unrest. The snake is the centre of this turmoil and acts as a sovereign god (Tanghe 1926:86). Tanghe asks about the Mongwande: *Tout y est plein de dieux, mais Dieu lui-même où est-il?* "Everything is full of gods, but where is God?" (Tanghe 1925:1). Maybe this statement answers Tanghe's question.

The snake cult concepts of faith, hope and love may differ from that of Christianity in that in Christianity we hope for salvation and redemption, whereas in the snake cult, as mentioned above, there are no such concepts.

The birth of twins may be compared to a sort of regeneration. The birth of a child is simply a birth, but the birth of twins is for the Mongwande something else altogether. It is a miracle. It is a double birth, a birth upon a birth, and quite unnatural. The name giving ceremony is one of the most important events in the life of the snake family. This ritual can take place anywhere from three days to several weeks or months after birth. It is at this moment in the life of the twins that a total change of nature, from animal to human being, takes place. The twins receive their civilian status and become humans, while their names are pronounced over their heads during the name giving ceremony (Moen 2005:120). The constellation animal – human or human – animal is an intrinsic part of the rituals of twins. It refers to the transference of the twin's status as animals into the status of persons. It has resemblance with the Roman Catholic concept of baptism in the Christian religion: transferring the baby from the realm of Satan into the realm of God. The thought and practice of the congregation in Christianity can be compared to the gathering of the snake families. As soon as a snake family learns about another twin snake family, they call upon them and they come together. Their gathering is not only a social meeting, but more a worship in the name of the snake, accompanied of course by singing and dancing. As God protects his children, so also the snake protects the family that has twins (Leyder 1935:40f).

The amulets are either worn by people or kept at particular places in order to exercise good or bad influence. A good many of them are natural objects such as beautiful stones, metals, teeth, animal claws and plants. But manufactured amulets of various forms and sizes are also used, such as small models of animals or utility articles. Medals and medallions, small skin bags containing formulas of incantations are not so common, and constitute an Arabic influence. The purpose of the amulets is the same among the snake people as they are for the cross in Christian tradition: healing, protecting, reminding and paying homage. But the amulets have also the power to reveal lies and truth. It seems that wherever amulets appear on the globe, they cover similar physical and psychological phenomena.

The cross expresses care for other people. Jesus died for us. We find the same attitude among the snake people. They take care of each other and help each other in time of distress in the same manner as the Christians. We might state here that people are just people with the same feelings and concerns.

With regard to dancing, there are differences both in the choreography and rhythm as well as in the melody and text. To build up a dance structure that pleases both the local culture and the missionaries may be a challenge, but not an insurmountable one. The Christians sing that the Lord is my keeper. The snake people are also singing that the snake is their keeper and protector.

The song book *Lembo na Sasaipt* was a translation of 133 western church songs. Only a couple of local songs have been accepted into this book. The songs were translated into Lingala, but the melodies were often not harmonized with the translated lyrics. For instance, the song "A mighty fortress is our God" is a beautiful hymn in the German tongue, but in Lingala it does not quite work. How can the church contextualize Christianity in its meeting with snake hymns? Could they adapt pieces of snake songs as for example:

Ngbo aga nzo lo – "the snake brings good things."

Ngbo aga pasa – "the snake brings happiness!"

I think here the churches are before a great challenge. But, perhaps this cultural encounter could be worked out and be a blessing to the parties involved in the process.

Both Christian and the snake people are seeking healing, and sometimes they are even seeking healing in a crisscrossing pattern. It is right here that many theologians may speak of split-level Christians. Maybe the two groups, the snake people and the Christians, could learn from each other?

Drugs are mostly used in order to attain a stage of intoxication when the Mongwande have their snake festivals and eat together in the name of the snake. In church, wine is used during communion. However, a state of intoxication is not the objective. Most evangelical churches serve a non-alcoholic beverage today.

Ecstasy is a well known phenomenon in almost all religions. It exists in Christianity as it does in the snake cult. The baptism with the Holy Spirit in Pentecostalism is connected with ecstatic experience, but it doesn't mean that all baptisms with the Holy Spirit should strictly conform to that movement. Worship is congruent on both conceptions of Spirit baptism. Though the content may vary, finding common ground when it comes to the somewhat variegated forms of worship and prayer among Christians should not be an impossible task.

As for the snake worshipers, prayers are usually filled with emotions. The object of prayer, however, ought to be changed from the snake to the Lord God. With regard to the question of guidance, the similarities between the snake cult and Christianity are revealing (Tanghe 1926:85). God guides the Christians and the snake guides the snake people. Still, a lot of work is awaiting the church leaders with regard to this issue.

A final point of comparaison is related to the question of worldview. The answer may be found in the fact that the Mongwande do not have a conceptual cosmology. However, there is in their philosophy no distinction between the material and the immaterial world. There is one world, god's world, and the Mongwande are part of that world. In my opinion, this concept whereby there is no distinction between the material and the immaterial seems very akin to the Judaic understanding of the immaterial and the material world, of "heaven and earth," as opposed to Greek dualism (cf. Gen 1:1; 2:7; Col 1:16, 20). This does not mean that there is no distinction between the Creator and his creatures.

This comparative evaluation ends with specific hamartiological, soteriological and eschatological concepts which have no equivalents in the Mongwande culture. The snake cult offers no salvation, justification or sanctification. The Christian's final goal, heaven, is also non-existent and so is biblical sin, although a social sin concept exists. Eternity and eternal life for humans do not figure in the Mongwande philosophy. As contextualization is a way of reinterpreting the Gospel in new cultural context, it must be biblically based, otherwise we could end up in syncretism.

5.2.3 Synthetic Table of Comparative Evaluation

Juxtaposing the following terms might be helpful for contextualization. In the juxtaposition column, the number (1) indicates some sort of continuity, while (0) signifies complete discontinuity. Let us remember that continuity is the basis for the missiological concepts of "points of contact" in cross-cultural communication. We must also remember that these points of contacts are only the beginning of the process. The discontinuities represent the elements which are subject to a more sustained reflection on contextualization. The question will be whether a functional substitute for these elements can be found in Mongwande culture.

Table 2: Synthetic Table of Comparative Evaluation

Snake Cult	Christianity	Juxtaposition
Snake	God, Christ	1
Snake as Keeper	God as Keeper	1
Spirits	Holy Spirit	1
Faith	Faith	1
Hope	Hope	1
Love	Agape	1
Snake mother	Mary	1
Snake father	Deacons	1
Birth of twins	Regeneration	1
Name giving festival	Baptism	1
Protection	Protection	1
Amulets	Cross	1
Fellowship meal: drugs	Communion: wine	1
Care	Care (symbol cross)	1
Supervision	Supervision	1
Dance	Dance	1
Snake gathering	Congregation	1
Songs	Songs (Hymns)	1
Healing	Healing	1
Ecstasy	Ecstasy	1
Worship	Worship	1
Prayers	Prayers	1

Supplication	Supplication	1
Guidance	Guidance	1
Cosmology	Creation	0
	Sin	0
	Salvation	0
	Justification	0
	Sanctification	0
	Heaven	0
	Hell	0
	Eternal Life	0
	Eternal Death	0

5.2.4 Conclusion

In accordance with the title of this book, I have sought to evaluate the Mong-wande culture in the light of Scripture. As we see, there are quite a few simi-larities between the two belief systems. These similarities will need to be ex-plored further to get beyond our initial impressions. Yet, many differences and challenges remain. The main challenge for contextualization may be that the Mongwande culture has no concept of sin, redemption and afterlife or is aware that such things exist and are a spiritual reality. Furthmore, the concept of salvation provided by our Lord and Saviour Jesus Christ in relation to this spiritual reality is altogether absent, and seems to be another major hinderance to appropriate contextualization.

Through trial and error, it has become clear for the Christian mission that con-textualization demands an understanding of the recipient culture, as well as of the Christian Gospel. In moving towards this goal, dialogue is of utmost im-portance. Through dialogue, one can ascertain what is acceptable in the Mongwande culture without compromising the Gospel or subjecting it to the threat of syncretism.

Many aspects of the snake cult should, in my opinion, be refused. The absence of the concepts of sin and salvation is a type of a worldview which is in direct opposition to the Gospel and the redemption by grace which Jesus Christ of-fers, and so must be refused. Still, there are certain aspects which can be "ex-ploited," for instance, the innate propensity of the Mongwande to believe in something. The Mongwande would be hard pressed to see the world as being totally without a spiritual dimension. A purely scientific secular understanding of the universe is quite unfathomable to them. There must be something be-hind it, *Nzambe*, a god if you will. So, much like Paul exploited the objects of

worship in Athens as an entrance into the Athenians' minds, we too can utilize
the Mongwande innate proclivity to believe in something as a channel through
which we can communicate the Gospel (Acts 17:22f). For this to happen,
modern missionary approach may have to be modified in quite radical ways.
Yet, it is pivotal to incorporate safeguards in any such modification and contextualization process. Hiebert's model offers certain elements which guard
against the above mentioned syncretism.

After this systematic and theoretical reflection on continuity and discontinuity
between the Mongwande snake cult and Christianity, in the following two
sections, we will look into very practical encounters between the two belief
systems, the Mongwande and the Christian, in the past and the present.

5.3 Past Encounters between Christianity and the Snake Cult

5.3.1 Experiences of the Norwegian Baptist Missionaries

Culture is universal. Wherever there are humans, there is culture, albeit variegated, all man made. Culture is an integral system of conceptions, beliefs and
practices. The values of cultures have to do with the evaluation of right and
wrong, true and false, important and not so important. Hiebert says that

> "... cognitive, affective and evaluative assumptions provide people with a way of
> looking at the world, to make sense of it, giving them a feeling of being at home,
> and reassure them that they are in the right. This worldview serves as the founda-
> tion on which they construct their explicit belief and value systems, and the social
> institutions within which they live their daily lives" (Hiebert 1985:47f).

The Hebrew and Hellenistic cultures are certainly part of the cradle that
formed biblical personalities like Abraham, Isaac and Jacob in the OT, and
Peter, John and Paul in the NT, as well as western missionaries in modern
times. Mongwande culture has produced cultural conceptions that are completely different from the Hebrew and Hellenistic worldview. Since this is the
case, we are faced with the crucial question of how evangelicals have reacted
to the Mongwande snake cult.

In the beginning of modern mission history, there seems to be little interest in
the question of the divine origin of the Christian message. But as time passed,
this intriguing question has come to the fore, followed by the question of the
comprehension of the Gospel. Local theologies sprang up in different parts of
the world, such as Kimbanguism in the Congo. Finally, the situation became
so intense that the mission societies acknowledged the necessity of redefining
their theology and of entering into conversation with those who received the
message. Dialogue was the word. In so doing, the question of now the receptor

understood the message emerged. The missionaries wanted the local people to comprehend the Christian values and in return the missionaries wanted to understand the values of the local religion. How about the values in the snake cult? Are there any values in the cult? What kind of values? How is it with the concept of right and wrong? By which standards can human actions be judged right or wrong? Does the cult encourage law and order? Could the church accept the snake cult as it is? Probably not!

There has been up to postmodern times no question about the sovereignty of Christianity. However, as the world changed, the mission did not, not until recently. The reality of sin, remission of sins and condemnation of sin had no place in the snake cult world. The perspective of heaven and hell was non-existent. Jesus says: "Heaven and earth shall pass away but my words shall not pass away" (Mt 5:18). It means that the word in the Bible can be changed under no circumstances. This view, supported by the great theologian Karl Barth with his *"Recht von oben"* approach, was common ground up to around 1970 when the idea of contextualization appeared on the theological scene (Kraft 2005:132f).

In Monga, we took neither to Barth's nor Troeltsch's new ideas. The Baptist missionaries regarded the whole idea of contextualization as being too close to syncretism, which would jeopardize the work of God. Their approach to the problem was rather to refuse custom. Nor was tolerance the order of the day. The entire church history among the Monga is fettered with conflict. Now, the situation has changed, as the church is faced with non-Christian ideas and movements. How is it to deal with these, as well as traditional religion, such as the snake cult? Do missionaries have to display some sort of permissiveness? Should the church modify itself and the message in order to meet the requirements of the Mongwande snake cult? The event which brought these questions to surface is the event which I have described in chapter 2. A young couple brought their twins to the church in order to get them blessed by the pastor. After the ceremony was over, they returned to their village, and there the name giving ceremony took place following the old traditional custom.

The international church community's reaction to the religious problems that emerged while spreading the Gospel through the years slowly but surely turned to dialogue, and then displayed an attitude of tolerance, acceptance and efforts to understand the deeper thoughts of culture. The pivotal insight has to do with context, namely: weaving together two worldviews into one without insulting, but rather enriching, and certainly not impoverishing one another.

5.3.2 Brief History of the Norwegian Baptist Mission in Monga

The history of the Norwegian Baptist Mission in the Congo will serve to illustrate some of the difficulties in contextualization. The Norwegian Baptist

Church started mission work in the Congolese district of Uélé in 1920. Bas-Uélé, or "lower part of Uélé," lies in the north-western part of the province of Haut-Zaire in the Democratic Republic of Congo. The work succeeded and five mission stations (Monga, Bondo, Buta, Bili and Likati) were established and several churches were planted. Monga is the northernmost of these churches and actually it was here that the first Norwegian Baptist missionary arrived in 1920 (Iversen 1946).

Bondo is the head station today and comprises a residence, a polyclinic, an optics workshop, a primary school, a teachers' college, a pastors' college, an engineering workshop, a sawmill, a Bible book shop, a dressmaker's work-room and a big church building.

Monga comprises a health centre, a residential area for missionaries and the personnel of the health centre, a commercial school, a church building, a small air field and a power station.

Buta comprises a residential area, a polyclinic, a primary school, a secondary school, a church building, an administrative building for the school and a development department.

Bili comprises a residential area, a polyclinic including a leprosy section, a primary school and a church building.

Likati comprises an agricultural centre, a secondary school, a polyclinic and a small air strip (Husby 1995).

The Baptist church in the Congo became member of the Church of Christ of the Congo in 1970 together with 52 other Protestant churches. By doing this, the church kept its independence and got a new name in 1973: *Communauté Baptiste du Bas-Uélé* (CBBU), the "Baptist Union of Bas-Uélé."

Evangelization and education have always been a priority for the Baptists. That is why the church built schools for pastors and evangelists. But their missionary vision included also health work and therefore they built clinics and dispensaries. They also had their own medical doctor for a while. But, even if the physical side of life was not ignored, the emphasis was of course on spiritual matters. Education of the young people was also made available as well as, for instance, engineering and optics work shops. Women were not forgotten, either: there were projects particularly set up for women, such as sewing and knitting.

The work went on smoothly until after the Second World War, when demands of national and religious independence emerged in the colonies. This surge of national and religious independence came also to the Congo, particularly the Bas-Uélé. In fact, a schism within the church took place between the followers of the missionaries and the leaders opting for independence. The reason for this rift within the church was, as already mentioned, the demand for independence of the indigenous Baptist Church in Bas-Uélé. In fact, their goal was full control over the church.

In the subsequent developments the Home Board in Norway met the demand for independence by turning over the leadership of matters concerning the internal affairs of the church to the Congolese pastors and evangelists. This move, however, did not change the mind of the separatist group. They left the church anyway, splitting it into two parts: one group followed the missionaries and another group, calling themselves the Fidels, followed some indigenous leaders accompanied by missionary sympathizers. This breakaway faction came to the open at the missionary conference at Likati in 1957. In 1959, it was legally recognized by the state of Congo with its own legal representative, under the name of: "Church of the Faithful Baptists in the World" (*Église des baptistes fidèles dans le monde*). It is quite large and works today independently from the Congolese mother church and the Norwegian Baptist Union.

This schism is quite important with regards to contextualization. The white missionaries, who followed the indigenous leaders, thought they were contextualizing, when in fact, what they were doing, was simply following the views of one, at that time, small extremist group, which moved out of the church both physically as well as spiritually. This shows how a concept like contextualization can be misused. It so clearly shows what Hiebert calls uncritical contextualization (Hiebert 1985:185). It is therefore imperative to be vigilant when doing contextualization work. I will delve more deeply into contextualization below.

A sort of contextualization was already introduced in 1960, when the part of the church, which was faithful to the mission, got its independence as a national church under the name of "Baptist Church in Bas-Uélé" (*Église Baptiste du Bas*-Uélé, EBBU). This name was changed in 1992 to the "Baptist Church in Northern Zaire" (*Communauté Baptiste au Zaïre du Nord*, CBZN). At this time, the leadership was transferred from the Norwegian Baptist Home Board to the indigenous church (Husby 1995:10). Even though this was not a theological contextualizing issue to start with, in my mind it was an initial contextualization procedure that also opened up the process of appropriate contextualization in the future.

Although there have been conflicts and uproar, the work of evangelization and church planting has gone on. Maybe these experiences between those who brought the Gospel and those who received it have been divine means to open the eyes of both groups in regard to the necessity of contextualization.

5.3.3 Theological Reflection on Evangelization and Conversion

In its effort to contextualize the Gospel, the duty of the church is to proclaim that the Kingdom of God is at hand (Mt 3:3). It will be helpful to look at some key words and concepts in the Scriptures in this connection. In regards to evangelization, the New Testament mentions the central concept of conversion expressed by the terms *metanoô* and *epistrephô* which mean "to turn around" and imply a "change of mind" (Acts 2:38; 3:19). Luther is, according to Niels Munk Plum in his *Dogmatics* (1941), not using *metanoia* "conversion" but "penance" with the meaning "showing sorrow or contrition for sin" and not merely a turn around (Ps 51:19). The way out of sin is a way of suffering, Luther maintains. This idea shows up in the English term "repentance" which is drawn from Latin.

In his book *Shame and Guilt* (2003), Hannes Wiher draws our attention to another way of looking at this question. Wiher points out that according to the Bible forgiveness should be a balanced concept of 1) repentance, 2) reconciliation and 3) reparation (2003:401f). Actually, we meet shame and guilt in the very beginning of the Bible. But before we get there, we are introduced to the happiest couple in the world: Adam and Eve (Gen 2:25). When we meet them again after their transgression, they are ashamed (Gen 3:10). God repaired the transgression according to his own plan, a plan that found its completion in Christ Jesus. This plan is called "plan of salvation," *ordo salutis*.

Missionaries have been given the keys of the kingdom (Mt 16:19). They are Christ's representatives on earth in His absence, so to speak, until His return. As mentioned above, the core of evangelization is to proclaim the Kingdom of the Lord Jesus Christ, which hopefully will produce a change of heart within a new convert or recipient culture. But this proclamation and the change that it brings cannot take place without the cooperation of those who receive the message. This happens within a framework of contextualization.

5.3.4 The Mongwande Perception of Conversion

In the Mongwande area, conversion means *kutia nkombo na buku* "put the name in the book." The primary purpose for the missionaries to go to Monga was to preach the Gospel. The missionaries came to a people who had not heard about Jesus. The Gospel was completely new to the Mongwande. They understood the message of love, but they also got the impression that they had to respond to the need for conversion. Their conception of Christ gradually grew and became more focused after a great deal of reflection over the issues of conversion, faith, baptism, communion and congregation. However, they noticed that their own culture was pushed aside and vanished to a certain degree. Looking at the development from the moment when a Mongwande accepted Christ until he/she was welcomed into the church will help us to better appreciate certain aspects of the conversion processus, which is connected with contextualization.

As already mentioned above, the missionaries held meetings at different places in the Monga district reaching a multitude with the Gospel. Many turned to Christ. Later the missionaries built churches and held meetings in them on certain fixed days. In Monga, services were held on Sundays and other meetings took place on Thursdays. It was on Thurday evening that those who wanted to take the step of conversion presented themselves. On that day, there was always a queue of people lining up in front of the pulpit on which there was a book. In this book, the names of the people who converted were registered. There was a mixture of people present at these meetings: some serious, some smiling, some weeping. Very few confessed their sins, probably because they did not acknowledge committing any sin. If you asked them why they wanted to follow Jesus or who was Christ, the answer was more often than not: "I want to go to heaven." A primary motivation for those wanting their names to be written in the book was that they wanted to be saved. It was not necessarily that they feared the snake cult or the medicine man, but rather that they had heard the Christian admonitions against going to hell if they were not saved and allowed that to weigh heavily when making up their minds. If you later met them and asked them if they were Christians, they would reply with a loud voice: "Yes, I put my name in the book." Why they answered in this way was probably due to the fact that they believed that having one's name written in this book was tantamount to going to heaven, and it was the prospect of going there that was the overriding goal rather than the actual act of being redeemed of all sins, which lies in the power of grace. As the reader might notice, the earliest Mongwande converts did not immediately grasp the fact that a prerequisite for entering heaven was the result of having one's soul cleansed of sin. These two aspects of salvation were understood eventually though. This way of conversion became customary all over the Monga area. The evangelists who were preaching the Gospel in the jungle followed the above mentioned pattern.

As mentioned above, the words for conversion in the NT are *metanoia* and *epistréphô* meaning "to convert, to change, to turn, to turn to matter" (Kittel & Friedrich 1985:639-641; Behm 1985:IV, 948-980; Wurthwein 1985:IV, 980-989). A Mongwande comes to the church in order to "put his/her name in the book." This was in line with conversion being an instantaneous experience. Likewise, the goal of the Thursday evening meetings was to facilitate such immediate experiences. However, when I tried to analyze the situation, it was difficult to find out whether it was a serious act or just a trend among the people. As previously mentioned, the converts did not always show signs of repentance. They were smiling and sometimes even showing obvious relief. It was rather seldom to observe any form of life crisis urging people to seek Jesus. It was also difficult to determine whether they were looking for mystical or spiritual experiences or not. Of course, conversion is a complex process. The people coming to Christ were in different situations. The most visible act during conversion was the handing over of different old objects to the missionaries, pieces of iron, wood and clothes representing spiritual powers.

It was a challenge to analyze why the Mongwande came to Christ and assess what their motif was. What did they mean by "coming forward" and becoming catechumens? I learned pretty soon that if I wanted to know anything about the Mongwande conception of conversion, I would have to interview them which I did. I asked my co-worker in Monga, Pastor Pierre Kembi, the question: "Why do Mongwande people turn to Christ?" He looked at me and gave me a rather interesting answer. He said: "The Mongwande feel a social lift when they can march to the church with the Bible in their hand." This response has its parallel in South Korea, where I served as a missionary from 1964-1975. I once interviewed the Director for the Emile Museum in Seoul, Dr. Zozayong, and asked him why the Koreans flocked to the churches. He looked at me and replied: "Social pride. The Koreans feel very proud when they can tuck the Bible under their arms and march to the church." I'm not saying that this is the only motif for seeking the church, but there are clearly surface level reasons for coming to the church such as looking for work as evangelist, teacher, carpenter or ordinary worker. Of course, there are fortunately also deeper reasons, such as to find out about life and death or other philosophical questions. Sundberg quite thoroughly elaborates this subject in his book *Conversion and Contextual Conceptions of Christ* (2000:185-217).

5.3.5 Two Worldviews: the Christian and the Mongwande

We have investigated the snake cult and the Gospel as presented to the local population. We have also looked at the new, independent churches that sprouted like mushrooms all over the Congo. Some of these are clearly biblical. Others carry unfortunately the mark of syncretism. It is not difficult to observe that the new churches have had serious problems with syncretism ever since the introduction of Christianity into the Congo. This to me is about the confrontation of two worldviews. John Mbiti wishes to depict African religion as a religion created by God as prelude to the Christian symphony with concurring and parallel tones with Biblical faith and doctrines. What he would like to show by this is that there is continuity between the African and the biblical religion in several important aspects (Mbiti 1980). Several researchers do not agree with him on that point. They purport instead what is usually termed discontinuity, i.e. that there is no and never has been any connection between these two religions.

After having been in the mission service in the Congo and South-Korea for over 20 years, I find the contention about the continuity and discontinuity between the African religion and the Old Testament a little off the mark. Yes, there are parallels between these two religions, but there are parallels between other religions too. I would rather ask the question: "Do not all the religions have typological similarities?" They all carry human wishes and hopes towards an almighty God. It is therefore, as I perceive it, more empirically valid to assert that there is continuity between all the major religions of the world rather than simply between two specific religions. I understand Mbiti as trying to show that the African system of religion is something the young generation should be proud and not ashamed of. The Christian culture they are now facing, so is his assertion, is only a continuation of the old traditional African religion. I agree with him that one ought to be proud of one's religious and cultural heritage and that, in these matters, one does not need to have an inferiority complex. Kwesi Dickson concurs with Mbiti when he argues that Christianity is a continuation of an already existing religion in Africa.

As far as the Mongwande belief system is concerned, my opinion on the matter is that it is a totally independent and self-developed religion. As a matter of fact, the religions in the Congo can hardly be developed anywhere else but there. It is through the geological and climatic conditions together with the psycho-social, religious-cultural and political forces seething in Mongwande societies that produced the Mongwande faith, and gave its form and meaning to the ancestral worship and the snake cult (cf. Käser 1997:51-58). It stands by virtue of its own energy. It has its own value and gives its adherents a feeling of security and community. It formed the Mongwande worldview. To speak of any conceptual Mongwande cosmology might be a little difficult, but somehow they believe in an almighty supernatural power called *Nzapa* "god." They know very little about him and consequently do not build houses of worship for him. If they had any kind of cosmology, it was quite simple and very practical. Suffice it to say that the Mongwande worldview was deeply rooted. The belief was that some force, *Nzapa*, is behind everything, yet that the lesser spirits, assisted by the ancestors, are those that take care of the daily inconveniences.

Is there anything left of the old Mongwande beliefs? Yes, there is and it is this old religion and the snake cult that the missionaries were facing when arriving in Monga. Out there in the forest and the villages, where a homogeneous community lives, the old indigenous religion will probably not vanish any time soon. After all, it concerns a view of life which has been inherited and fostered for generations. As Reverend Kumbowo Manzinga says in an interview presented below, people are still mindful of the snake cult and respect some of its traditions. For example, people still avoid killing snakes. So the snake cult has proved rather tenacious and it will not disappear without leaving some traces in cultural life. But today, the snake cult is a very closely guarded secret. Even I stumbled across the snake cult by accident, and when I tried to get people to talk about the snake cult, it turned out to be very difficult. There seemed to be two reasons for that: one was the feeling of inferiority. The Mongwande did not like to appear inferior to the Europeans with their highly developed civilization. Secondly, the snake phenomenon could not match the religion of the missionaries. Even though it is a religious-cultural phenomenon largely tucked away in the forests today, the snake cult might reappear on the scene in a new setting, for instance, when the old system blends with the new religion into one local church creating syncretistic or pagano-Christian strains of religion. Nor must we forget that the old cultic traditions might be a possible avenue for those who go back to the old roots and an unbroken African identity.

The Christian worldview with God creating the earth and organizing the world from chaos to cosmos maintaining the world in His hand and guiding people from day to day, is an unbelievable proposition for the Mongwande. If this is difficult to grasp for the Mongwande, it does not get any easier when Christ comes into the picture. A mediator between God and men who saves humanity from their sins is a notion that seems strange to them. And on top of that, they hear that salvation and entry into heaven is contingent upon believing in this mediator, i.e. Christ, if not, an eternal perdition awaits them.

So far, their own system has met their daily requirements and has given them a coherent and meaningful perception of the universe. The snake cult must be looked at as an attempt of the Mongwande to understand the universe, the creation and the structure of this world. Although, in Africa one did not know anything about causality as a working concept, it didn't mean that life as such was incoherent and chaotic. On the contrary, the whole world system is explained according to quite different observations than ours and these are just as logical. We must be aware of this when working with contextualization, whether in relation to the snake cult or the Korean *toro*-ancestor cult.

While I was a missionary in South Korea and was resident director of the Pearl S. Buck Centre for Mixed Race Children in Seoul in the period of 1969-1975, I wrote a book on the plight of mixed race children: *The Amerasians: A Study and Research on Interracial Children in Korea* (1974). One day I invited the director of a large secondary school to dinner. As he entered my house, he suddenly stopped and bowed with reverence and clasped his hands in front of a statue of Buddha I had in my study. Seeing my surprised face he said: "You look at me wondering how I as an intellectual can bow and pay respect to a statue. But it is not the statue as such I pay respect to. It is the spirit and the power this statue represents." Upon my inquiries he continued:

> The Christians also have their statues and pictures. You make images of Jesus and Mary from wood and stones, paintings and plaster, and put them up in your churches; and for us it looks like you are praying to them. But the Christians feel mortally offended if we tell them that you pray to the pictures. We feel also mortally offended when you assert that we pray to the picture of Buddha and his heavenly entourage.

This woke me up. Equipped with this information from outside the Christian world, I made several field study trips, among others to Nairobi, Kenya (1978). I focused on the question of worshipping inanimate objects. I found that it was not the picture, as such, made of wood or stone or iron, the African or the Mongwande worshipped, but the power and authority these objects represent in the world order. This is nothing new in the studies of religion. Käser is specifically discussing the spiritual double of material objects (Käser 2004:107-119). Most of the objects are not artwork, but this is probably due to the fact that the maker was not an artist. If he was some kind of an artist, the final object could be nice. The utility articles that are inherited from the ancestors are pure religious relics.

In any case, whether the objects are artistically made or not, the aim is the same, namely to get in contact with powers represented by the statues, relics or the snake. The power incarnated in the snake might from time to time appear in the human world in the disguise of twins. But, it is misleading to talk about nature worship of any kind. Adoration of the sun is perceived as adoration to the sun-god, and worship of rain as adoration to the rain-god, but it is not quite so among the Mongwande. As mentioned above, it is not the object itself which is venerated but the power it represents. As far as the snake cult is concerned, the represented power comprises all aspects of life. The snake and the worshipping of him are not only for the twins, but it concerns also the daily bread, hunting and the wellbeing of the entire village (see snake song no. 7 in Moen 2005:68f). What I am trying to say here is that we as missionaries are dealing with deeply rooted emotions, deep level beliefs, worldview if you will (Rommen & Corwin 1996:223). We westerners have our own worldviews and easily neglect and even ignore that the local people have theirs. They also have their deeply rooted worldviews. It is just that they are different from ours and might be difficult for us to grasp. In their book *Missiology and the Social Sciences* (1996), Edward Rommen and Gary Corwin say:

> Anthropology has enabled missiologists to know that each culture has its own worldview. We know that in every culture there are assumptions made about the nature of reality and about the nature of a person, his relations with other people, and his place in what he defines as his world (Rommen & Corwin 1996:223).

These conceptions and assumptions are called worldview. Ortiz defines worldview as follows: "A worldview provides a people with a structure of reality; defines, classifies and orders the 'really real' in the universe, in their world, and in their society" (Ortiz 1992:234 in Rommen & Corwin 1996:223; cf. also Käser 2004:59-64).

Studies of worldview have taken us deeper in our awareness that beliefs, values and symbols must be understood within the context of a particular culture. There are implicit and explicit assumptions that underlie specific beliefs and norms of people or groups (Hiebert et al. 1999:45-72; Hiebert 2008). In short, each group of people has its own worldview. Even though the Mongwande might not have any idea of the creation or of God, their worldview is still valid for them just as our worldview is for us. It has been developed based on observation of the world around them. It may not stand up to our scientific scrutiny, but it has served them well during centuries. Our task will be to acknowledge this fact and work with the local community and church in a cooperative and cross-cultural way.

5.3.6 Conversion and Identity

The Mongwande had no great difficulties in understanding and accepting the Christians' God, but they had problems with some other postulates of the Gospel. For instance, the concepts of sin, salvation from sin, the Saviour, the Son of God, and eschatology were questions they found difficult to fathom: that God had a Son and that God the Almighty sent his Son to the earth in order to save the world were unacceptable thoughts. What does sin and salvation from sin mean? It was difficult for the Mongwande to see the reality of love at work in salvation. To them these were incomprehensible elements.

Ecclesiastical services like baptism and communion were understandable because, as mentioned above, there were points of resemblance. The efficacy of the sacraments, baptism and communion, and their elements (water, corn and oil) were understood in continuity to their own rituals. According to my fieldwork, resurrection from the dead (being raised physically from the grave) had no parallel in the Mongwande comprehension of the world. However, some theologians like Mbiti have argued in their publications about African religion and philosophy that there is a certain continuity between African religions and Christianity (e.g. Mbiti 1980). According to Mbiti, these religions prepared the way for the Gospel (*praeparatio evangelica*). He interprets it as evidence that the African traditional religions contained elements of the revelation of God and thus formed a platform which the Christian message could build on. Mbiti's assertion is that the God of the Bible is none other than the God who is already known by African traditional religion. According to Mbiti, the missionaries did not bring God to Africa. It was God who brought the missionaries to Africa. Furthermore, Mbiti sees a difference between the mission of God that is revealed in African religiosity and the Christian mission introduced by the missionaries in that the African god was a god of power. The concepts of forgiveness and reconciliation were not a part of his existence and purpose, whereas they are, of course, the driving force of the Christian God as He seeks to bring His people back to His Kingdom.

When I use the expression "African Traditional Religions," I understand with John S. Mbiti (1980) and E. E. Evans-Pritchard (1956) that this expression comprises a myriad of definitions such as animism, fetishism, totemism, polytheism, zoolatry, paganism or snake cult. The missionaries seem to have found points of resemblance in the African Traditional Religions: anguish, fear and veneration. The Africans are mostly warm, accepting and light-hearted people. But here comes the Christian message emphasizing surrender, renunciation, even disowning his own tribe or family if they rejected conversion to Christianity. In the eyes of a Mongwande, the fact that the message was brought by white missionaries, was a guarantee for its truth. But if they didn't accept the call to salvation, the missionaries told them that they would be punished by the All Mighty Christian God.

Furthermore, there is another psychological factor coming into play, i.e. faith. In his old religious world, the Mongwande had no particular conception of faith. God was there up high and unapproachable. But the spirits and his ancestors were around him. Confronted with the claims of the Gospel, he felt himself alienated from his family and tribe. If he accepted the Gospel, then his former life was emptied of ancient ideas and thoughts. He was alone, but a new creature in Christ (2Cor 5:17). The anguishes of getting lost followed the new experience of conversion. This type of fear pertains to the fear of isolation and ostracism from the others when one decides to become a Christian. Though we should beware of equating religion to culture, it is by all practical purposes closely linked, and hence it has great bearing on a person's identity. When a person, whose identity has been closely linked to a religion, for example the snake cult, is converted to Christ, his identity concomitantly becomes redefined as a Christian. Yet this transition is far from immediate. It takes place over time. And in the meantime, the convert is in a cultural limbo, in a religious bi-culture (Hiebert 1985:238). The convert may feel like he or she no longer completely belongs to his primary culture, but has not yet become comfortable in his new culture and his new identity as a Christian. There is no easy solution to this challenge, but one thing which can be of help if wisely used is time (Trobisch in Hiebert 1985:177). One must allow for time in order to give space for the transition to take place to the point where the first identity releases its grip and the second identity is more firmly in place. This may even take generations. This poses a second challenge. Which aspects and elements of a primary culture, identity or religion can one take care of and bring into the new identity and which should one do away with? Hiebert's model of critical contextualization may be of help here. After having assessed one's old culture and identity in the light of the Bible one must either accept, reject or modify aspects of one's old culture and identity, or even create new elements.

But fear and anguish also pertain to other aspects of a person's life and his belief in afterlife. The Mongwande did not have a concept of hell and were not afraid of spending eternity punished for their lack of faith. The doctrine of eternal punishment was quite a new concept for the Mongwande. One of my evangelists, Kimbangu, told me about an experience which illuminates this point. Once he was attacked by a hippopotamus and was in mortal danger. I asked him: "You must have been very frightened?" "Afraid? No, that happened before I became a Christian. I wasn't afraid at that time, not the way I am now anyhow." I am simply putting in writing what Kimbangu said. What is quite sure anyhow is that he had got a different sort of fear after his conversion and became an evangelist. His utterance was so special that I felt it ought to be mentioned here in the book.

5.3.7 Experiences of the Christian Mongwande: Split-Level Christianity

The influence of the snake cult among the Mongwande is overwhelming. It cannot be ignored. In my ministry in Monga, I observed this fact time and again. In his work on the Mongwande, Basile Tanghe writes about a Banzyville council member who said: "God is in the church. The snake is for us what God is for you" (Tanghe 1926:86). As I delved into the matter, I found that to be true. It was not superficial strands of thoughts, but deep-rooted faith harboured in the heart of the Mongwande. Their concept of god was rather vague. Therefore, no temples or prayer houses were built. But they did build small shelters for the ancestor spirits. Most of their dances, however, are consecrated snake dances. Men and women get up and tell stories about the snake. Direct prayers to the snake are practiced very often. The observance of the snake took especially place when twins were born. Twin birth was considered dreadful and mysterious. The sole explanation was that the snake with his forked tongue was at the root of this mystery. If we know a little of the religious life and the grip the snake cult has on people, it is not so difficult to understand the behaviour of the Mongwande. Why do they behave as they do? The following stories may shed some light on their reaction towards the Christian mission, and especially exemplify the concept of split-level Christianity. They show very well the reaction the villagers have to the Christian mission.

5.3.7.1 Christian Dedication and Snake Name Giving Ceremony

Again I feel the necessity to mention the couple who called upon their pastor in order to have their twin babies prayed for and given names. This couple had joined the church just a few years earlier. They already had a few children and were now blessed with twins. A Sunday was chosen and the dedication ceremony set to be held at 11 a.m. The couple appeared at the agreed upon time with their family and the twins. The ceremony took place with the blessing and name giving. When all was over, the couple left the premises seemingly very happy.

On the very same day in the afternoon, a deacon from the church appeared outside the house of the pastor. He was extremely upset and could hardly talk. He said with a trembling voice that he had heard that the couple participated in the "snake name giving ceremony" in the village. The deacon adamantly reminded the pastor that those rituals are pagan. The deacon begged him to go to the village and investigate the matter, which he did. The inquiries led him nowhere. The couple admitted no wrong doing and they were fully supported by the whole village. They insisted that they did this voluntarily. They asserted that the initiation into the community, the change of identity and name had to be carried out in the old way.

5.3.7.2 On Trial for Christ

One evangelist was accused of adultery. He was married and denied any immoral conduct. The entire village was upset. The elders did not accept empty phrases. They insisted on evidence to back up his position. The only way of obtaining the truth was to swear a solemn oath. The evangelist was willing to swear on the Bible to asseverate his innocence. This, however, was not accepted by the chief and the elders sitting in the council of judges. They would only accept an oath sworn in the old way. Swearing in that way meant that a series of old consecrated objects, such as ashes, crocodile teeth, leopard hide and pieces of iron were put in a bowl of wood. The most important ingredients were the skin, the teeth and the head of a snake. The accused was asked to strike the objects and swear by the name of each animal that he was innocent. This was impossible for the evangelist. On one hand, his pride and honour were at stake, and on the other, he did not want to be labelled as a conjugal infidel. If he complied with the condition of the elders, he would be exonerated. If he insisted on swearing on the Bible, the elders would not believe him, even if he was innocent. Actually, they would interpret his choice as token that he had committed sexual offence against said woman. He could of course get the blessing from the church by swearing on the Bible, and be religiously and socially acquitted. But by doing so, he would incur the condemnation of the council judges and the villagers. The social pressure was too heavy on him. He swore in the traditional way by the head of the snake and the teeth of the crocodile. It was this broken-hearted man who knocked at my door in the middle of the night.

5.3.7.3 Elisabeth

This story shows the influence of the snake cult on Christians. Elisabeth was the wife of chief Bela, not the above mentioned chief. She was a church member. During an interview I had with her concerning cultural and religious life at Monga, I brought forth the same iron piece *Yenda-Gazoroma* that I had shown chief Fakula. Elisabeth screamed and covered her eyes with her hands and ran out of the house. For some considerable time, I did not see her so I had to ask her to come. She came and we continued our conversation. I asked her why she had run away. She looked very intensely at me and said: "The snake people worship the snake out in the forest. They are fearsome of the snake and usually follow all its instructions. When twins are born, the snake is in command and there is unrest in the village."

5.4 Present Encounter between Christianity and the Snake Cult

While working on this book, I have pondered upon going to Monga to see for myself how the situation is today and to find out the present state of contextualization practices at our former Baptist Mission field. The political circumstances in DRC have been very much out of control and have gone from bad to worse in these latter days. It is as of today a general restriction for foreigners and tourists not to enter the north-eastern part of the Congo. Travelling in Congo nowadays might involve mortal danger. I refer here to the two Norwegians who have been sentenced to death in autumn 2009. However, with kind assistance from the Norwegian Baptist Union, I got the telephone number and the e-mail address of the headquarters of the Mission in the Congo. With their help, I obtained good communication with the president of the Baptist Independent Church in Congo (*Communauté Baptiste au Zaire du Nord*, CBZN), the Reverend Robert Kumbowo Manzinga. Below is the result of the e-mail interviews, better expressed as a correspondence stretching from June 10, 2009 through July 3, 2010. His correspondence is very instructive and shows that the contextualization process is going on. In the following section, I will seek to summarize the most important information resulting from our correspondance about the snake cult.

1. Question: Is any kind of snake cult or worship found at the present time in the former mission field of the Norwegian Baptist Mission?

   Answer: The people who practiced the snake cult in Monga do not live any longer, they are dead.

2. Question: Does the practice of snake worship exist in other places in the Bas-Uéle area?

   Answer: No! I hear no more talking of the snake cult in the Bas-Uélé territory.

3. Question: Do you think that the cult has vanished?

Answer: One might still find the snake cult scattered in the forest, here
and there, but those who worship the snake don't appear to be numerous.

Before continuing, allow me to interject. In emphasizing the assertions of Rev.
Manzinga that practitioners of the cult are dead and that there is no more talk
of the snake cult in the Bas- Uélé territory, one might be tempted to think that
the snake cult has disappeared. However, if we consider the fact that he does
not categorically rule out the possibility that the snake cult still has a certain
impact on the Mongwande society, at least in rural areas, as stated above, we
must acknowledge the possibility that the snake cult still has not disappeared
completely, but still plays a roll in the Mongwande society and psyche. Furthermore, one must allow for the possibility that in these postmodern times the
snake cult might in fact have gone underground, much the result of uncritical
contextualization. Upon request through intermediaries, I got similar answers
from Mongwande living at Bangui, Central Africa Republic:

> Everybody still knows of the reality of the snake cult, still everybody honours
> twins and twin parents, but mature evangelicals go with twins to the pastor to get a
> blessing. Only 'immature' evangelicals and Catholics still organize ceremonies.
> With the charismatic renewal in the Catholic Church this changes also. Generally
> snakes would not be killed except by mature evangelicals (Vungbo 2009).

Baring in mind the behaviour of so called immature evangelicals and Catholics, we return to Reverend Robert Kumbovo Manzinga, who rounds off his e-
mail correspondence by stating that:

> The contextualization process faces big problems both with older religious tradi-
> tions as well as with secular customs, being as much a separatist as a unifier. As a
> matter of fact, the problems are a natural part of the contextualization process it-
> self. This is the reason that the church should work as a divine institution which
> has a vision that is different from the secular life. The difficulties vary according
> to milieu and customs within each tribe. I do not need to remind you [Sveinung
> Moen] that we have many cultures here in the Congo and that the church meets
> them and should cope with them according to the rule of contextualization. We
> should always strain ourselves to make the Gospel understandable and a homoge-
> neous whole. At the same time as we got to appropriate the word of God to each
> milieu, it is this effort we call contextualization (Manzinga 2009).

I find it appropriate to continue this study in the light of Reverend Manzinga's
suggestions. First, he states quite firmly that it is the preaching that is most
significant in contextual theology. We are dealing in this process of contextualization with religious and socio-cultural questions. He is emphasizing the
preaching of Christ (*kerygma*) and asserts that they are making great efforts to
avoid certain old popular traditions to be adapted into the new system of faith.
He continues that it is the people who should adapt their culture into the Gospel. He also spells out that they must be aware of syncretism creeping into the

church. As I understand Reverend Manzinga, he appears to be on the alert to the problems they are facing in their contextualization process. We know that contextualization captures the challenge of relating the Gospel to culture in method and perspective. We may also say that it is part of an evolving stream of thoughts that relate the Gospel and the church to a particular context.

Second, as already said above, he is not afraid of criticizing the local culture for not letting go of its old traditions that are opposite to Christian teachings. The biblical critique might sometimes turn out to be offensive to people. The history of the church shows that good contextualization enables the church to offend people for the right reasons, while bad contextualization offends them for the wrong reasons. I assume that we are touching here on sensitive questions that require a great deal of wisdom. It appears to me that the contextualization process carried out by the new leadership in the African Baptist Church is being implemented in the best way possible.

As we have noticed, there are at least three functions the church in Monga has to be aware of: first of all the communication of the Gospel, secondly a sort of critique of local culture, and last the creation of communities. These communities are somewhat newer and wider than the old ones. Missionaries should be equipped with all kinds of techniques in language, history, psychology, sociology, cultural anthropology, not to mention the science of religion. Most people dealing with foreign people and cultures have neither the talent nor the opportunity to attend all the required education. However, the most important thing though is the divine call. I have no doubt that missionaries face cultures that are quite complicated to handle and to interpret.

5.5 Conclusion

In the Bible, the snake is the tempter and killer, but also is symbolic of the healer. He is responsible for the Fall of man and represents the evil forces: destruction, deceit and slyness. Furthermore, the snake is the impersonation of wickedness, which is supposed to be vanquished by man. It represents both good and evil. He is the Dragon and Satan (Job 3:8). But he is also the snake in the desert elevated by Moses to protect the Israelites from mortal snake bites (Num 21), a type of Christ, triumphant over the forces of evil (Rev 12).

At the same time, the snake is the central feature in the Mongwande culture around which all Mongwande life turns. It constitutes the basis of the Mongwande worldview and influences behaviour in all sectors of life. Even Christian Mongwande showed reactions based on the traditional worldview built around the snake cult. They usually developed split-level Christianity demonstrating the double allegiances in the parallel worldviews.

Today, the prevalence of the snake cult in a largely Christianized society has much decreased and is restricted to marginal forest areas. However, the so called "immature" Christians will still refrain from killing snakes and show allegiance to the snake cult in their everyday behaviour. This indicates the presence of two parallel worldviews manifesting themselves through the phenomenon of split-level Christianity.

In the next chapter, we will reflect on a better contextualization of Christianity in regards to the religious context of the Mongwande in order to prevent or even solve the problems of split-level Christianity and hidden syncretism. We will also seek to apply the contextualization models to Mongwande religious life, and work out guidelines for a contextualized missional theology and practice.

Chapter 6
A Better Contextualization Practice

6.1 Rethinking among the Missionaries

Missionaries went to foreign countries with the opinion that the local people were pagan. Arriving in villages, the missionaries thought the villagers needed the word of God. Churches were planted. In the beginning, local people accepted the Gospel as the word of God and believed. As time went on however, it became more and more clear that the church was not the only institution with a claim to be heard. The local culture, specifically the religion, did not remain silent. A claim for contextualization arose. The missionaries accepted slowly that they lived in cultural contexts. The Gospel had to be translated into form and meaning that the indigenous people understood.

Like all humans, missionaries and cultural anthropologists have worldviews. From time to time, these views need to be changed. The first cross-cultural encounter of any significance with foreign people during the modern period took place in the so called colonial era. Western governments, especially European, sent soldiers in order to conquer land. Traders followed and missionaries felt God's calling and went to fulfil their vocation. It was in this context of cross-cultural encounters with the foreign land and people that the science of cultural anthropology emerged during the twentieth century. Alongside with it, epistemology armed with positivism or naïve realism appeared including the belief that science was a new and unique type of knowledge (cf. Hiebert 1994:19-51).

After the colonial era, in the 1950s, people all over the world, the so called Third World, rose and started fighting for their independence and identity. The churches of the Third World stood also up and claimed their human rights. Cultural anthropology as science had a different approach from that of the church. It accepted other people as fully human, with their cultures and religions. The church had a quite different view. The receptors of the Gospel message were people all right, but their culture and religion could not be accepted without evaluation.

Paul Hiebert writes about this era of non contextualization which lasted according to him from 1850 to 1950. Mission authorities regarded the non-Christian cultures as of no value and to be replaced. Fortunately, not all the missionaries adopted this view. If we shall talk about contextualization, we need to recognize the right and the responsibility of the church in each culture and historic setting to interpret and apply the Scripture to its context. First, the

Bible needs to be translated into new languages. Second, old customs must be dealt with. Third, the church ought to become a new socio-cultural centre. Fourth, the church should develop its own theology. This theological process, already gone through in different socio-cultural contexts, is in fact bringing us to the formulation of a supra-cultural theology, a meta-theology (Hiebert 1985:193-225; 1994:93-103).

6.2   Critical Contextualization among Folk Religious Beliefs and Practices

6.2.1   The Critical Model Made Practical

In the first centuries, Christianity was a kind of folk movement, a gathering of ordinary sinners who had turned to Christ. The Gospel does not consist of a collection of abstract religious-philosophical systems building complex institutions or organizing large programs. Its main concern is to bring people, common people, into direct relationship with God through our Lord Jesus Christ. It then engages people to live out the implications of the Gospel in human culture. As soon as the church becomes a haven for the powerful, educated, high-ranking elite, its identity as the church is jeabodized. Eugene Peterson writes: "It is important to note that a Christian response to folk religions should not be an attempt to stamp out folk religions" (Peterson in Hiebert et al. 1999:91).

Folk religions consist of all kinds of beliefs. Researchers disagree as to the origin of beliefs. Some assert that beliefs give rise to behaviour. Others insist that behaviour generates beliefs. The explanations are causal in their logic and reasoning. There are dependent and independent variables. Hiebert et al. analyze the relationship between beliefs and behaviour in folk religion, and examine how the practices and organizations are related and may reinforce people's religious beliefs. They ask five questions: 1) How do people express their religious beliefs through signs and symbols? 2) How do people tell their cosmic stories through myths? 3) How do people enact their beliefs through rituals? 4) How do people organize their religious activities? 5) How do people transform themselves through religious movements? (Hiebert et al. 1999:230).

Additionally, it is particularly important to examine the beliefs in relation to some central questions to which people seek answers. For example, how do people find meaning in life on earth? And how do they explain death? These questions are naturally followed by questions like, how do people try to attain a good life, and how do they deal with misfortune? An important question in this research is how do people seek to discern the unknown in order to plan their lives? The last, but equally compelling inquiry is, how do people maintain a moral order, and how do they deal with disorder and sin? (Hiebert et al. 1999:95).

One Christian response to these questions might be a phenomenological one, i.e. to try to understand the world as the people in the host community see it without passing judgement on their beliefs. This attitude would enhance open syncretism. Another attitude would be to reject all culture with the consequence that the people would "save" some essential cultural elements by "going underground," creating a hidden syncretism. A better attitude would be to critically evaluate the culture in the light of Scripture and look for appropriate solutions faithful to the Bible and relevant to culture as Hiebert's model of critical contextualization foresees (Hiebert 1985:186-190).

When analyzing a religion using the critical contextualization model, four steps should be undertaken:

1) Before anything can be done the researcher must study the local culture or a particular phenomenon. This might be difficult depending on time and place or personalities involved. The meaning of secular objects may be a bit more overt, but religious items and rituals are often kept very secret.

2) In order to test the claim of truth of different beliefs and values, Christians must go beyond phenomenology to ontological evaluation.

3) The congregation must critically evaluate their beliefs and customs in the light of the new understanding. An understanding brought about by cooperation between local people and missionaries.

4) By this step we have arrived at the final process, which Hiebert calls the passage for transformative ministries, meaning that ministry helps people move from where they are to where God wants them to be. One cannot expect people to abandon the old ways and adopt new ones immediately. People can only move by a process of transformation. Let's now turn to the various elements that may be part of any given folk religion.

6.2.2   The World of Sacred Symbols and Myths

In the following discussion, I will attempt to link the theory with the world of symbols, signs and rituals in the snake cult. According to Ernst Cassierer, only humans create mental worlds by means of symbols. He writes: "Man lives in a symbolic universe. Language, myth, art and religion are parts of this universe (Cassierer in Hiebert et al. 1999:232). How do signs enable humans to think, create culture and communicate their thoughts to one another? Signs represent, signify, typify, denote and refer to something. A sign is a vehicle for a conception of perceived reality (Hiebert et al. 1999:232). Man makes an insensible world sensible by creating categories, order out of disorder, cosmos out of chaos. In the case of the snake cult, the name giving ceremony is an example of a ritual that re-establishes order out of chaos. In daily life, signs can communicate cognitive information in two ways: denotatively, which means indication, or connotatively, which means implying additive attributes. We have furthermore expressive meanings such as dance and music, and evaluative meanings, for example red lights and uniforms. Many symbols belong to more than one cognitive domain (Hiebert et al. 1999:238).

Symbols have two important functions: communicate information and transform reality. If we look at Charles Pierce's triadic model of signs (Hiebert et al. 1999:232), we see that there are three parts: (1) the sign (signifier), an external form, the spoken or written word, the sound of a bell, (2) a mental concept or image (the signification), and (3) the reality which the sign refers to (the signified). The signs connect the outer world to the inner mental worlds, like the iron snake represents *Ngbo* in this world. Ideas, feelings and values are transmitted to persons by encoded signs. Understanding signs in the Bible is the ability to exegete the biblical symbol systems. Being knowledgeable in hermeneutics is very useful. Of course, the contextualization of the Gospel in other cultures must begin at the level of signs and symbols.

According to Hiebert, Scripture is the best remedy for salvaging people in distress. In this book, I am attempting to illustrate how this is also true for the snake cult. By understanding rituals like the name giving ceremony or the symbolism of the iron cross, missionaries can use these as starting points to bring across the message of the Gospel.

Messages are often brought across by narratives and myths. Throughout history, myths have been used and misused. Myths were seen as stories that were not true or half true as an attempt to explain the world as the forefathers believed it to be. Actually, myths are the opposite of all that. Myths are stories believed to be true, which serve as paradigms people use to understand the bigger tales in which ordinary lives are embedded. They are master narratives. Their function or purpose is to give meaning to human existence. They were used to convey moral truths in literary form (Hiebert et al. 1999:260). They have great power. They explain reality in ways people can understand. They are prototypes for life and they give people a sense of identity. The identity forming master narrative in the snake cult would be the story of the twins as snakes that have come into the world and created chaos, a chaos which is remedied by the name giving ceremony. There are apocalyptic and eschatological myths not to speak of sacred myths. I did not encounter any such myths during my observations among the Mongwande snake cult.

The Mongwande spirituality is characterized by the here and now. Their stories give interpretations of the religious rituals themselves, the name giving ceremony for example. That's why telling a story, whether orally or by way of drama, is still an effective method to capture the people's attention. Missionaries should adapt biblical stories to this style of communication (Hiebert et al. 1999:268). One of the most dominant myths is the battle between God and the devil. The biblical view of the warfare between God and Satan is a moral encounter. The fight is between holiness and evil, justice, love and hate. The story in the Bible should be told, but it is recommendable that people also tell their story.

6.2.3 Religious Rituals, Leaders, Institutions and Movements

Central to formal as well as folk religion are rituals. According to Hiebert et al. (1999), formal religions have a higher and more sophisticated ritual system than folk religions have. But the personal experience of the participant is, in my opinion, just as valid. There is always the question of oscillation between order and freedom. If imbalance occurs, the cosmic rules might break down and chaos ensues. Rituals have important functions in societies ranging from handshakes to highly structured religious ceremonies. Many rituals combine diverse and contradictory meanings in a single set of symbols, for instance in the rites of passage where the recipient both dies and rises up again as a newborn (Hiebert et al. 1999:292).

Yet, rituals are limited and operate within a certain framework. They may be embodied in dramas. There are social dramas, religious dramas, cultural dramas and even cosmic dramas, re-enacting of cosmic myths. We operate with three kinds of rituals: rites of transformation (they create a new order and move individuals and groups through life), rites of intensification (to reinforce the existing order) and rites of crisis (to enable people to survive emergency situations) (Hiebert et al. 1999:302-318). In the case of the snake cult, we find that the name giving ceremony of twins comes into play. For their birth produces chaos. The ceremony seeks to recreate order and can therefore be classified as a rite of transformation. It re-enacts a cosmic drama, but it also rectifies a crisis, hence it can also be viewed as a rite of crisis. Signs, myths and rituals can be viewed as road signs by the missionary, indicating how most appropriately to respond. They should be put to good use in the contextualization process.

Hiebert et al. point to the fact that the Bible is an important source of information on how to deal with rituals that deviate from biblical views. Missionaries should observe their own rituals and keep them alive. Conversion should be made publicly known. Furthermore, church leaders must help local Christians develop meaningful, evangelical rituals. In relation to the snake cult, a Christian response might be to analyse for example the name giving ceremony to see if it is totally unbiblical or if there are elements that can be utilized with

Christian meaning. In any case, it might be necessary to allow for time in order that the transition from the snake cult name giving ceremony to a Christian ritual or practice goes smoothly and does not create grounds for revolt or split-level Christianity. Split-level Christianity refers to the phenomenon where people come to church on Sunday, but seek the medicine man on Monday (Hiebert et al. 1999:15-30).

Old beliefs and traditions persist long after people have become Christians. Even though a local person accepts Christ as her Lord and Saviour, the convert retains the ways and habits that belong to the pre-Christian culture and religion. The reasons could be many. Either the convert is unaware that he/she is still following the old traditions or he/she is either unwilling or unable to give them up. So, the challenge for a missionary will be to know how to respond to and deal with that phenomenon. Hiebert's suggestions as to a response strategy are helpful and I will get to that, but first let me say something more about leaders and institutions.

In the section "Religious Leaders and Institutions" of his book on folk religion (Hiebert et al. 1999:323-346), Hiebert examines which groups of people structure religious activities (religious leadership), and how these structures shape and limit the religious life of the people. According to Hiebert, there are a great number of leaders in religious activities: shamans, diviners, healers, magicians, astrologers, priests, prophets, preachers, evangelists, mystics, saints, gurus and sadhus. We can divide them in two different groups. One is concerned with this world and the other with the other world. Healers, exorcists, doctors, sorcerers, magicians, astrologers are occupied with this material world, but priests, prophets, saints, evangelists, mystics, monks, ascetics, dervishes, sannyasins and bikkus are concerned with the other world. The men and women in the first group are ordinary people, but villagers think they have special gifts like healing or divination. Healers and diviners are just such persons.

In the snake cult, the religious leader is the medicine man, sometimes referred to as the witchdoctor. In Lingala, a medicine man or witchdoctor is called *monganga*, but so is also a European medical doctor. In Mongwande, a medicine man is called *kókóró*. In the eyes of the local people, these persons play an important role in their lives. Another way of viewing their role is to see them as diviners, exorcists and, of course, witchdoctors. In these capacities, they fill very well the role of spiritual advisors.

Among the first specialists to emerge in the history of mankind are the religious leaders. Maybe the diviner was the first to appear on the scene, then the prophets and the priests, whom we find in formal religions. The prophets calling people to God are God's special servants. They receive their authority from God. The priests are the more bureaucratic leaders. They sustain the religious life of the community by exercising religious rituals, law and order. They erect temples, churches, mosques and monasteries, and came as an answer to the need for being together or coming together as groups. Corporate activities require social organizational structures. Without them there can be no corporate worship or relationship between the members. However, institutions undergo changes from time to time. The first generation is made up of the "founding fathers and mothers," those who started it all. By the fourth and the fifth generation, the corporation has become an "establishment." An institution has its advantages, but also its disadvantages. One advantage is in terms of creating spiritual fellowship, while a drawback could be in terms of a growing inclination to resent criticism and a tendency to display power. The Christian response to this challenge is to encourage the members of the church to get involved in the diverse activities of society. Sometimes, it looks like it is easier to contextualize the Gospel than to make an impact for Christ in the cultural context (Hiebert et al. 1999:339).

A missionary or leader has to take responsibility in helping the new believers cope with the transition from non-Christian to Christian living. One needs ministries of transformation. Church history shows that it is not enough to only plant a church. The church needs trained leaders and biblical scholars, Bible translators, theologians, and also specialists in other ministries. These people should be well educated and trained, and last but not least, be of good standing and reputation lest they should be scorned by the people. The new churches need both prophetic and priest-type ministries. They should complement one another.

Like other cultural systems, religious systems are constantly changing. These changes are caused by internal social pressures, environmental changes or foreign ideas. Some of the old religions have been revitalized and completely new religious movements have emerged. Deterioration is not an unknown phenomenon in the cultural or physical life, but if that process is left unchecked, the object, whether it is cultural or physical, may crumble. Revitalization is then necessary and this often begins with a prophetic vision of things. This often allows a renewed community to emerge more forcefully and actively. Harold Turner (1981) provides a useful taxonomy for understanding religious movements based on the solutions they offer to crises they face (see the figure in Hiebert et al. 1999:351).

Native movements seek to solve a crisis, improve the temporal lot of the people by returning to traditional roots and reviving aspects of the people's religious past. I do not hesitate to call the snake cult a native and original movement that reflects the above mentioned traditional, cultural and religious aspects. There is no doubt that the snake cult is the oldest knowable religious phenomenon among the Mongwande. A contextualization process will require quite a lot from the missionaries, but also a great deal from the local Christians. In the so called accommodationist response people react to crisis by skipping old fashion cultural structures or systems and instead build a new identity.

Missionaries believed that the superstitions of tribal people should be replaced by Christianity. This has not always been so easy to do. Traditional religions often persist as undercurrents after people have become Christians and we often see split-level Christianity. An alternative reaction is the emergence of new religious movements (Hiebert et al. 1999:353). Several independent movements have emerged out of the encounter between Christianity and African traditional religions. A case in point is the Kimbanguist church in the DRC Congo. Other examples of new religious movements in the RDC Congo are the *Fidèles*, *Kulinga and Kundima*, the "Love and Faith" movement; the two latter had strong footings in our region. Sub-Saharan Africa, Latin America as well as Asia have also been witnesses to various new religious movements. The number of these new religious movements is said to be around 23,000 with some 57 million followers.

Turner calls a set of independent movements Hebraists (Turner in Hiebert et al. 1999:359). These movements break with traditional African religious aspects, but are not Christ-centred. Their status as Christians may therefore be questioned. These movements stand for a more indigenous oriented religious movement, yet they are not followers of any African traditional religion. They are at best oriented towards the Old Testament. Some of the African Initiated Churches (AIC) are examples of this (Turner in Hiebert 1999:359-364). These movements represent attempts to bring the Gospel into the African culture. They are trying to express the Gospel in images familiar to the African people. They preach the Old Testament prophesies of the coming of the Messiah. Therefore and perhaps inadvertently, they have given rise to mass movements in which whole families and communities have turned to Christ. These movements are mostly to be found in group-oriented societies.

Another type of revitalization movement is renewal in established religions and churches. Revivals of new religious vision and fervour often occur on the margins of the institutional structures. One ought to pay attention to the fact that tensions between folk religious movements and formal establishments may sometimes arise that can be difficult to resolve (Hiebert et al. 1999:365).

6.2.4 Conclusion

Above I have suggested that the snake cult can be categorized as both folk religion as well as animism. I have described various elements that are part and parcel of all cultures and religions, namely signs, myths and rituals. I have also looked at religious institutions and their leadership. And I have presented some religious movements which have sprung up in Africa and around the world. The main objective is to find strategies for Christian responses to various challenges such as split-level Christianity, Hebraist and nativist tendencies and, in particular, the snake cult.

6.3   The Models of Contextualization Applied Critically to the Snake Cult

In this section, I will apply some models of contextualization to the snake cult and make them practical. Many theologians and missionaries have struggled with the problem of contextualization. In his work, Stephen B. Bevans documents many names of the missiologists who have published in this specialized area. However, in what follows, I will build my argument primarily on my own experiences and understanding (Moen 2005).

6.3.1   The Translation Model Applied to the Iron Snake

In this case study on the iron snake, I will take into consideration what has been done in contextualization and give some suggestions of what to do in the future. I have previously written about the snake songs but in this case study I seek to go deeper in the investigation of contextual theology. I agree with Hesselgrave that contextualization is not facultative but is a missiological and theological necessity (Hesselgrave 1980; Hesselgrave & Rommen 1989). But before we launch into the depth of the contextualization process, we will look at the case of the iron snake cross. I will, as best as I can, follow the translation model as a first approach.

In the snake songs, we find the *Yenda-Gazoroma*, the snake god, the snake cult and the snake sticks. The snake sticks are holy and are worshipped. They have different functions within the cult, such as property defence. During the birth of twins the blood of the twins was given to the village. The iron stick seems important to the Mongwande. They pray to it. They worship it. They expect answers from it to daily questions, in times of sorrow and death.

We could certainly consider many things concerning the Mongwande religion and the snake cult, but one issue would surely be very important and that is faith in the *Yenda-Gazoroma*, the snake god. We noted above that Pope John Paul II has shown a real interest in culture (Bevans 2008:49-53). After he became pope, he has emphasized the necessity of dialoguing with the different cultures. The dialogue between faith and culture has been a constant subject of his voluminous writings. We have here two dimensions in the question of faith: faith and culture, and faith to faith. The way this interest is formulated, seems to indicate some kind of opposition between faith and culture. I do hope that this is not the case. In my eyes, they ought to be co-workers, people working together in harmony with one another. While the faith side of the equation certainly has to do with theological and dogmatic questions, culture concerns the social life per se. In bringing the two together, the prime question would probably be: Is the faith ready to reformulate some of its doctrines in light of a given culture? The answer is not simple.

Be that as it may, the problem of faith to faith deserves some attention. As far as can I observe, the translation model's primary concern is the preservation of Christian identity and at the same time to seriously take into account cultural views, social change and historical events. A starting point in this discussion could be the expression "from faith to faith" in Romans 1:17. I notice that the Bible in some French, German, Bangala and Norwegian versions is very close to the Greek version which reads *ek pisteôs eis pistin* "from faith to faith," while the English NIV version is paraphrasing. In the French, German, Bangala and Norwegian versions it seems more like a transcription from the original Greek text. In the English NIV version, the verse is a mixture of word-for-word translation and an accommodation of the particular language. By doing this, the translators seek to render the verse more comprehensible and meaningful to the reader. The problem question, in my view, as already mentioned above, is the expression "from faith to faith." What does Paul mean when speaking about faith? Does he speak of God as giver of faith and that the said faith produces in turn faith. In other words, the object of our belief produces belief. But there is an insertion in NIV that instead of "from faith to faith" goes "faith from first to last." This is, as I see it, a paraphrasing addition. In the eyes of the translators, the purpose this paraphrase is to clarify and give the readers a meaningful understanding of the context. But, could there also be another explanation of verse 17? Faith can be manifold. The theologians in earlier days used to talk about "believe in" and "believe on." These concepts have been more or less abandoned today. In accordance with the science of psychology, in this postmodern time, theologians are asking themselves, what a soul is and what belief is? The answer from psychiatry is: "The entire life of our consciousness is insolubly tied up with the functions of the body and must therefore cease when the body dies" (Sheldrup 1971).

Today's common view among theologians, I presume, is that spiritual or mental functions, in relation to the soul and faith, depend more or less on one's sensory organs and brain. This view however must be balanced with the fact that God has created the human person in every aspect of his being. Furthermore, there exists one subjective and honest belief deeply rooted in a person which directs the person towards a transcendental object. So it seems reasonable to think that personal faith is a good and honest thing. However, the object or objects of one's faith might be wrong or false. This may explain why Paul writes that God is producing faith in humans so that they in their belief can grasp God's salvation.

We are in process of analyzing the snake iron cult in relation to Christianity. I would like to return to a particular experience I had in Monga which illustrates well the faith of the Mongwande in the snake. I met a person, who lived in the village nearby, on one of my walking tours around the mission station. He stood beside an orange tree and was in the process of clearing the site around that tree. I saw also that he had placed sticks around the tree, sticks that were carved to look like snakes. As far as I knew, this man was the spokesman of religion and belief among the Mongwande. The distinction between magic and religion is a European distinction, introduced by the church. It is not a Mongwande conception. The snake is paramount to all. I found out that the person standing beside the tree believed in the snake cult to the extent that he used carved sticks, symbolic of the snake, in order to protect the orange tree he had taken for himself. I started to talk to him in order to find out about his faith in the snake. Our conversation in Bangala took place at Monga in the form of questions and answers in the middle of the day and went like this: "What are you doing?" "I am cleansing around my tree." "Why have you blocked the path to the tree?" "The sticks are set up in order to protect my tree. They look like snakes. The snakes are watching my orange fruits." "What are the basket and the bunch of twigs doing?" "There are powerful medicines inside that watch over my orange fruits."

In what way are they watching? The Mongwande believe in the snake. The villagers know the purpose of their rituals. After a while, I understood that my interlocutor did not like to continue our conversation. So I had to turn to others in the village to learn more about his actions. The man wanted to have the tree for himself as a supplement to his daily diet. The only way to preserve the fruit of the tree was to claim it in the name of the snake. He knew that if he hang up some sort of ressemblance of the snake, people would shun the place. So, when I asked him what the reaction from the people was, he replied that they believed in the snake like he did. Here was a case that clearly showed that the villagers were believers and that their own belief kept them at bay. The snake's presence casts a spell over the tree and the tree was called *ndeti na dawa* "the bewitched tree." Here I had met an individual who knew witchcraft and without scruples utilized the religious technique egotistically. In this case, the faith kept the villagers outside, while it kept the man at the tree inside. Nobody wished to do harm to the man and the tree because they believed, if they did, they could lose their eyesight or fall ill or in some way be hit by a catastrophe.

Could this situation invite some sort of contextualization? We know that cultures are made up of systems of beliefs and practices that are built upon assumptions that people make about themselves, their fellow humans and about the world around them. Could we agree upon the assumption that the Mongwande's faith has similar concerns as ours? Is this subjective, personal yearn-ing for truth the same as ours? If it were so, we could stand on a very firm basis together in our common belief towards the same object of our faith: the Christian God. There are several other elements in the religious culture that concern individuals as well as the group. Common to them all is a personal faith that is underlying the practices.

6.3.2   The Anthropological Model Applied to Worship

It is not difficult to see that worship is the primary concern of a religion. Prayers are the foundation of it. The Mongwande pray to the snake, to their ancestors, to the ashes, to the moon and so on. I would like to present here an example of a Mongwande morning prayer.

Every morning a Mongwande wife warms some water which she pours into a bucket or a hand washbasin. She gives her husband a piece of wood that is split at the end so it looks like a brush, a toothbrush. The husband takes the toothbrush and dips it into the water and puts it in his mouth to brush his teeth. He then spits out the water while saying:

> Oh you Mbonga, you Yayo, you Nzapa, you Nomo, you Ketua,
> May I be in good health!
> When I go out may I not steal the property of others!
> If I should find something in my father's property which he has given to me but which does not belong to him, I shall give it back to the owner.
> I am not cheating.
> Those who know, that I do not know it. [Meaning: she is ignorant of her future life.]
> I will have a long life, but not those who wish me a bad life.

Then he rinses his mouth and spits the water on his child saying:

> My child, do what I am doing.
> Never insult anybody.
> Associate with people and show veneration.
> And you will have many children.

After the wife has poured water for her husband, she saves a little for herself. Then she takes a piece of wood out of the fire and throws it into the water and says:

> I am the lawful wife of my husband.
> I have no medicine to kill people.
> I have no evil spirit in me.
> I kill no-one in the village.
> On the contrary, I honour old and young people.
> I also honour the other wives of my husband.
> I do my best for them.

I nurse my husband and take care of him.
I do not give him things that are stolen, because the curse from those I have robbed can kill him.
You Nzapa, God, Yayu, Sese, Banga, Mbongo, Ketua, Nomo,
May those who wish me evil die at an early age.
But I shall live long in the service of my husband.
I shall have children (Zakalembe).[5]

Then she takes a piece of wood and carves the end of it up so that it becomes a toothbrush, with which she rinses her teeth and mouth and says: "May I stay sound and healthy."

In order to reinforce the fact that Mongwande people are actively praying, I will also quote a prayer song to the snake:

We ought to honour the snake.
He has given us twins.
They [the villagers] are drawing their knives and wish to cut the head of the snake.
I am moaning and grieving from pain.
The people have only contempt for the snake.
What is the snake bringing us?
Oh Yes! Happiness!
So let us sing and danse of joy because the snake wanted to visit us.
What is the snake bringing us?
Oh yes, only joy and happiness! (Tanghe 1929:53).

We presuppose that there is a basic religious emotion that is common to all human beings on earth (A in Figure 3 on the next page). It is from this original basis that faith and view of life is formed which is in harmony with other social and cultural expansions of people. Then we get the African religiosity (B) to the left of the figure and the Euro-American religiosity (D) on the right side. The African and the Euro-American meet in C and form a new African religiosity that is a cultural novelty. Below follows a graphic representation of the above thoughts.

---

[5] Zakalembe was a teacher at Mongwande Primary School.

Figure 3: Neo-African Religiosity

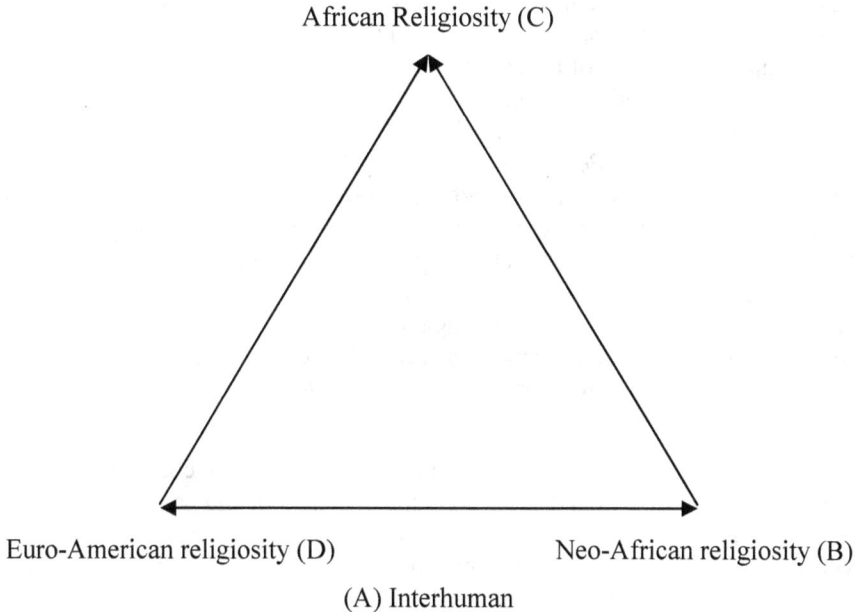

African Religiosity (C)

Euro-American religiosity (D)   Neo-African religiosity (B)

(A) Interhuman

Analyzing the morning prayers of the husband and his wife is as if we were looking into the deepest layers of the African soul. We remark the despair of the father of the twins when he discovers that the people of the village have killed their own happiness, the snake. The husband stresses his own loyalty and integrity. He has not committed anything wrong and if his father has, he shall straighten it up. He wishes to live long. The wife stresses her intact character by telling that she is not hurting anybody. On the contrary, she is honouring even her fellow wives and doing her best for them. She is caring for and nursing her husband. She is concluding her prayers by pronouncing her wish to live long and be blessed with children.

Both are praying to *Nzapa* "god" and all his spirits. It is important to avoid the wrath of god and his spirits. The African religion is characterized by the fact that there is no borderline between the material and immaterial world. The two merge into each other in a way that the dead can be living and live together with the living. In this line of thought, John Mbiti talks about the "living-dead." It is an insurmountable gap between the African traditional religion with its ontological comprehension of god and the spirits, and Christianity with its doctrine of sin. If one wanted to be free from sins, one had to accept a hidden God who is not identical with the Mongwande universal supra-human god. The Mongwande regards the universe as a whole. His view of life is holistic. The universe is one and the salvation is not to fight against nature or the power therein but to live in accordance with nature. Thus, the Mongwande has found other ways of coping with the world than the Euro-American. The Euro-American's philosophy of religion has its roots in the Judeo-Christian world of ideas with its conceptions of sin and guilt, punishment and reward, heaven and hell, and a material/carnal world that is evil and must therefore be broken down and punished (1Pet 2:20). Christianity has its roots in a culture that is separating the notions from one another in order to express them in universal abstracts. But, as said above, the Mongwande world of ideas comprises entities. There is also distinction, but all aspects of reality participate in the whole. Thus, there are two different views of life that are confronting each other. If we evaluate these two views of life against each other, we will find both positive and negative traits. So actually a conclusion would rather be that they are both products of their own particular cultural context with their own particular solution for the enigma of life.

Let us have a look at Figure 4 (on the next page). A is the collective original macro-soul where the individual micro-soul has its root and point of departure. Salvation in the African worldview is collective and holistic, i.e. it is the whole that shall be saved. From this socio-religious original power, all individuals can get their strength. The husband steps up from the original soul as a positively charged anode. When he is psychologically and even physically discharged, he (or his soul *anima* B) returns back to the original source (A) deep in his soul as a negatively discharged cathode. The same is valid for his wife (C) and the father of the twins (D) who get their strength from the African macro-original soul. Through their prayers, they mount up into fellowship with *Nzapa* "god" and sink down into the same depth of collective fellowship in order to gain strength and courage. As long as the Mongwande keep this mytho-pneumatological canal open, the snake cult will live on. I learned this from a conversation with Zakalembe, a teacher at the Primary School in Monga in 1960.

Figure 4: Collective Original Macro-Soul

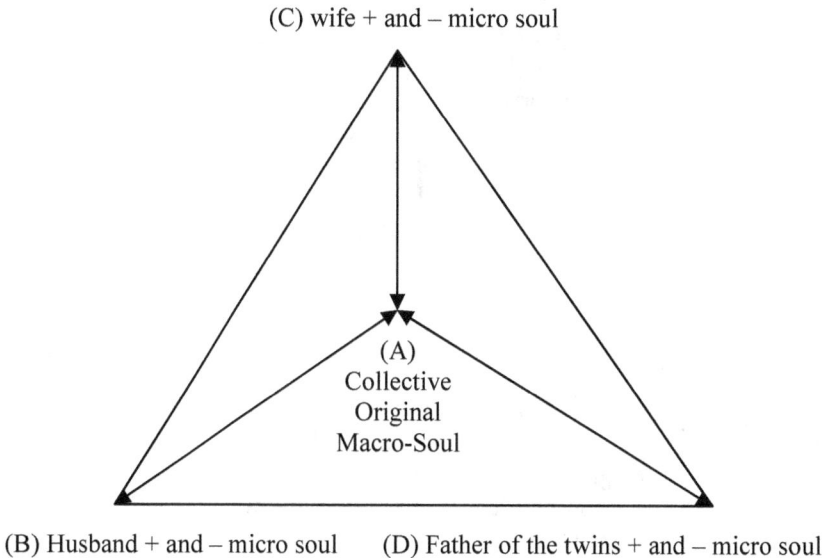

(C) wife + and – micro soul

(A)
Collective
Original
Macro-Soul

(B) Husband + and – micro soul   (D) Father of the twins + and – micro soul

Now let us have a look at a survey of a more personal approach to the religious life of the Mongwande. In the example that follows, I cannot but see an echo of the story of Rachel who stole her father's household gods (Gen 31:19). It appears that Rachel stole the gods from her father, Laban, in order to have something to rely on when she left home and went with Jacob as his wife. It was during an evangelical meeting on the outskirts of Monga that a woman came forward and placed a pitcher full of small wooden sticks carved with all sorts of figures or symbols on them. She burst in tears and said that bringing these gods was a real offering. But, as she now had accepted Christ as her Saviour she would not have this household altar and these household gods in her house. It was obviously no sacrifice too great to become a believer of Jesus. This event was not the only one that I witnessed as a missionary in the DRC. The proclamation of Jesus was followed by a clear cut distinction between the old life and the new life in Christ.

But what about her tears? What about her emotions? We do have elements of emotions in Christianity also, fortunately! Do we have here another reason to be a little more cautious and do we have an opportunity for contextualizing? In my view, the religious feeling is the basis (*Grundsatz*) in all religions. There is nothing wrong with her emotions. The problem may be with the object of her emotions. Is the target, her old faith, actually worth her tears? On the other hand, are her tears signs of breaking with the past?

We notice further a series of old faith objects of worship. The moon, ashes, Banga, the ancestors, the rainbow, Yenda and Gazoroma, the twin name of the snake (*ngbó*), the river god Kilima and the forest god Kaina. What do these different religious exercises show us else but deep felt yearnings for spiritual experiences? Worship comprises characteristics like praying, adoration, devotion and so on. Instead of going against this complex and deep-seated desire to worship, should we not capitalize upon it? We have the eternal message. Why do we not plant it in the already fertile soil of local culture? The longing for divine answers through the tripod (*mbeti*), for example, can be changed to folding of hands in prayers to God instead of using hands to rub the *mbeti* "tripod" instrument.

6.3.3   The Anthropological Model Applied to Initiation Rites

The subject of circumcision is relevant to the Mongande culture. The circumcision of boys was well known in Monga, but I did not find any evidence regarding excision of girls. I am sure it took place. The circumcision of boys was actually so common that it was often executed with the help of the local health services (Moen 2005).

The circumcision took place within the framework of a ceremony of initiation. First, it took place in isolation. The boys stayed in small huts made for this kind of activities. Second, it took place under scorn and acts of contempt. Third, the boys were between the age of 14 and 16 and abstaining from sexual intercourse with females and from different kinds of food, and sometimes full fledged fasting. Fourth, the youngsters had to pass through certain bodily encroachments, such as filing of the teeth or pulling the teeth. Fifth, the final act of these rituals was the circumcision. The prepuce, the foreskin, was cut off and thrown in the woods. The boys suffered a great deal after the operation because the wound was not properly cleansed. After the operation, the circumcised were presented as initiates in a new scheme of life, the adult world. Upon returning to their village, these neophytes were received with dancing and singing. However, something unexpected emerged. Those who were not circumcised were subjected to scorn from the circumcised. Everything touched by the uncircumcised was considered unclean (those out of the ritual boundaries of Mongwande society, see discussion below and Douglas 1966).

The Mongwande have created their own rituals in order to mark biographical events such as birth, initiation, marriage, and death. Status changes follow these events. Ordinarily, the rites of passage are performed in connection with the life crises. However, researchers like the French anthropologist Arnold van Gennep (1873-1957) have emphasized the significance of ceremonies that are both social and cultural. The rites of passage have a strong taint of local religiosity in Monga. The rites for the most part mark a transition from one status to another like the name giving ceremony of the twins and the circumcision for ordinary boys. There are a lot of rites to be found in Mongwande society: rites of passage, symbolic rites, initiation rites, funeral rites, and healing rites. These rites follow all the changes of life places, social positions and ages. Mary Douglas (1966) helpful study on Leviticus 11 and 15 deals with the purity of priests and common people. She argues that human society seems to have difficulties in accepting the in-between situation, the intermediate positions of particular subjects. The society insists on well defined boundaries. Douglas maintains that what is unclear and contradictory in a social and religious context is regarded as ritually unclean. In the light of this hypobook, she points at the prohibitions of eating certain animals and fish and the need of washing and anointing. The animals or fish that cannot be clearly and unequivocally classified as belonging to one group are considered unclean. Well, it was just that kind of conception, clean and unclean, that emerged in Monga, expressed in the concrete form of circumcision. Circumcision was an answer to the identification of the boys and their integration into society. They had passed through the prescribed rituals and were declared to be clean. Those who had not gone through the rites faced the scorn of the community.

6.4   Guidelines for Critical Contextualization

6.4.1   Theological Responses to Traditional or Folk Religion

Hiebert and his co-authors have tried to understand folk religion phenomenologically through key questions. They provide guidelines for evaluating old beliefs and practices in the light of biblical truth and discuss general principles for developing a missional theology and practice and what they call a Christian folk religion (Hiebert et al. 1999:367ff).

Hiebert and his co-workers have pointed out some of the problems and possible answers in the process of critical contextualization. I find their argumentation pertinent to the situation in our church at Monga when dealing with issues surrounding the snake cult. The first, and foremost helpful step, is to investigate phenomenologically people's beliefs and practices. And in so doing, one must be conscious of the reality that no effective communication can take place before language is learned and some local cultural characteristics have been understood and adopted. As I have sought to demonstrate, good contextualization is neither a matter of uncritically rejecting ancient systems nor uncritically accepting the old traditions. It is incumbent upon the missionary and the local congregation to assess each and every aspect of the host culture and judge prudently whether it should be discarded or kept, albeit in a slightly altered form. To pass wise judgements requires deep knowledge of local culture, and this takes time. It should be noted that no culture is a problem to be solved, even though it may be a challenge for one's understanding. Further-more, each culture should be dealt with theologically. Old traditions, be they religious or social, ought to be handled with consideration. Contextualization should not, at any cost, be forced, but allowed to sprout as naturally as the flowers in the springtime. The criterion for evaluating human social, cultural and religious systems is, of course, the Scripture. It is supra-cultural as a ma-trix for appraising culture.

In their general theological principles, Hiebert and his co-authors develop a series of guidelines which they recommend for contextualization (Hiebert et al. 1999:370-377). Firstly, they insist on the importance of a "theology of the invisible" based on the insight that an important dimension of the real world is in fact invisible. In biblical perspective, the invisible world deals with angels, Satan, and demons. In psychological perspective, we deal with people and their dreams, character and beliefs. In anthropological perspective, the invisi-ble world deals with spirits. The snake cult should, of course, be taken seri-ously. Furthermore, in theological perspective, one should take the trinitarian understanding of God seriously.

Secondly, Hiebert et al. advocate a "theology of worship and submission." Christians should not struggle for control and power. Self-centredness and self-possession are great temptations in human life. Humans are called to submit to God. Faith, and not control, is their compass.

Thirdly, the notion of a "holistic theology" needs to be kept at the heart of all theologizing for Christians. The planet, the heavens with its sun, moon and stars, in a word, the entire cosmos is the work of God. Neo-Platonic dualism is unknown to Hebrew thought.

Fourthly, the message in the Gospel is about the Kingdom of God. After the Fall in the Garden of Eden came sin, sickness and suffering. Christ came to proclaim his kingdom and to make known to the entire world that salvation and redemption is at hand.

Fifthly, the Christians should emphasize a biblical "theology of power and the cross": God's love and His power are demonstrated on the cross. The church shows God's power in transformed lives and in Christ-like confrontation of evil.

Sixthly, a "theology of discernment" is necessary when Christians are dealing with traditional or folk religion. How can the Christians discern the work of God from the work of Satan? Hiebert et al. give the following guidelines and guiding questions: 1) Give the glory to God; 2) The Bible recognizes the Lordship of Christ; 3) Is the evidence of God's power through the Holy Spirit emphasized? 4) Does it conform to scriptural teaching? 5) Are the leaders accountable to others in the church? 6) Do those involved manifest the fruits of the Spirit? 7) Does the teaching and practice lead believers toward spiritual maturity? 8) Does teaching and practice seek the unity of the body of Christ?

Hiebert continues by highlighting some theological pitfalls (Hiebert et al. 1999:377-381). There are many dangers lurking in the church and in the contextualization process. One of these is syncretism, meaning that Christianity and folk beliefs have been combined in a way that the Gospel has more or less lost its identity. The Gospel has changed to the extent that the result of that change is somewhat a new religion: Christo-paganism. Fighting syncretism and magical mentality as well as not becoming captive to non-Christian worldviews is very important. Christianity fights human-centeredness. Be cognizant of the snake cult and deal with it patiently, but firmly, calling believers to a theocentric and biblical worldview.

Another pitfall is experience-based theology: "Folk religiosity is existential and experience-based. The result is a pragmatic concern for power rather than truth" (Hiebert et al. 1999:379). There are traits in the modern church that reveal old traditions that are not necessarily biblical. These should also be evaluated and dealt with in the most biblical way before they develop into secularism. Those with prophetic and priestlike gifts should also possess the gift of discernment, knowing how to judge between the work of God and the work of Satan. Showing imbalance here could be fatal. In their treatment of this issue, Hiebert et al. have examined some principles that might be helpful in critical contextualization. Exalting a particular leader, for example, may be the result of allowing a gifted person to dominate and force his opinion upon the congregation. However, a biblical remedy for avoiding such abuses is to place the gifts of leadership, healing, guidance and other ministries in the church beside one another. Some members may have particular gifts, but, they should be used for the common good of the congregation as we are reminded in 1Corinthians 12:7-10.

Through their analysis Hiebert and co-workers attempt to provide a critical response to traditional and folk religion and split-level Christianity. They deal with evaluation in the light of biblical truth, and follow the transformation of believers and churches from unbiblical ways to an authentic Christian life as witnesses in their particular milieu (Hiebert et al. 1999:381).

We have examined possible Christian responses and strategies missionaries might employ when faced with challenges. These missiological responses are strategies which take the invisible aspect of reality seriously, submit the believer to the will of God who desires to incorporate all mankind into His Kingdom. Imperative to these strategies is to emphasize the transformative power of the cross and develop the ability to discern. The variation from culture to culture is great. We ought to handle these variations with care and sensitivity. Churches should be taught how to deal with culture. They should also be taught how to do theology and contextualization in their own context. Hiebert says: "The first principle of a biblically based meta-theology is that it is rooted in the acceptance of Scripture as divine revelation" (Hiebert et al. 1999:383f). The Holy Spirit must guide believers, because the understanding of truth is partial. The church must be accepted as the centre of truth, the centre of learning about the Lord, and the centre of hermeneutic expounding the Scriptures. The first important step is to be committed to the truth as Scripture reveals it. After some discussion and debates, critically evaluating their own standpoints, the new congregation, under the guidance of the Holy Spirit, agrees to create new practices that are both Christian and native. This process of contextualization takes the Bible as the rule of faith seriously (Hiebert et al. 1999:387). Earlier, the Christian response was at times characterized by uncritical contextualization. For example, missionaries were expected to burn fetishes. We have studied the negative consequences of uncritical contextualization, i.e. open or hidden syncretism. Therefore, let us look once again at critical contextualization.

6.4.2 Ministries of Transformation

Let us now take a closer look at one aspect of step four in Hiebert's critical model, the ministries of transformation. Transformation is total conversion. The apostle Paul talks about being a new creature in Christ (2Cor 5:17). This transformation, if it is authentic, should appear in daily life. The transformation starts in the church but manifests itself in society. It is an ongoing process that leads to a total renovation of the converts' beliefs, worldview and life. Based on Ephesians 4:11, Hiebert proproses four such ministries (Hiebert et al. 1999:387-391). We are adding a fifth one which is missing in his presentation:

Apostolic Ministry: The church sends out pioneer missionaries who communicate the Gospel and plant and nourish new churches.

Evangelistic Ministry: Evangelism is central to the church's ministries of transformation. Churches are sending out missionaries to call people to God. That is the greatest thing that happens to people.

Pastoral ministry: Pastors and missionaries go out to help those in psychological and physical need.

Teaching ministry: The New Testament speaks of Paul as an ardent teacher and expounder of the Bible. He is an example of a person full of thoughtful consideration for people.

Prophetic ministry: Prophetic calling belongs to the church. It represents the ministry of discernment. It is the critical voice which evaluates the life of church and society. It brings the good news that creation will one day be restored and that sickness and death will vanish, that heaven is waiting on everyone who has turned to the Lord.

6.4.3 Conversion and Church Planting

In his reflections on church planting, Hiebert takes us back to the question of conversion (1994:107-135). Can a person become a Christian after hearing the Gospel only once? What essential change takes place when a person responds to the Gospel? He has heard of Christ and his redemptive work on the cross, his death and resurrection. But his biblical knowledge is still minimal. The convert Papayya, presented by Hiebert (1994:108-110), seems to have a lot of trouble in his attempt to live in harmony with his Christian identity. The congregation accepts him without further ado. But he doesn't understand much of the message being preached. The cultural differences are too big to be ignored. Papayya is very much the same after his conversion as before, says Hiebert.

What does it mean to be a Christian? Before we can answer this question, we need to look more closely at how we form categories such as "church" and "Christian." There are many categories, such as "intrinsic sets" formed on the basis of the essential nature of things. There are "bounded sets" having sharp boundaries, and "fuzzy sets" having fuzzy or no boundaries. Western cultures are usually bounded sets. We make Christianity a bounded set, meaning that we draw sharp lines between Christian and non-Christian. In Western cultures, the church becomes also a bounded set. A church is a gathering of people, like a club, a voluntary association of like-minded people. The theology of a "bounded set" church tends to be ultimate, universal, and unchanging. The church maintains clear boundaries. It is inclined to be democratic. In principle, all members have an equal say. Mission societies as bounded sets want to win persons to Christ, stress the difference between the religions, fear incorporating ideas and practices into Christianity that are taken from other religions.

Like all societies, the church organizes its conceptual worlds by creating cognitive category systems of logic and basic belief. In short, the West organizes its social worlds, personal and institutional, by assigning authority and prescribing proper ways to behave. This view of order is based on our Western concern with the intrinsic structure of things. We believe that life and events are highly predictable. We want to know the world in order to rule the world. This concept of structural order is also rooted in our belief in hierarchy. We find this structural order very much in our churches. In addition to order, societies need relationships. Parents, children and people organize groups. Communities and institutions are established. Without relationships societies collapse. Where people are, relationships are to be found. It looks like the Westerners know how to keep everything in order, but they do not emphasize

relationship to the same extent. Westerners rarely open their homes spontane-
ously to visitors. Western missionaries are also products of their culture and
should be aware of this fact in order to help build credibility in other societies.
Hierbert reminds us that "we need to look below the surface-level cultural
differences to the deep worldview assumptions we bring with us (1994:145).

6.4.4   Renewal of the Church

There will always be the question of the mission and the renewal of the church.
Of course, new churches must be planted, but the old churches must also be
revived. There is no such thing as a church that is not in need of renewal. All
forms of life are involved in the laws of health and illness, of reinvigoration
and decay. Thus, from time to time, the church must be woken up. That being
the case, we must not forget that spiritual renewal is ultimately the work of
God. The emphasis here is on the human dimensions of personal conversion
and transformation. There could be a question of renewal for the entire church
or of just personal salvation.

The question of renewal and transformation can be raised at the level of rites.
Rituals play an important role in all religions, including Christianity, as the
Roman Catholic Church amply shows. Protestants have never been eager to
observe many rites. But that depends on how close their doctrines and practices are to the Catholics. Can we talk about the need for restoration of certain
rituals in the Christian church? What about the most common ones, those we
call basic, such as the Lord's Prayer, songs and hymns, and special clothing?
Transformational rituals are to be found in all religions of the world. They
include practices such as pilgrimages, camps and retreats. In crucial ways,
transformative rites are the opposite of restorative rites. First, they are characterized by what Victor Turner calls liminality. Transformational rituals are to
be found both in the Judeo-Christian life and in the Christian church. Indeed,
the Christian church has a lot of rituals that should not be forgotten, such as
festivals, religious fairs, pilgrimages, and rites of passage as birth, initiation,
marriage, and death. Church planting and church renewal are two central tasks
of mission.

Restoration is also needed in what Hierbert calls the "excluded middle" in a
Christian worldview. When Hiebert speaks about this excluded middle he
seems to have no special answer to it (1994:189-201). We deal relatively easily with the questions of science and religion, but the questions of the uncer-
tainty of the future, the crises of present life and the unknown of the past are
somewhat in the middle and are complicated. Platonic dualism and a science
based on materialistic naturalism killed the idea of a middle world of uncer-
tainties and unexplainable phenomena. Hierbert reminds us that when Christianity excludes the middle, it provides few answers to the everyday questions

of man. Hiebert concludes that in confronting animistic worldviews, our central message should always focus on the greatness and power of God, whether in cosmic, human or natural history (1985:201).

6.4.5 Spiritual Gifts

When the Pentecostals arrived on the scene in the beginning of the twentieth century, a new emphasis was brought into the Christian world. They highlighted the spiritual gifts such as speaking in tongues, prophetic gifts, words of knowledge and wisdom, and healing. Many churches have their focus nowadays on healing, exorcism and words of knowledge. This charismatic phenomenon seemed to be new, but the history of the church shows otherwise. We find charismatic elements in the church from the time of the NT (Acts 2:1) up to the twentieth century with the emergence of the Pentecostal movement in 1905.

With the Enlightenment, many new thoughts appeared like the modern dualism and the deification of the self: placing of humans at the top of nature and thereby considering them as the gods of the earth. During the last decade of the nineteenth century, the focus on the self became the dominant theme in Western society (Hiebert 1985:221). The modern worldview changed and showed great concern for psychic and physical health. However, today it seems that the church is going backward, back to some sort of animism and animistic thinking. In the midst of this thinking, the New Age emerged. The New Age seems to be a western response to animistic thoughts and puts emphasis on the promise of holistic health. There is no need for anyone to be sick, poor or unsuccessful.

Hiebert is recognizing the dangers of the above mentioned movements. The practices of speaking in tongues, healing, and exorcism are not necessarily positive experiences for the church, they may turn out to be negative. It could be a danger, if we stretch the Gospel to suit us instead of living to the glory of God. Satan is always on the alert to tempt us and sometimes even imitates God's miracles. The question must always be: "Is the miracle what it pretends to be? Is it glorifying God? If not, then it is not of God." In the closing passages Hiebert is warning the churches to be careful and to apply a theology of discernment (Hiebert 1985:182).

6.4.6 Contextual Biblical Strategy

The great leaders in human history have usually made strategic plans for their work and our Lord Jesus Christ was no exception (Mt 16:21). He knew that God had a plan for Him and he was determined to follow that plan to the end. When the time came, Jesus presented his strategy to his disciples. He himself followed his Father's plan when being baptized by John the Baptist (Mt 3:13-17). He regarded baptism as ordered by God. Because he knew that he was sent by God, he had to be obedient to the law of God. After his baptism, he began to preach and his sermons had the same emphasis as those preached by John the Baptist: "Repent for the kingdom of heaven is near" (Mt 4:17). This message has essentially not changed throughout the life of Jesus. He changed, however, the contempory Jewish understanding of God from ruler and protector of the Jewish nation to the father of each particular individual. He taught them to pray: "Our Father in heaven" (Mt 6:9).

Shortly after his baptism and the temptation, which also was in accordance with the will of God, Jesus called his first disciples: Simon Peter and his brother Andrew. Then he got sight of James and John, sons of Zebedee, and he called them. I see here the first strategic plan of Christ, the plan of working in groups, which we find again in the organization of the church.

After having called the twelve disciples, he sat down with them and explained the plan that he followed through his life. It appears that he examined the faith of the disciples and then he told them to go out to serve and to preach to the people (Mt 10:5-15): 1) they should not go to the gentiles; 2) they should not enter any town of the Samaritans, but rather 3) go to the lost sheep of Israel; 4) they should preach the same message he did: "The kingdom of heaven is near" (Mt 10:7). As we notice, Jesus is pointing out to the disciples certain areas and certain groups of people as target for their mission. And as soon as they have come to the places, they should remain there. The reason for this way of acting was to establish good contact with the people so they would listen to the word of God. This last point is the most important one: the message that the kingdom of God was near and that redemption of sin could be obtained through conversion and baptism.

This was the first part of the strategy. Then came another one: 1) healing the sick; 2) raising the dead; 3) cleansing those who have leprosy and 4) driving out demons (Mt 10:8a). In so doing, Jesus demonstrates that his is eager to meet the needs of the people, without financial considerations. So he encourages the disciples to do all this without asking for money. As he says: "You have received the gift of healing freely, give it freely" (Mt 10:8b). This means that one must not ask for any payment.

Although it seems that the message Jesus preached did not differ very much from that of John the Baptist, there are indications in the NT that the Lord Jesus Christ, modified his strategy with time. In Mark 13:10, we read the following: "And the Gospel must first be preached to all nations." We observe here that the Lord Jesus did not limit his ideas concerning evangelization to the Jewish people. He had also the non-Jews in mind, but didn't reveal this part of the plan to the disciples immediately. Jesus is here taking a long step away from his somehow prudent expressions in Matthew 10:5-15, where he tells his disciples not to go to the non-Jews. Throughout the Gospels, we see Jesus entering into contact with non-Jews, as though he was preparing the disciples for their future mission. In his last meeting with the disciples, he emphasizes the need to go to all nations: "When you go, make disciples of all nations" (Mt 28:19). If we, as simple Bible readers, should have any resistance towards changing our strategy when necessary, we shouldn't hesitate. There is no doubt that the Master himself changed strategy, when he felt the need.

We have analyzed part of Jesus' strategy in the NT. But we need to investigate the role of the missionaries and the sending agencies too. When Jesus is instructing his disciples he is at the same time instructing the Christians, the missionaries, the mission agencies and today's preachers. Much has been said and written about what missionaries should do in the contextualization enterprise, but very little about the role of mission agencies. Of course, the liabilities and duties of the missionaries are in focus because they usually are in the forefront of this work. But the different mission agencies should also be taken into account, as their role of decision-making is considerable in the matter. However, in many cases, mission organizations seem to shun their responsibilities and often let the missionaries carry the burden.

But strategy is also about spiritual equipment: Jesus gives the Holy Spirit to the disciples (Jn 20:22). According to 1Corinthians 12:1-11, eight different gifts are bestowed upon the believers by the same Spirit. The plan of Jesus is that the believers shall be filled with the Holy Spirit and equipped to engage in the fight against flesh, the world and the devil. We know that the Holy Spirit is working with us, but we know also that the Holy Spirit can work against us in some cases. Paul for example was hindered by the Holy Spirit to leave for another place. On the other hand, tied by the Holy Spirit, Paul had to stay in a place he did not want to be (Rom 1:13; 15:12).

Servanthood is also part of the plan. In John 13, Jesus wraps a towel around his waist and washs his disciples' feet. By so doing, Jesus gives his disciples a personal example on how they should behave in daily life. Jesus is actually demonstrating by this action the very core of the Gospel, the non-egoistic mind of a servant which was thought to be an example for all mankind. To serve one another has become a single event once a year in a Vatican ceremony. If the action had been practiced as intended, maybe many of today's world problems would have been unknown.

Another part of Jesus' strategy for his disciples is found in his encouragement to be very diplomatic in their mission among the people; he even shows a way of doing that. He says: "I am sending you out like sheep among wolves.

Therefore be as shrewd as snakes and as innocent as doves" (Mt 10:16). A better word of wisdom has never been said.

At the end of this section on contextual Biblical strategy, I would like to mention one person who has followed the strategy and plan of Jesus closely, namely the apostle Paul. When we talk about contextualization, Paul serves as a very good example of how to do it. Wherever he arrived, he picked up the cultural and religious similarities and differences between Christianity and the local people. He has left excellent examples in Acts 13, 14 and 17 of how to approach various cross-cultural situations. In Acts 17, he starts by talking about an "unknown god" the inhabitants of Athens did not know but wanted to know (Act 17:23). However, Paul was a special man. As far as the rest of us are concerned, it is imperative that we do not act alone. We should not only go out into the world two by two, but also have fellowship with other believers in order to allow the Holy Spirit to recharge our spiritual batteries, so to speak.

Though instant spiritual transformation and rebirth are realities, as it happened to Paul on the way to Damascus, we must also take into account that sanctification is an ongoing process. Therefore the spiritual fruits of patience and endurance are important parts of the missionaries' character, equipment and strategy.

6.5 Conclusion

In conclusion of this chapter, we have to mention that contextualization is a relatively new approach to theology. It is at the same time a departure from the old way of looking at the Scripture, and also a continuation of traditional theology. I am in agreement with the necessity for more freedom and a more independent way in biblical interpretation, but at the same time I warn against unfaithfulness towards Scripture. If we regard Scripture as our first and last authority and are committed to pursuing a biblical strategy, we should have no fear.

What alternative do we have to the worldviews offered by consumerism, animism, and New Age, all of which are deifying the self? A theology of God's work in human affairs must begin with an understanding of God Himself as Father, Son, and Holy Spirit. Constantine thought of God as a ruler over the political as well as the religious life. Likewise, a trinitarian theology takes into account the presence of the Son. The Son is the Saviour for all mankind. A trinitarian theology never forgets the Holy Spirit either. We need the experience of the Holy Spirit that is manifest in the preaching and power of the Gospel. In developing a theology of God's work in our days, we must reject the modern dualism that restricts God to otherworldly matters and leaves the natural world to science.

Chapter 7
Conclusion

As mentioned at the outset of this book, my intention was at least twofold: a desire to investigate and clarify as much as possible some of the problems that may arise when Christianity encounters the snake culture among the Mongwande people in the Democratic Republic of Congo, and secondly trying to make the subject more understandable to missionaries, to the Mongwande church, and to other interested people like government officials, students, medical personnel and businessmen.

I understood quickly that the task ahead required a great deal of research. Fortunately, being a missionary in the middle of the snake cult area for many year, I was able to collect and study the phenomenon on site. The results which I have presented in this book have been collected from empirical studies consisting of interviews, narratives, participant observation of rituals and cult practices, and analysis of legends, songs and poems. During the research colloquia at the International Baptist Theological Seminary, Prague, between 2006 and 2010, it appeared that a suitable main title would be: "The Mongwande Snake Cult: A Case Study in Contextualization." This title conveys the fact that contextualization was the focal point of the study. The Mongwande snake cult was the subject matter on which the theory and practice of contextualization was to be reflected on.

In line with the above, I have dealt with the different arguments forwarded by Hiebert, Bevans, Kraft and others in relation to the various models of contextualization and their application. Regarding the application of the models, I found that the critical model, the translation model and the anthropological model were most applicable to my subject. The outline of the book follows logically the steps of Hiebert's critical contextualization model.

I have tried to give this study a natural development beginning with the Mongwande culture, dealing with the social and religious life, particularly the snake cult. Then continuing with the method of contextualization, I discussed the various approaches to this question. In agreement with several authors, the authority of Scripture is indisputable for me. Contextualization of theology is an attempt to understand Christian faith in terms of a particular context. This is a theological imperative. It is both traditional and new, because it has been practiced in some form throughout church history, starting in the NT.

In my reflection on the models of contextualization, I followed Gilliland's and Bevans' typologies (Bevans 2008:37-127; Gilliland 2000). I have highlighted all of their models and ploughed through the different points in some detail. Even though three of the models seem to fit best my case (the critical model, the translation model and the anthropological model), I must admit that there is no one completely adequate method to be followed in all situations. I have therefore chosen to analyze each case with the model that seems to be the most appropriate. It is to be noted that Bevans and Guilliland have concurrent views in some areas but different views in others.

I concluded that contextualization equals appropriate Christianity. I agree with Kraft who asserts that contextualization of theology is an attempt to understand the Christian faith in terms of a particular context. The snake cult in Monga has been our particular context in this book. In an evangelical perspective, the evaluation of the particular practice in the light of Scripture is a crucial point in the method of contextualization. Hiebert's critical model has been foundational for my work, and I have therefore followed his four steps in my analysis.

After the analysis of the Mongwande culture, I have evaluated the biblical material on the snake concept. Then I sought to assess thirdly the Mangwande culture in the light of Scripture by analyzing the continuities and discontinuities between the two. Fourthly, I proposed on a theory (theology) and a practice that seem faithful to Scripture and relevant to culture.

Dealing with the snake phenomenon in the Mongwande culture, it was necessary to look at the question concerning the place of the snake in Scripture. Is there any continuity between these two religious traditions? There is no doubt that the snake is an old tradition in the Bible and so is also the snake tradition among the Mongwande. Just as the study of the snake cult among the Mongwande requires a thorough research, so also does the snake phenomenon in the Bible. We started this research with lexical studies of key words and concepts and their semantic domains. Then we continued with the study of the different passages that mention the snake or cognates. Finally, we looked at some key passages in the OT and NT. The result of our biblical analysis is that the snake concept is ambivalent in the OT and develops towards a mainly negative concept in the NT.

The next step in critical contextualization is a serious evaluation of the Mongwande snake cult in the light of Scripture. Firstly, I launched into a theoretical comparative study of the two cultural and belief systems in order to discern elements of continuity and of discontinuity. While there are many elements of Mongwande religious life where some form of continuity with the corresponding biblical concept can be detected, there are essentially soteriological and eschatological concepts in which we can find no correspondence. Secondly, we presented some past and present encounters between the snake cult and Christianity. It has become apparent that the Mongwande worldview, which is moulded by the snake cult, has survived for a long time and has had continuing influences on Christian life in a way that Hiebert calls split-level Christianity. This means that Mongwande Christians still seem to function very much according to their old worldview. The result is a sort of hidden syncretism among the Mongwande people that call themselves Christians.

In the contextualization quest, we have also searched for the best missional theology and practice. This quest reveals the necessity of being faithful to Scripture and relevant to the Mongwande culture at the same time. There are many elements in a missional theology that are regarded as necessary tools, such as appropriation and contextualization. However, one issue in the interest of best practice seems to have been forgotten. The relationship between the mission agency and the national church seems to have been largely glossed over. Mission boards, and especially the protestant mission boards, ruled the mission societies and their missionaries on the field independently up to World War II. An almost total break between the mission agencies and the local churches took place after the war was over. The mission situation had all of a sudden changed. The local people demanded full control over their church, both in leadership and cultural expression.

Our church responded slowly but accordingly. It did not happen without many sufferings on both sides. The situation required great adjustments of the local congregation, of the missionaries and the home board. The contextualization process was picked up somewhat and is moving forward today as my interview with Reverend President R. K. Manzinga shows well. It appeared that the missionaries needed to rethink certain things. After the colonial era, people all over the world, the so called Third World or Global South, rose up and started fighting for their own identity, and the churches also stood up and claimed their human rights. The missionaries understood as well that they needed a better education, especially in the anthropological field. The way things were done had to be stopped and replaced by dialogue. Missionaries understood that studying the language only was not enough. There was the need also to study social, cultural, and religious life as well.

In chapter seven, I have described, to the best of my knowledge, some much needed approaches for a better contextualized practice of mission. I have pointed to the need for missionaries to rethink the notions of conversion and church planting. Considering the social, religious and cultural features, what does it mean to become a Christian and how does one go about planting churches? The church organizes its worlds by creating cognitive category systems of logic and basic beliefs. To become a member of the church, a conversion is required. That is, one needs to accept what the church stands for.

The church is planted and consists of people who believe in Jesus Christ and look at the missionary as their model. The shift from traditional religion to the Christian faith may have a psychological and social price attached to it. Social shame, a feeling of inferiority and punishment from the spirits may be too much for the Mongwande. The inferiority complex goes deep among these people. To get a Mongwande to reveal what he is religiously bound to is very difficult. For a foreigner it is almost impossible. If a person has a background in the snake cult, the missionary has to be careful in dealing with him. The convert should not depart from a meeting with the feeling that he has given too much nor should the missionary have that feeling.

To sow the word of God, start a church and create a community of believers cannot be dissociated from one another. Church communities are networks of relationship. To build these networks as a missionary might be quite difficult as the difference between cultures is usually far-reaching. Both the receiving culture and the giving culture are looking for identity. The church has become a real community when the bi-cultural church starts to live out the experience of her bi-culturality.

Church renewal is another matter. Planting a church refers to the very beginning of a church, while renewal of a church is normally renewing of rituals, songs and worship service. In order to go further in the contextualization process among the Mongwande, it might be nessary to incorporate host culture traditions, such as songs, dance or theatrical performances.

I have also mentioned the place of spiritual gifts in renewal. With the rise of the Pentecostal movement and its emphasis on tongue speaking, prophetic gifts and healing, our church in Monga has not been spared with dealing with this aspect of church life. But it seems that the church is tackling the situation very well and is marching forward in the name of the Lord.

Is further research needed on the snake cult from a scientific point of view? Is more investigation required into the meaning and practice of the contextualization of the Christian faith in relation to the snake cult? Does the snake cult still exist or is it vanishing? Do people still worship the snake? It is no secret that snake worship is known all over the globe. However, the snake cult among the Mongwande was not well known until the catholic missionary Basile P. Tanghe published his books and articles on the snake cult among the Mongwande between 1920 and 1930. His work on the snake phenomenon in the Congo seemed to have inspired another Belgian, Jean Leyder, who published his book on the snake cult and primitive ideas in 1935. The third researcher, as far as I know, Louis Molet from France, published his work on the snake cult and Mongwande culture in 1970. My book on the snake cult was published in 2005. Even though a great deal has been achieved, there is much more to be done concerning the snake cult. It might be useful to study further the mythological world of the Mongwande, trying to find out more about the mysteries that surround the roots of the snake cult. Studies of this phenomenon from other points of view can be useful. But in my analysis, it will be impossible to agree to conclusions that are opposite to biblical teaching. A better contextualization cannot be one that is more in accordance with scientific views but contrary to biblical faith.

When a church is facing a situation where contextualization is needed, the first thing to be done is to work out a plan. Above I have pointed at the necessity of having a good strategy. I pointed out that even Jesus himself worked according to a well orchestrated strategy. A biblical contextual strategy contains several elements. First, the word of God must be preached in all possible situations. Jesus and Paul are the best models of good strategists. They knew how to approach people. They knew how to make the Gospel pertinent and acceptable by proclaiming an appropriate message. Besides, we have an arsenal of spiritual tools in the Bible. The apostles used these spiritual means whenever an appropriate situation presented itself. Well-planned work always bears fruit in the material world, as it does in the spiritual world.

Bibliography

Behm, J. 1985. *Theological Dictionary of the New Testament.* Abridged in One Volume by Geoffrey William B. Bromiley. Grand Rapids: Eerdmans, p. 948-980.

Bergmann, Lorenz. 1947. *Kirkehistorie I,* Kjøbenhavn, Danmark.

Bevans, Stephen B. 1992/2008. *Models of Contextual Theology.* Rev. and expanded ed. Maryknoll, NY: Orbis.

Bietenhard, H. & Budd, P. J. 1986. "Dragon, Serpent, Scorpion, Sting." *NIDNT.* Vol. 1, p. 507-511.

Burssens, Herman. *Les peuplades de l'entre Congo-Ubangi. Ngbandi, Ngbaka, Mbangia, Ngombe et gens d'eau.* Reprint. Tervuren: Musée Royal de l'Afrique Centrale.

Carsten, J. & Hugh-Jones, S. 1912/1993. *Lévi-Strauss and Beyond: Bodies, Houses, Kinship and Architecture.Towards an Anthropology of the House.* Cambridge: Cambridge University Press.

Clercq, A. de. 1958. *Notes sur la Langue Mongwande.* Tervuren: Musée Royal de l'Afrique Centrale.

Coe, Shoki & Sapsezian, Aharon. 1972. *Ministry in Context.* London: Theological Education Fund.

Cooper, J. C. 1993. *Symbol Lex.* Second printing. Oslo, Norway: Hilt & Hansteen. First Printing: London, 1978.

Douglas, Mary. 1966. *Purity and Danger.* London: Routledge & Kegan.

Durkheim, Émile. 1976. *The Elementary Forms of Religious Life.* London: Allen & Unwin (1st ed. 1915).

Evans-Pritchard, E. E. 1956. *Nuer Religion.* New York: Oxford University Press.

Evans-Pritchard, E. E. 1963. *Witchcraft, Oracles and Magic among the Azande.* New York: Oxford University Press.

Evans-Pritchard, E. E. 1965. *Theories of Primitive Religion.* New York: Oxford University Press.

Foerster, W. 1985. "exousia." *Theological Dictionary of the New Testament.* Abridged In One Volume by Geoffrey William B. Bromiley. Grand Rapids: Eerdmans.

Frost, Michael & Hirsch, Alan. 2003. *The Shaping of Things to Come: Innovation and Mission for the 21st Century Church.* Peabody: Hendrickson.

Gilliland, Dean S., ed. 1989. *The Word Among Us: Contextualizing Theology for Mission Today.* Dallas: Word.

Gilliland, Dean S. 2000. "Contextualization." *Evangelical Dictionary of World Missions.* Ed. A. Scott Moreau. Grand Rapids: Baker, p. 225-227.

Grimberg, C. 1978. "The Shipwrecked Sailor." In *Menneskenes liv og historie: Egypt – Forasia.* Vol. 1. Oslo: Cappelens Forlag, p. 288-289.

Hesselgrave, David J. 1980. *Communicating Christ Cross-Culturally.* Grand Rapids: Zondervan.

Hesselgrave, David J. & Rommen, Edward. 1989. *Contextualization: Meanings, Methods, and Models.* Grand Rapids: Baker.

Hiebert, Paul G. 1984. "Critical Contextualization." *Missiology* 12: p. 287-296. Reprint: 1985. In *Anthropological Insights for Missionaries.* Grand Rapids: Baker, p. 171-192. Reprint: 1994. In *Anthropological Reflections on Missiological Issues.* Grand Rapids: Baker, p. 75-92.

Hiebert, Paul G. 1985/2006. *Anthropological Insights for Missionaries.* Reprint. Grand Rapids: Baker.

Hiebert, Paul G. 1989. "Form and Meaning in the Contextualization of the Gospel." In *The Word Among Us: Contextualizing Theology for Mission Today.* Ed. Dean S. Gilliland. Dallas: Word, p. 101-120.

Hiebert, Paul G. 1994. *Anthropological Reflections on Missiological Issues.* Grand Rapids: Baker.

Hiebert, Paul G. 1999. *Missiological Implications of Epistemological Shifts: Affirming Truth in a Modern/Postmodern World.* Harrisburg, PA: Trinity Press International.

Hiebert, Paul G. 2008. *Transforming Worldviews: An Anthropological Understanding of How People Change.* Grand Rapids: Baker.

Hiebert, Paul G., Shaw, Daniel R. & Tiénou, Tite. 1999. *Understanding Folk Religion: A Christian Response to Popular Beliefs and Practices.* Grand Rapids: Baker.

Husby G. 1995. *Det Norske Baptistsamfunns Mision I Zaïre Gjennom 75 År.* Oslo, Norway: Det Norske Baptistsamfunn.

Iversen, F. 1946. *Fem og Tyve År I Kongo.* Oslo: De Norske Baptisters Kongomisjon.

Käser, Lothar. 1997. *Fremde Kulturen: Eine Einführung in die Ethnologie.* Bad Liebenzell: VLM.

Käser, Lothar. 2004. *Animismus. Einführung in seine begrifflichen Grundlagen.* Bad Liebenzell: VLM.

Kittel, G. & Friedrich, G. 1985. *Theological Dictionary of the New Testament.* Abridged in One Volume by Geoffrey William B. Bromiley. Grand Rapids: Eerdmans, p. 639-641.

Kraft, Charles H. 1979. *Christianity in Culture: A Study in Dynamic Biblical Theologizing in Cross-Cultural Perspective.* Maryknoll: Orbis.

Kraft, Charles H., ed. 2005. *Appropriate Christianity.* Pasadena: William Carey Library.

Lekens, B. P. 1952. *Dictionnaire Ngbandi. Francais-Ngbandi-Francais.* Tervuren: Musée Royal de l'Afrique Centrale.

Leyder, Jean. 1935. *Association primitive d'idées. Serpent-jumeaux, arc-en-ciel au Congo belge.* Bruxelles: Hayez.

Lonergan, Bernard J. F. 1972. *Method in Theology.* New York: Herder and Herder.

Maessens, M. 1952. *Notes de Discours. Institution Primitive.* Bruxelles: Hayez.

Manzinga, R. K. 2009. Personal Communication. E-mail Correspondence and Telephone Conversations between June 10th, 2009, and July 3rd, 2010.

Mbiti, John S. 1980. *De Danser Livet. Introduksjon til Afrikansk Religion.* Viborg, DK: Nörhaven Bogtrykkeri. Original English version: 1969. *African Religions and Philosophy.* London: Heinemann.

Moen, Sveinung J. 1961. Fieldnotes 1951-1961.

Moen, Sveinung J. 1974. "The Amerasians: A Study and Research on Inter-racial Children in Korea."

Moen, Sveinung J. 2005. *The Mongwande Snake Cult.* Falköping, Sweden: Swedish Institute of Mission Research, Kimpese Publishing House.

Molet, Louis. 1965. "Kanga et Sangere, Génies Yakoma." In *African Systems of Thought.* New York: Oxford University Press.

Molet, Louis. 1970. *Aspects de l'organisation du monde des Ngbandi.* Tervuren: Musée Royal de l'Afrique Centrale.

Mowinckel, S. 1971. *Religion og Kultus.* Oslo, Norway: Land og Kirke.

Murphy, Nancey. 1996. *Beyond Liberalism and Fundamentalism: How Modern and Postmodern Philosophy Set the Theological Agenda.* Valley Forge: Trinity Press International.

Murphy, Nancey. 1997. *Anglo-American Postmodernity: Philosophical Perspectives on Religion, Science and Ethics.* Boulder, CO: Westview Press.

Murphy, Nancey. 2004. *Theology in a Postmodern Age.* The Nordenhaug Lectures 2003. Prague: International Baptist Theological Seminary.

Mørland, Henning. 1990. *Latinsk Ordbok.* Oslo, Norway: Cappelen Forlag.

Newbigin, Lesslie. 1986. *Foolishness to the Greeks: The Gospel and Western Culture*. London: SPCK.

Newbigin, Lesslie. 1999. *Trinitarian Doctrine for Today's Mission*. Reprint. Milton Keynes: Paternoster (1st ed. 1963).

Nida, Eugene A. & Taber, Charles R. 1969. *Theory and Practice of Translation*. Leiden: Brill.

Renfrew, Colin & Bahn, Paul G., eds. 2000. *Archaeology: Theories, Methods and Practices*. London: Thames & Hudson.

Richardson, A. 1958. *An Introduction to the Theology of the New Testament*. London: SCM.

Rommen, Edward & Corwin, Gary, eds. 1996. *Missiology and the Social Sciences: Contributions, Cautions and Conclusions*. Evangelical Missiological Society Series No. 4. Pasadena: William Carey Library.

Scheldrup, Harald. 1971. *Innføring i Psykologi*. Oslo: Gyldendal Norsk Forlag.

Schreiter, Robert J. 1985. *Constructing Local Theologies*. Maryknoll: Orbis.

Scohy, A. 1949. *L'Uélé secret*. Bruxelles: Office international de librairie.

Stallman, Robert C. 1996. "*nahash.*" *NIDOTTE*. Vol. 3, p. 84-88.

Stallman, Robert C. 1996. "Reptiles." *NIDOTTE*. Vol. 4, p. 1129-1132.

Stott, John. 1975. *The Lausanne Covenant: An Exposition and Commentary*. Minneapolis, World Wide Publications.

Sundberg, Carl. 2000. *Conversion and Contextual Conceptions of Christ*. Uppsala, Sweden: Swedish Institute of Missionary Research.

Tanghe, Basile P. 1925a. "Le culte de Dieu chez les Ngbandi." *Congo* II, 3: p. 435-438.

Tanghe, Basile P. 1925b. "Une page de philosophie congolaise. Chefs, serpent, jumeaux." *Congo* 14: p. 562-565.

Tanghe, Basile P. 1926. *Le culte du serpent chez les Ngbandi*. Brugges, Belgique: Les Presses Gruuthuuse.

Tanghe, Basile P. 1929a. *De Ngbandi. Geschiedkundige Bijdragen*. Brugges: Moderne Druk.

Tanghe, Basile P. 1929b. *De Ngbandi. Naar het leven geshetst*. Brugges: Die Gruuthuuse Presen.

Tanghe, Basile P. 1930. "Le droit d'aînesse chez les indigènes du Haut-Ubangi." *Africa* III, 1: p. 78-82.

The Holy Bible. 1998. New International Version. London: International Bible Society.

The New Encyclopaedia Britannica. 1988a. Vol. 3, s.v. "Congo."

The New Encyclopaedia Britannica. 1988b. Vol. 5, s.v. "Zaire."

The New Encyclopedia Britannica. 1988c. Vol. 25, s.v. "Occultism: magic."

Turner, Harold. 1981. "Religious Mouvements in Primal Societies." *Mission Focus* 9: p. 45-54.

Turner, Victor. 1992. *Blazing the Trail: Way Marks in the Exploration of Symbols.* Edited by Edith Turner. Tuscon, Arizona & London: University Press.

Vungbo, Jacques. 2009. Personal Communication. Information transmitted by Hannes Wiher.

Waardenburg, Jacques. 1973-1974. *Classical Approaches to the Study of Religion: Aims, Methods and Theories of Research. Vol. 1: Elements of The Science of Religion. Introduction and Anthology.* Paris: Mouton.

Webster's Third Dictionary. 1988. Vol. 1, s.v. "G. & C. Merriam Company, Publishers Springfield, Massachusetts, U.S.A. ."

Wiher, Hannes. 2003. *Shame and Guilt: A Key to* Cross-*Cultural Ministry.* Bonn: Culture and Science Publications.

Würthwein, E. 1985. *Theological Dictionary of the New Testament.* Abridged in One Volume by Geoffrey William B. Bromiley. Grand Rapids: Eerdmans, p. 980-989.

Appendix

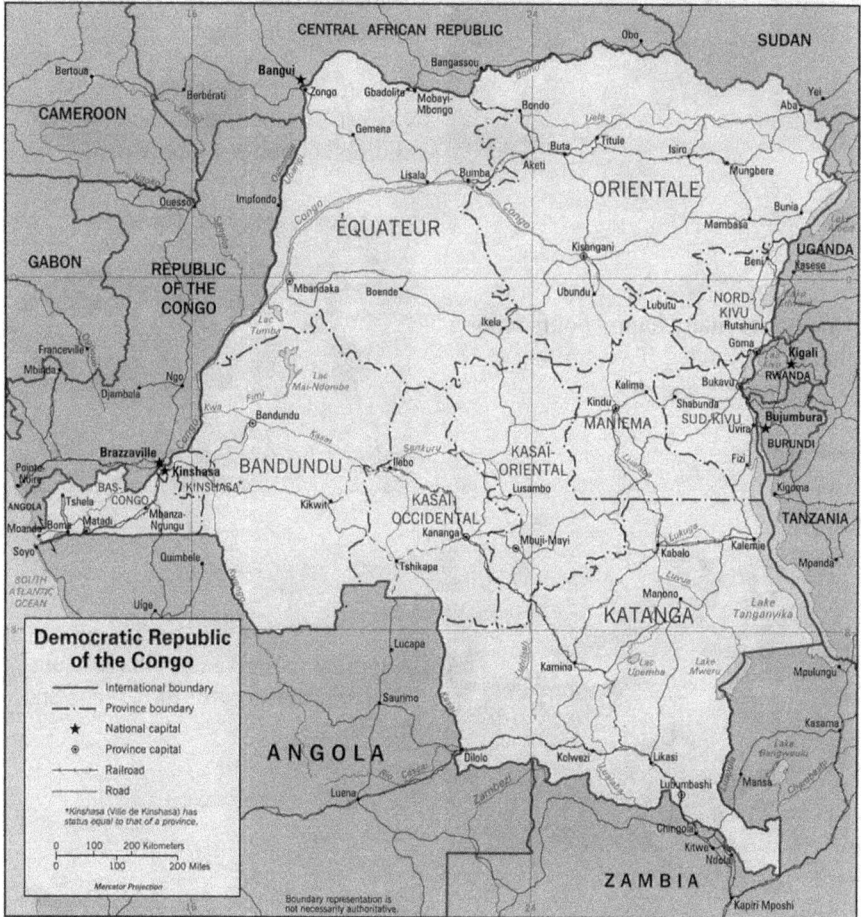

Map of the Democratic Republic of Congo

Sveinung J. Moen with four of his informants on the Mongwande history, culture and religion.

Standing: Head nurse Gaspard Boya and pastor Dundaloma.

Sitting: Sveinung J. Moen, parish worker Elisabeth and leader of the church council Yanzere Ernst.

One of the many happy hours among the Mongwandes. Two smiling Mongwandes and me.

A typical mongwande village. I am here told the story of the village and the people.

A well made pitcher from Monga.

Mbeti the answering tripod.

Folk religion and gods – spirits.
Animated objects.

Snake sticks. See 2.8.6.

Four wooden pieces and two iron
pieces. Animated objects.

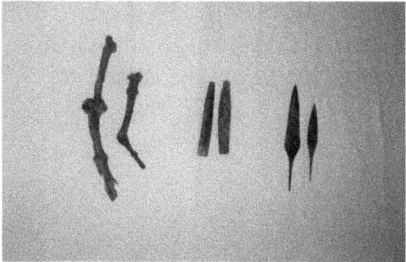

Especially made box for smaller animated objects.

Animated necklas as protection against bad spirits formed as necklas.

A handy made taburet. It is made of one piece of wood.

Leopard skin and the medicinman's paraphernalia, drums, taburet etc.

Glossary

Akotara	Ancestors
Banga	Ancestral spirit
Dawa makasi	Strong medicine
Gegi	Atmosphere
Kaina	Jungle / forest god
Kilima	River god
Libanda	Open place, yard, market place
Lingala	One of the four national languages in Congo DRC Swahili, Kikongo and Tshiluba are the other three, besides French
Lora	Heaven
Mokili	World as an entity
Molimo	Spirit or soul
Mpozo na nyoka	Snake skin (Lingala)
Mpozo na Zanza	Moon skin (Lingala)
Mpozo	Human skin and animal skin (Lingala)
Nda ngbò	House of the snake
Nda ntolo	House of the ancestors / spirits / the soul, shelter
Nda	House
Ndibere	Poisonous ashes
Ngbò concept	Power and authority of legislation, cultic sphere
Ngbò	Snake, twins
Ntolo akotara	Soul of the ancestors
Ntolo ngbò	Soul of the snake
Ntolo	Soul, power, shadow, image or picture
Nyi	Children (Mongwande)
Nzambe	God (Lingala)
Nzapa	God (Mongwande)
Nzoto	Body
Paka Nzambe te	No one else but God (expression of fatalism)
Poro	Human skin and animal skin (Mongwande)
Sese	Earth
Tà	Mother
Tá ngbá	Mother of the snake (twins).
Tó ngbò	Father of the snake (twins)
Tó	Father
Wali	Woman
Ya	Wife, married woman (Mongwande)
Yenda-Gazoroma	Snake god, stilistic figurine
Yolo	Poisonous ashes

Index of Authors

Index of Subjects

The Author

Sveinung Johnson Moen was born in Oslo in 1924. He studied theology at the Baptist Theological Seminary in Oslo from 1945 to 1949. Following a year of language studies in Brussels, Belgium, he and his wife went to the Monga district in the northern part of the Democratic Republic of Congo (former Belgian Congo), where he undertook anthropological studies of the Mongwande snake cult (among other things). Here the family spent ten years, from 1951 to 1961, until the turmoil of independence made leave all the expatriate personnel. In 1964 he was asked to go to South Korea where he remained with his family until 1975. In Pusan, South Korea he built a psychiatric clinic, the first of its kind in Korea. Later on, Pearl S. Buck called him as director for her Centre for mixed raced children to Seoul, South Korea. In 1975 he joined an American refugee organisation until he accepted a position in the administration of his home town, Halden, Norway, in 1979. From 2005 to 2010 he upgraded his theological studies at the International Baptist Theological Seminary in Prague, Czech Republic. His publications include The Amerasians (1974) and The Mongwande Snake Cult (2005).

www.ingramcontent.com/pod-product-compliance
Lightning Source LLC
Chambersburg PA
CBHW072238270326
41930CB00010B/2182